IN THE FOREFRONT

IN THE FOREFRONT
Alloa At War 1914–1919

ANDREW HUNT

Reveille PRESS

Reveille Press is an imprint of
Tommies Guides Military Booksellers & Publishers

Gemini House
136-140 Old Shoreham Road
Brighton BN3 7BD

First published in Great Britain by
Reveille Press 2018

For more information please visit
www.reveillepress.com

© 2018 Andrew Hunt

The right of Andrew Hunt to be identified as the author of this
work has been asserted by him in accordance with the
Copyright, Designs and Patents Act 1988

A catalogue record for this book is available
from the British Library

All rights reserved. Apart from any use under UK copyright law no part of this publication may be reproduced, stored in a retrieval system, or transmitted, in any form or by any means, without prior written permission of the publisher, nor be otherwise circulated in any form of binding or cover other than that in which it is published and without a similar condition being imposed on the subsequent publisher.

ISBN 978-1-9998900-5-6

Cover design by Reveille Press
Typeset by Vivian@Bookscribe

Printed in the UK

The cover illustration is Matania's painting of John Crawford Buchan's heroic last stand in March 1918. It is printed with thanks to the Clackmannanshire Heritage Collection for permission to use this picture.

Contents

	Introduction	7
Chapter 1	Alloa and the Declaration of War	11
Chapter 2	Alloa's Industries	18
Chapter 3	The Landowners and Industrialists	44
Chapter 4	The Impact on Schools and Education	62
Chapter 5	Sport and the War	89
Chapter 6	Women at War	108
Chapter 7	Daily Life in the War	121
Chapter 8	Churches and the War	160
Chapter 9	Local Politics	182
Chapter 10	The End of the War	189
Chapter 11	Commemoration	195
Chapter 12	The Impact of the War	220
Chapter 13	Alloa Soldiers in Battle	236
Chapter 14	Remembering the Brave	246
	Conclusion	269

Dedication

This book is dedicated David Henderson (JDH), a true son of Alloa and my old friend and colleague of almost 40 years, who died in September 2017.

For over 25 years we were the History Department at Alloa Academy. Teaching the First World War and commemorating it was our shared interest; we ran 8 Western Front trips together and never tired of creating teaching resources for it. He shared his views with me on every chapter of this book and always encouraged me to dig deeper. He read and approved a rough draft but illness overtook him before he could see the final published version.

This is for him.

INTRODUCTION

This book had its beginnings a long time ago, when I was teaching Standard Grade History Investigations at Alloa Academy in the 1990s. All S3-S4 History pupils had to conduct an Investigation as part of their course, and write up their findings. It would have been far too great a task, both for pupils to manage and teachers to oversee and advise, if pupils were allowed to pick whatever topic they liked, so I made it my job to provide a wide range of primary sources on a single topic – 'Alloa at War 1914–1918' – and let the pupils pick whichever aspect they wished to study. In this way they had a chance to do genuine research and were not likely to run short of at least some useable evidence on which to base their conclusions. Meanwhile, I discovered vast amounts of information about a topic that I became fascinated by and which became my continuing research hobby. However, an ongoing frustration in trying to build up this picture is how few photographs survive of what was going on in Alloa at that time. Did no-one have a decent camera then?

Standard Grade Investigations died the death, as many ambitious educational endeavours do, but I always felt that there was a book in it somewhere. No one else seemed to have collated their researches into a general and over-arching review of the impact of the war on Alloa, and I always regarded 'writing it up' as my retirement task, indeed my retirement **obligation,** since probably no-one else had collected as much material as I had, and it would all go to waste if I did not do something with it. So, almost twenty-five years later, here it is.

What, then, did I find out about the way just over four years of war affected a small town and how was all this information to be organised? All historians 'classify' their information; by placing what they have researched under headings, it helps give it order and coherence. I therefore broke down the impact of the war on Alloa and its people into fourteen chapters. It's not as easy as that however; many chapters overlap, the same people and institutions crop up again and again, making different contributions depending on what theme is being discussed. The town of Alloa was composed of a complex set of inter-connected and overlapping social groups; for example, a worker in Paton's Mills could feature in the chapter on the industrial development of the town, but might also be a keen cricketer appearing in the sport chapter, then join up and become a casualty statistic in the war service chapter and/or, finally, have a growing family whose life stories contributed to the social impact chapter. It was my job not only to try to sift and make sense of all this under the fourteen chapter headings I had set myself, but also to allow the threads binding it all together to show through as a true reflection of a small town's triumphs and sufferings.

In this book I have kept my focus solely on Alloa, a small industrial town on the north bank of the River Forth, with a population of around about 12,000 people, according to the 1911 census. This book is not about wider Clackmannanshire; there are just a few references where good parallels can and should be drawn [eg prominent landowning families in the local area and nurses], but, in all my researches, my eyes rarely looked beyond about a mile radius from the Town Hall!

It is clear that some evidence is contradictory (eg. the number of dead on Alloa's War Memorial differs from the number of dead listed in the Burgh of Alloa Roll of Honour). This is not enough to ruin the telling of a good story, but enough to make you realise that, in some cases, people producing the documents at the time were working from the best information they had, which was not always 100% accurate. In other cases they had their own agendas, wanting to sell a view of how people would think it was, rather than how it really was. This was not just connected with wartime papers and censorship (either official or voluntary, self-imposed) but sometimes just the sensibilities of the people from that age, about not always giving out 'the full picture'; about protecting people from harsh truths. Some conclusions therefore have to be tentative; I **think** this was how it was, rather than I **know** this was how it was. People with greater knowledge than me and/or more research on a particular topic may dispute my findings. That is their prerogative and, to help them, I made a decision from the outset to use footnotes. Any reader can, therefore, see exactly where I got my information from and check it for themselves to see whether, when I made judgements, they were indeed justified. In fact, in most cases I have not actually included a chapter conclusion; I have just recorded what I've discovered, with a commentary. It's up to you, the reader, to reach a conclusion on how great the impact was. Despite the 'academic' tone of using foot-notes, this book is intended for the general reader: it's a mixture of economic, social and military history; telling the most comprehensive story possible about real people's lives in a real town during extraordinary times, hopefully written in an accessible way.

INTRODUCTION

The title of this book was of course chosen because it is the Burgh of Alloa's motto and it seemed to lend itself as a heading to any discussion of the part the people of Alloa played in the war. However, readers seeing a sub-title like *Alloa At War 1914–1919* should not expect a story of continuous death and destruction. No bombs fell on Alloa (in either war); there was no shelling from the sea, as in Hartlepool in 1914 and no Zeppelin bombing like that on Leith in 1916; but the four years of war shook up this small town in many different ways. The impact fluctuated; it was serious and intense, but 'ordinary life' went on. Indeed, there were many continuities from Alloa's peace-time experience, but by the end of 1918 no-one could say the town had stayed the same.

There are no Alloa folk alive now to remember that time, but there must be a few of the children and certainly the grandchildren of that wartime generation still around, who heard some of this stuff from their parents and helped to pass it on themselves as family stories. For all of these people it's up to me to 'get it right'; a tribute to those who experienced it and to the next generation who heard about it. The rest who followed on can only wonder how well they would have coped with something like that themselves.

Andrew Hunt
June 2018

CHAPTER 1

ALLOA AND THE DECLARATION OF WAR

World War I started for British people on Tuesday 4 August 1914 at 11.00pm, but did it catch the people of Alloa by surprise? Were there any signs before that date to give them a warning of what was coming?

It was the assassination of Archduke Franz Ferdinand in Sarajevo six weeks earlier on Sunday 28 June 1914 that had triggered the countdown to war, and the *Alloa Circular*, being a mid-week paper published on 1 July, was the first local newspaper to be in a position to comment. Sure enough, it noted that the Archduke and his wife had been assassinated on the previous Sunday and accurately reported that there was a bomb attempt followed by another attempt involving 2 revolver shots.[1] It came to no conclusions as to what the impact of this event might be, and, following that report, the *Circular* contained nothing remotely connected to the idea that Europe was heading for a war until the day after war broke out.

The *Alloa Journal* likewise did not show much advance recognition that an event had happened which might lead to a war. Saturday 4 July would have been the first occasion that it could have commented but it said nothing; the *Journal*'s editorial was only interested in the Irish Problem.[2] Even by 18 July it was still only reporting important local news like the death of the brother of the Earl of Mar, Greenfield House being destroyed by fire and a long piece on the problem of dealing with Ulster.[3] On 1 August, although there was a report on the Territorials of the 7th Battalion of the Argyll and Sutherland Highlanders (the local regiment) and their successful summer camp at Machrihanish, there was no hint that they might soon be needed elsewhere on more serious business. The *Journal*'s parliamentary column was still totally concerned with Irish Home Rule.[4]

The *Alloa Advertiser* was just that little bit better informed about the significance of international events. On 4 July, the first item in its editorial column was entitled *The Assassination of the Austrian Heir*, followed by a 225 word article offering condolences to Emperor Franz Joseph and regretting the 'assassination committed in the name of anarchy'.[5] However, there was not really much more on this story over the next few weeks. Its 18 July issue focused on the terrible fire which saw Greenfield House gutted,[6] and its 25 July issue echoed the *Journal* with its concerns for Free Trade and the Ulster Crisis.[7] However, on Saturday 1 August, under a by-line of 'War Clouds', the *Advertiser* commented on 'growing anxiety' and it was believed 'that warlike actions were imminent' although there was also the view that they might be 'localised' despite 'grave fears that Russia may be compelled into action.'[8] All in all, it was quite an intelligent review of the impending crisis, which erupted into European war three days later.

Published on a Wednesday, the *Circular* also had the luck to be the first local paper to be issued following the actual outbreak of war on 4 August, and it did not miss the chance of some epic language; 'The blow has fallen. Europe is in a conflagration, the end of which no-one can possibly foresee.' It then offered a balanced account of what the Germans had done and what the Russians had done to help provoke war, followed by some doom-laden comments on what its impact might be, along the lines of 'The suspense is terrible. At any moment word may come of some sanguinary conflict which will send a shudder through civilization.'[9]

Once war was declared, all the local newspapers were fairly full of speculation on how it might affect the people of Alloa. The first wartime issue of the *Journal* on 8 August made a strongly patriotic rallying cry in its editorial, where Germany was accused of 'The wanton breaking of solemn treaties' and expressed the view that Britain would save 'small but sturdy independent states'. It went on to warn that people who hoard or 'deplete the nation's gold reserves' would not be helping matters.[10] It now had a 'War Column' which reported on a wide-ranging set of news items on how the war was likely to affect Alloa; there was everything from a run on newspapers to get information and a feared run on the banks, to worries about food supplies, the seizure of two German vessels lying off South Alloa and watching the local Territorials head off for Stirling (and subsequently Bedford for training) following their mobilisation.[11]

The *Advertiser* for 8 August [and for the following three weeks] covered its front page with a big warning notice called 'Notice to Mariners', of the public traffic regulations that had been put into place by the Admiralty over the whole River Forth. It echoed the *Journal* in commenting on the rush to buy foodstuffs and the calling up of reservists, but, with memories of the Boer War not so distant, it also included an article addressed to boy scouts (chiefly about their use as signallers, message boys and making their push bikes available if needed).[12] The *Advertiser* clearly had feature writers who were more prepared than those in the *Journal* to get their teeth into some dramatic imagery, for their editorial on 8 August[13] described, with remarkable foresight after only four days so far of war, how 'We are in the midst of what is believed to be the most sanguinary war in the world's history' and blamed it on the fact that the 'war dogs of Austria and Germany were let loose', making us 'honour-bound to protect Belgium'.

By the time the issues of 8 August were published, the papers were already including sizable adverts or cartoons under the heading 'Your King and Country Need You', for the 'Call to arms' encouraging local recruiting.[14] By 22 August this had been supplemented with adverts more specifically laying down the conditions for enlistment. While the lower age limit was an unsurprising nineteen years old, the height limit was a

'Vacant place for you lad' cartoon (*Alloa Advertiser*)

rather lowly 5ft 3in with a chest measurement of 34in. This hardly seems to suggest that the nation was planning on calling up a breed of supermen even in the first flush of war when our fittest and finest might have been expected to volunteer.[15]

The *Journal* of 15 August reported that the women who were involved in Alloa's suffrage societies had announced that any political work they would have done was now suspended 'for the time being'.[16]

The same column saw the announcement that telegrams would be censored and the interesting point that Alloa's Territorial soldiers, both officers and men, had followed the national pattern by almost all of them volunteering for foreign service, even though their original terms of enlistment specified home service only.

The Prince of Wales' Fund for relief of distressed servicemen was set up, mostly with the support of the wealthier local families (as evidenced by the names on the subscription list).[17] A more extended subscription list seen in the *Journal* on 22 August confirmed further that this was a fund that the upper echelons of local society all felt they had to contribute a few guineas to.[18] No one could match the directors of Paton's Mills who subscribed £1000; the Earl of Mar and Kellie was next with £25.[19]

Many other aspects of local news show that the war must have had a marked effect, at least on some. Menstrie Games was called off; there was concern that coal miners faced hard times due to lack of pit props which came from the Baltic states, and it was noticed that there was a shortage of cars on the streets, although whether this was due to worries about being commandeered or shortages of petrol in unknown.[20] However, by 26 August the *Circular* was already getting used to the idea of war, and commented that 'The first feeling of excitement and alarm caused... by the outbreak of war has to a considerable extent subsided' and that people had become 'reconciled to the dread state of affairs existing'.[21]

By 29 August, both the *Journal* and the *Advertiser*

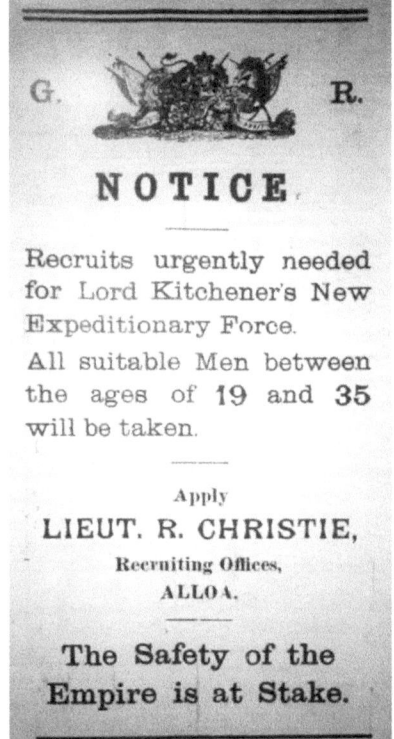

Recruiting poster
(*Alloa Advertiser*)

had a note of urgency about getting recruits. This could be seen in their publication of the government's recruitment notice, stating that the upper age limit had stretched to 35.[22] Meanwhile, there was plenty of information about different work parties being set up to make clothing for soldiers and their families, and the Burgh Council still seemed heavily preoccupied with setting up a committee to administer the Prince of Wales' Fund, which was clearly regarded as the big thing of the day.[23] By 5 September in the *Journal*, there was clear evidence of a big rush [over 400 men so far] to join up under Kitchener's scheme [join at the Drill Hall], but that Alloa also wanted 200 men to join the local Territorials [so that it had its full complement and could be sent fairly promptly on its overseas service].[24] Enlistment for the Territorials was in the Unionist Club and the Liberal Club.[25] The enthusiasm to join was fairly widespread, with forty or fifty men a day being sworn in, and the local papers had several stories of the numbers of sons from prominent local families who had joined up. There were two or three articles and letters about the wish (emanating from London) to set up an Athletes Volunteer Force (or sportsmen's battalion). It was noted that '8 of Clackmannan County's regular team' [*cricket*] had joined the colours[26] and this zeal for joining up was widely praised. However, Capt. A.P. Moir wrote a letter to the *Scotsman* discouraging the creation of these sportsmen's battalions.[27] He argued that they should all just join the Territorials.[28] The question was asked about whether football should be stopped. It seems St Johnstone FC had abandoned its matches; and there was a feeling in the *Advertiser* that Alloa should follow suit; it 'would bespeak the highest motives' as the paper quaintly put it.[29]

The *Advertiser* for 5 September had its own poster specifying the need for 200 recruits [30] and backed up its plea with a note about 'German Barbarities' in Louvain, where a historic Belgian town of about 45,000 people had been more or less burnt to the ground.[31]

The *Advertiser* also started to put in 'lists

Recruiting poster
(*Alloa Advertiser*)

of heroes' containing the names of all the local men who had joined up; to help encourage the rest.³² Despite the references to the German atrocities, there is little sense of jingoism in the local press; it seemed more a call to duty than anything else and there was no indication of any high hopes of an early and easy victory. Lady Mar, in a letter to her son on 1 October 1914, regretfully told him that 'The Russians don't think they can be in Berlin before Christmas',³³ and the recognition that this might be a hard war and a long slog was fairly widespread.

By early 1915 active recruiting was still going on in Alloa, but there was a sense of resigned acceptance along the lines that almost everyone who had wanted to go had gone already. This led to some local citizens noting the unconscious humour in the positioning of the latest large recruitment placard: right outside the local cemetery was a great big notice which read 'Wake Up... Your King and Country needs you'.³⁴

ENDNOTES

1 *Alloa Circular* 1 July 1914 p. 2 col. 3
2 *Alloa Journal* 4 July 1914 p. 2 col. 4
3 *Alloa Journal* 18 July 1914 p. 2 col. 7, p. 3 col. 2, p. 4 col. 2
4 *Alloa Journal* 1 Aug 1914 p. 2 col. 2, p. 4 col. 3
5 *Alloa Advertiser* 4 July 1914 p. 2 col. 4
6 *Alloa Advertiser* 18 July 1914 p. 3 cols. 2+3
7 *Alloa Advertiser* 25 July 1914 p. 2 col. 4
8 *Alloa Advertiser* 25 July 1914 p. 2 col. 4
9 *Alloa Circular* 5 Aug 1914 p. 2 col. 6
10 *Alloa Journal* 8 Aug 1914 p2 col3
11 *Alloa Journal* 8 Aug 1914 p2 cols6+7
12 The Boy Scout Movement didn't start till after 1908 when Robert Baden-Powell wrote *Scouting for Boys*; however the actions of the Mafeking Cadet Corps at the Siege of Mafeking [1899–1900] during the Boer War, are largely credited with being the inspiration and model for the later Scout Movement. Don't under-estimate the role of Alloa's boy scouts during World War I; two of the pictures of the nursing staff and convalescing soldiers at Arnsbrae Hospital [see Chapter 7] clearly had scouts in uniform sitting in the front row, so there must have been some use for them even by mid-1915.
13 *Alloa Advertiser* 8 Aug 1914 p. 2 col. 4

14 *Alloa Journal* 8 Aug 1914 p. 2 cols. 1+2
15 *Alloa Journal* 22 Aug 1914 p. 2 cols. 1+2
16 *Alloa Journal* 15 Aug 1914 p. 3 col. 4
17 *Alloa Journal* 15 Aug 1914 p. 3 cols. 2+3
18 *Alloa Journal* 22 Aug 1914 p. 2 cols. 3+4. A guinea is one pound and one shilling. Since this is the first reference to money it is worth reminding readers that Britain's currency in those days was pounds, shillings and pence; 12 pence to a shilling and 20 shillings to a pound. An average wage which would have supported a family was around £2 10s a week.
19 *Alloa Journal* 15 Aug 1914 p. 2 col. 1
20 *Alloa Journal* 22 Aug 1914 p. 2 col. 8
21 *Alloa Circular* 26 Aug 1914 p. 2 col. 5
22 *Alloa Advertiser* 29 Aug 1914 p. 1 col. 3
23 *Alloa Journal* 29 Aug 1914 p. 2 col. 2, p. 3 col. 2
24 *Alloa Journal* 5 Sept 1914 p. 2 cols. 5-7
25 *Alloa Journal* 5 Sept 1914 p. 2 col. 5
26 *Alloa Journal* 5 Sept 1914 p. 3 col. 1
27 As an old soldier, Captain Moir was the Secretary of the local Territorial Forces Association. He was the father of Archie Gifford Moir and Robert Gifford Moir.
28 *Scotsman* 1 Sept 1914
29 *Alloa Journal* 5 Sept 1914 p. 3 col. 1
30 *Alloa Advertiser* 5 Sept 1914 p. 2 cols. 4+5
31 *Alloa Advertiser* 5 Sept 1914 p. 2 col. 5
32 *Alloa Advertiser* 5 Sept 1914 p. 3 col. 4
33 National Archives Mar and Kellie Muniments GD 124/15/1852
34 *Alloa Journal* 27 Feb 1915 p. 3 col. 8

CHAPTER 2

ALLOA'S INDUSTRIES

Information available for investigating industrial developments in wartime Alloa includes the histories written in the 1940s and 1950s by professional writers like J.L. Carvel, though the obvious support for management and criticism of any workers who demanded better conditions - a consequence of the company sponsorship of the studies – make them less than wholly reliable. The National Archives in Edinburgh holds business records for Paton's Mills, Younger's Brewery and the Alloa Coal Company, all of which give revealing insights, but there is not a great deal of detail on their wartime activities. The Alloa press was quite informative, especially on 'special interest' items as they occurred, but was better in its end-of-year review, usually called 'Industrial Retrospect' or 'Local Retrospect', of what it thought had happened on the industrial front. The Central Regional Council oral history projects in the 1980s, which were taken from interviews with the last few surviving Alloa workers who remembered that far back, are also useful.

The Retrospects gave a moving account of the general impact of war on local industry. The first wartime comment was on 2 January 1915, when it held the view that 'On the whole, the prospects in our local industry and work are fairly bright at present'.[1] The next one in the *Advertiser* on 30 December 1916 noted that 'It is a cause of universal thankfulness that in the midst of the greatest war the world has ever seen, and in spite of enormous sacrifices... the public business of the county has been carried out without interruption..'[2] The *Journal* echoed this by commenting that 'the industrial wheels have been kept going very briskly by the war conditions... the local factories have been working overtime for most of the year.'[3] By 29 December 1917 there was the balanced view that 'There is no part of national activity which has been more affected...by the abnormal conditions brought about by the war, than that of industry. Some firms have enjoyed a prosperity undreamt of either by employers or employees, while others again have suffered.'[4] The general tone of its last Retrospect on 28 December 1918 was slightly depressed, but it ended more optimistically with the view that 'The ordinary trade of the county has been dislocated and public business has been restricted. The exigencies of war have made large demands upon the industrial resources of the nation, and all over there have been evidences of prosperity. The year drawing to a close has largely shared in that prosperity, and while the cost of living has naturally increased, wages have advanced to such an extent to more than counter-balance that increase, without any personal sacrifice whatsoever being rendered on the part of the wage earner.'[5] The overall mood of the Retrospects suggests that Alloa actually did quite well economically as a result of the demands of the war on its local industries.

This chapter focuses on the industries in Alloa which had a major wartime impact, but it should be remembered that Alloa had a host of smaller industries that just continued their business during the war without rising to any great prominence. These included cooperages, maltings, ropeworks, woodyards and Messrs G. Sellar and Son. This last company made agricultural machinery in Huntly, Aberdeenshire, but had moved its entire operation from Huntly to the site of the old Sun Foundry in Kelliebank, Alloa in May 1915 and operated there throughout the war. It had organised a special train of twenty-seven vans to bring all the household effects of its employees to Alloa, while the workers and their families, numbering over 100, travelled to Alloa by passenger train via Larbert.[6] Most of the workers moved to the Forbes Street/Medwyn Place area of the town. The company must have made a reasonable start, because the *Advertiser* commented in December 1916 that it had 'enjoyed a large amount of industrial prosperity'.[7]

COAL MINES

The Alloa Coal Company (ACC) was the most prominent of the local coal companies. It was founded as a private company in 1898, with fourteen shareholders owning the 16,000 shares valued at £10 each. By 1914 that had risen to 30,000 shares and there were now twenty-one shareholders, including five women. Every year during the war the Company filled in its *Form E* to describe its capitalisation and shareholders; these show that it retained the same five directors for the entire war. The deputy chairman, Lieutenant Colonel Alexander Mitchell, was the largest shareholder, with 8,750 shares – over 25 per cent of the total.[8] The Alloa Coal Company had pits in Bannockburn, Carnock and Pirnhall , south of the River Forth, as well as Craigrie, Meta, King O'Muirs,

Dollar, Zetland, Whins, Tillicoultry, Melloch and Devon, north of the river. There were other mining companies with their own pits around Alloa, but the story of how the Alloa Coal Company developed during the war years is, in many ways, typical of them all.

The ACC was on the brink of extending its operations by buying the Carnock No 1 pit in July 1914.[9] The outbreak of war delayed this, but only until May 1915, when just over £34,000 changed hands for the purchase of the rich seams lying between Bannockburn and the River Forth. The directors may have wished they had not bothered, because the coal industry in Alloa suffered great disruption and difficulty during the years of the war.[10] The government demanded the greatest quantity of coal possible at the very same time as there was a rush 'to the colours' from the pits, by young men who were fit to serve. The fact that Lieut. Col. Mitchell was also the commander of the local territorial association and had encouraged his miners to join up also made matters worse. He offered, from the start of the war, free rent and free coal for their families at home to any married men who joined up, which made enlisting quite attractive. Within a few months of the war beginning, 650 employees had joined up, which made it very difficult to maintain the rates of coal production. In fact, output dropped sharply. The *Journal* reported the government figures; by mid-1915 there was a drop of 21 million tons in national coal production, and there were almost a million fewer miners on the national payroll.[11] The situation was made worse for the company by the fact that the port of Alloa was closed for normal business for the duration of the war and it had to find new means of getting its coal out to buyers. The *Journal* reported in October 1915 on this concern, commenting that Alloa, 'which had at the same date last year shipped 57,077 tons of coal, has not shipped a single ton this year,'[12] The general shortage of coal due to the great demand from munitions factories resulted in a price rise, followed naturally by the miners asking for a pay rise. They were awarded, without much of an argument, an 18.75 per cent pay rise in May 1915 and[13] by midsummer 1915 miners were earning 9s 6d a day, which was the highest wage since 1873.[14]

Another worry that the ACC faced was the shortage of pit props. It had usually obtained them from Scandinavia, but these markets were now cut off, due to the North Sea being a war zone. More home-grown timber had to be used and some imported from Canada. Prices for this timber were higher.

Carvel argued that friction and unrest in the wartime mining industry was quite high, but that Alloa and Clackmannanshire were generally free from this. One example of this was when the local miners agreed to work a six-day week to help the war effort.[15] Nevertheless, the government took all mines under its direct control in March 1917 and this both held back profits and regulated wages, though it did not prevent the ACC buying further, fairly limited, coal-bearing lands in 1917, at Dunmore, south of the Forth.

During the War, the ACC made contributions to many good causes; the Red Cross, returning/wounded soldiers, disabled men and their dependents, and encouraging employees to buy War Bonds by having a payment deducted from their wages each week. By February 1917 they had contributed £6,120 to the War loans.[16]

In the years after the war there was major disruption in the coal industry, as the issue over whether or not it should be nationalised was fought over. In June 1919 the *Advertiser* produced a very informative, if slightly anti-worker, article which attempted to set out the record of what Alloa's coal industry had achieved during the war. It was not very favourable.[17]

	Tons of coal produced in Clackmannanshire	Persons employed above and below ground
1913	342,546 tons	1,264
1914	296,773	1,192
1915	309,945	981
1916	309,718	1,026
1917	303,967	1,061
1918	282,972	1,086

These figures show that wartime production had dropped and by quite a lot by 1918, even with a slightly increasing labour force.

Curiously, in the Industrial Retrospects of the Alloa press there was almost no mention of the coal industry.

THE GLASS WORKS

Things were going well for The Alloa Glass Work (AGW) in 1914. Annual output of bottles was eight million and a Glasgow brewer had offered to take the whole production. The outbreak of war caused a change for the worse. Lieut. Colonel Alexander Mitchell, as mentioned above, already a Deputy Chairman of the ACC, was also one of the chairmen of the AGW. He encouraged the workers to join up and it was hard for the rest to keep up rates of production. Carvel generously observed that 'The number of men, particularly in the bottle-house, was seriously reduced by the operation of the Military Service Acts, but those who were left rose to the occasion and gave of their best.'[18] The AGW had to fight hard to retain the rest of its workers; in June 1917 it asked the local tribunal for conditional exemption for nineteen workers, arguing that it had so severely pruned its work force already since 1914 that it could not do without them. Its plea was upheld.[19]

However, Carvel noted that 'A tremendous fillip was given to bottle-making during the war';[20] because there were no imports from Austria and Germany there was an increased demand and by 1915, with its new Owens machine, the AGW was producing 8.4 million bottles a year. There was a decrease in demand from distilleries due to government policy limiting their production, but this was compensated for by an increase in public demand for different types of lemonade.

By 1918 there was pressure on the AGW to release some of its Forth frontage land for ship building but it resisted this. The situation did not improve after the war: the lost demand for whisky bottles was never recovered and the soaring excise duty on whisky, the building up of replenished stocks in distillery warehouses and American prohibition all combined to limit the demand for bottles in this sector.

The Retrospects did not have very much to say about the AGW either.

TEXTILES

The local textiles industry benefitted right from the start of the war; by January 1915, it was reported that 'The boom in yarn and clothing material set most of the County factories working at full pressure...'[21] The Local Retrospect for 1916 recognised the significance of the war for Paton's Mills, commenting: 'It is fortunate that Kilncraigs factory, which for many years has been the sheet-anchor of the town's industrial prosperity, has been largely engaged during the war in the production of materials for the making of comforts for our soldiers and sailors, and that, as a consequence, there has been no lack of employment for the many workers. In order to keep pace with the demands...Messrs Paton's have been obliged to run both a day shift and a night shift and workers have been fortunate this year, as last, in participating in a substantial war bonus.'[22] The details of this 'third war bonus' were in the Directors' minutes in April 1916:[23]

> 1/- per week to all female workers
>
> 1/- per week to all male workers whose wages apart from bonuses are under 20/- per week
>
> 2/- per week to all male workers whose wages apart from bonuses are 20/- or more weekly

Two more bonuses came in 1916-17 and the Directors also gave a 10 per cent pay rise to everyone as from 1 September 1917.[24] Paton's may have employed as many as 1700 workers in total during the war years, so that was quite a lot of bonus pay.

Certainly Paton's Mills seem to have done very well in the war. In her book on the company, Isobel Grant Stewart recounted carefully that 'During the period of World War I, the company's works were engaged almost entirely in government contracts and the years 1914-1918 saw many changes in hours of labour, cost of living and remuneration of employees brought about by the exigencies of the time'.[25] Paton's Mills were in fact doing a greater deal better than that. The minute books of the Board of Directors are still available to study, and they shed interesting light on the progress of Paton's Mills during the war years and their decisions on some war-related issues. Firstly, the directorship of Paton's Mills was an incredibly small and close knit, inter-related group which really seemed to own most of the shares in the Company and gave themselves large rewards during the war.[26] In February 1915 they raised the pay of one of the directors when 'it was agreed on the motion...that the remuneration of A.D. Thomson, on account of the countless demands which had been made on him since the outbreak of the war, should be in the order of £2000 (pa) from August last...'; this was a pay rise backdated for six months.[27]

The Company was making a lot of money. In May 1916 'It was resolved to recommend that £112,500 be applied to paying a dividend of 15 per cent and bonus of 10 per cent, on ordinary shares, both free of income tax...' and they still managed to carry forward £72,000 to next year's account.[28] In fact, some of the spare cash was used when the directors authorised the Company to invest in a War loan; but, it was not British. In July 1916 'It was agreed to purchase a further 200,000 francs worth of the French war loan at 5 per cent through the agency of the Credit Lyonnais...'[29] In December 1917 the directors discussed the accounts and still announced a dividend of 15 per cent and bonus of 10 per cent, plus carrying forward £48,000 to next year. Business must have been going very well, since in their budgeting the directors noted that they were 'not... aware of any contingencies that now require to be provided for...'[30]

In August 1918 the directors of Paton's Mills held an extraordinary meeting to deal with a financial matter; they had a spare £225,000 in the Company's reserve fund and had been wondering what to do with it. They had seen, in July 1917, how the Distillers Company in Edinburgh had 'capitalised' a spare amount of cash which they had, by turning it into shares to give as a bonus to their shareholders.[31] Paton's directors, being in charge of a private company with very few shareholders, wondered if they could do the same. In November 1917, the Company's lawyers wrote to a senior King's Counsel (HP Macmillan), making the somewhat understated comment that Paton's was '... quite successful in business' and asked him if there were any problems in making this sort of financial transaction.[32] He replied that it was acceptable. The Company then borrowed a copy of the completed procedural form that Distillers Company had used so successfully, changed all the names, dates and figures to suit Paton's intentions and the directors of Paton's then approved a big cash transfer. They decided to turn £180,000 of their reserve fund into 18,000 shares worth £10 each, which would be divided between all shareholders in proportion to the number of shares they held already. The Company had been informed in July 1918 that HM Government did not object as long as it 'allows for proper provision of Income Tax, Excess Profits Duty and the Munitions Levy.' From August 1918 the share value of Paton's Mills therefore rose from £750,000 to £930,000, but all the wealth of the Company still remained in the hands of that very small clique.[33] The directors were in a position to make themselves very rich and didn't miss the opportunity. However, they also donated to worthy causes; in 1916 'It was decided to give the following... *viz* £250 to Princess Louise's Hospital for Limbless Soldiers and Sailors, £100 to Royal Blind Hospital Edinburgh for Blinded soldiers and sailors.'[34] No doubt they could afford it.

Moving from the directors, there is also evidence of the daily working life at Paton's Mills from the reminiscences recorded in The Hillfoots Textiles Oral Project between 1985 and 1988. One interviewee remembered the poor lighting which hindered her chances of weaving properly the tartan cloth for the Black Watch soldiers' uniforms. She also mentioned that they did a lot of khaki...'but we never got naval or airforce or anything like that. It [the khaki] was heavy stuff, especially the privates' cloth.'[35] This same worker remembered that they somehow 'improved' the officer's khaki cloth... commenting that 'We didnae do much to the khaki that the privates wore, we did more to the officer's cloth...they had finer stuff, lovely stuff they had.'

Another interviewee remembered that 'The war years were all khaki and Black Watch tartan and Argyll and Sutherland Highlanders tartan and Gordon tartan.

We had two looms going then with the khaki. It was solid work you see.'[36] Several interviewees remembered the changes in their work and lifestyle brought about by the war; 'Quite a lot of women went back to work. There was stacks of work, you couldn't get enough workers. Och aye, you could leave one factory and walk into the next one the next morning. You got 38s 7d a fortnight.'[37] Another remembered that 'We got the khaki work and it was big money. We made good money because there was never a thread broke. It was awful good work.'[38]

BREWING

It is sometimes hard to find sources for brewing which are specific to the development of the industry in Alloa. One assumes that some of the generalisations about the Scottish industry as a whole must have applied to Alloa. In 1914 Alloa had seven breweries, of which the largest and most famous was George Younger's. They found their business disturbed by the war. Sales abroad were reduced and transport problems at home limited their ability to reach their markets. Sales of bottled beer and stout remained fairly steady during the war years but even they declined.[39]

A photograph from just before the war of some of the raw materials for Younger's Brewery being unloaded at Alloa Wet Dock[40] (*Scottish Brewing Archive*)

There may have been a war in progress, but Younger's was always trying to do business and consolidate its markets. Back in 1896 it had set up a partnership with Dundee spirit merchant John Robertson and Co., to provide the beer and spirits for George White and Co.'s pubs in Newcastle upon Tyne. By 1914, Robertson's was trying to get out of this somewhat profitless deal and wanted to liquidate the co-owned company; they offered to sell their share to Younger's for £10,000. James Younger thought that was far too much. Younger's Brewery's lawyers also thought that Robertson's was using a bit of sharp practice in its accounting techniques and trying to change George White's balance sheet to make it look more favourable to them by re-valuing its property. Negotiations dragged on and somewhat acrimonious letters passed between the two partners on the ethics of their accountancy methods, until Robertson's made an offer to sell up for £8,000. On 25 November 1914, four months into the war, Younger's lawyers advised that 'We suppose that in the present exceptional times through which we are passing, you do not wish to buy out Messrs Robertson, particularly at such a price as £8,000...'; but Younger's had negotiated a slightly better deal and on 31 March 1915 they bought out the three shareholders in Robertson's for £7,000.[41] Younger's certainly did not let the war get in the way of what looked like a reasonable business deal.

Younger's Brewery faced a short strike of seventy-five of its bottle workers in March 1915. They wanted recognition for their union,[42] but the response from management was the traditionally patriotic assertion that this was an 'inopportune time when the country was engaged in a life-or-death struggle'.[43]

It seems that in late 1915 Younger's considered how else they might guarantee their supply of bottles, and contemplated going into partnership with Glasgow's Fountain Brewery to actually become a bottle maker. However, evidence in a letter from their lawyer shows that he advised against them doing this, since the Memoranda of Association which set up Younger's Brewery Company did not permit them to make this sort of co-ownership deal, as brewing was the only thing the company was set up to do.[44] It was recognised that breweries could have cooperages and therefore produce their own barrels, but not that they could also make bottles.

Alloa's breweries must also have suffered from a loss of manpower when their workers joined up. The *National Guardian* was the publication of the licensed trades and it published 'rolls of honour' right through the war, of workers in its related industries who had joined up. From Alloa, the roll for September 1914 included three men from Maclay's Brewery, and eleven from Calder's Shore Brewery.[45] There must have been some sort of standard response from the local employers towards their workers who either

Younger's bottle works in 1920. It would not have looked any different during the war.[46]
(*Scottish Brewing Archive*)

volunteered or were called up. In January 1916 it was noted at Arrol's Brewery that '2 clerks at Alloa, William Ross and William Syme, each £6 10s a month, have joined the forces. They desire to know whether, in the event of their safe return, their places will be kept open for them and any allowance will be granted. It was resolved to treat them in the same manner as other clerks... their places will be kept open for them and if the army pay and allowances be less than the amount they receive from the Company then the Company will make up the difference.'[47] That echoed what Alloa Burgh Council was doing for its employees. The idea that the employers had a collective approach is supported in May 1916, when the issue of calling up married men emerged, and the Alloa manager of Arrol's was instructed 'to ascertain what other breweries in Alloa are doing and we must fall into line with them as much as possible'.[48]

Maclay's Brewery found that 'the restrictions on raw materials and output imposed by the government [meant] the range of beers was greatly reduced'.[49] The availability of raw materials was always a problem for wartime brewers, and over the war years, Scottish beer production slumped to almost a third of its pre-war level[50] (1.85 million barrels down to 0.72 million barrels). In the case of Younger's, it was not quite so dramatic; by 1920 there was only 12.5 per cent less barrelage than in 1913.[51]

Arrol's was a local brewery but it was run from Newcastle upon Tyne. They had problems getting a good Head Brewer for the Alloa Brewery during the war and went through four of them. There is evidence that in 1915-16, Alloa Brewery was also having problems guaranteeing the quality of its beer; a letter from Edinburgh commented that the causes of the problem may be in dirty plant, poor quality hops and dirty barrels.[52] However, it was not clear if this was anything to do with the war itself.[53] There were certainly no references in the Alloa press to brewing issues and the Company must have kept it pretty quiet, because the Directors noted in their minutes that the beer 'was deplorable' and dumped a fair amount of it; so much so that they received £1,309 in returned duty from the Customs and Excise in 1918.[54] This did not seem to stop Arrol's turning in a fair wartime profit. Its printed Company balance sheet each December recorded:

1914	£8,700 profit
1915	£9,400
1916	£7,000
1917	£22,000
1918	£48,000

The dramatic increase in these profits bears a direct comparison with those of George Younger's shown below. Arrol's 1918 profits were considered so great that they were ordered to pay £12,000 in excess profits duty. Maclay's Brewery also seems to have been doing quite well towards the end of the war. At their first post-war Annual General Meeting, held in August 1919, they agreed to give a 'further dividend of 11 per cent less tax...' and to 'carry forward a balance of £5770 to meet Excess Profits Tax and depreciation'.[55] It looks as if they were having the same problem as Arrol's with excessive profits.

The brewing industry was greatly affected by government measures and regulation, what the *National Guardian* euphemistically called 'exacting conditions imposed by the Treasury',[56] where the Chancellor, Lloyd George, wanted to impose a beer tax of an extra penny per pint. The government took a major role in controlling drink retailing, including introducing licensing hours and regulating the specific gravity.

Brewers found they could not produce strong ales and this hit smaller breweries. Arrol's directors, in their 1918 Annual statement, noted 'the numerous difficulties caused by the War regulations and restrictions'.

Larger companies, with economies of scale, might be expected to weather the tougher economic conditions better, but later evidence from Younger's Brewery reveals the dramatic rise and equally dramatic fall in their fortunes during and as a result of the war. At the end of January 1923 George Younger wrote a note to the Company's Edinburgh lawyer, Mr Prosser, entitled 'The Value of Ordinary Shares'.[57] He complained about the lack of present financial reward from brewing and backed up his point with a note on the historic dividends of his company:

1914	2.5% dividend
1915–1917	2.5%
1918	5%
1919	10%
1920-21	5%
1922	nil

He then moved on to specifying the Company's historic net profits:

1913	£31,314
1914	£42,096
1915	£34.976
1916	£40.397
1917	£86,558
1918	£85,982
1919	£47,755
1920	loss of £10,908
1921	£8,575

It can be seen that Younger's, like Arrol's, had two terrific years at the end of the war, where profits doubled and dividends rose dramatically. They may not have been in the same league as Paton's Mills but like Paton's, Younger's Brewery was distributing those dividends among a very small number of major shareholders, almost all of whom were in the family.[58]

There is no record in Younger's Brewery archive of any big wartime bonuses for its employees, but Arrol's Brewery at least did them justice. At the end of December 1917 Arrol's directors noted that '£1500 had been reserved for the purposes of paying an additional remuneration. Mr Church [Alloa General Manager] and Mr Montgomery [Alloa Head Brewer] got £100 each, and the staff and foremen at Alloa got 'a sum equal to 10 per cent on their salaries and wages, paid to them... on 1 January 1918 in National War Bonds and War Savings Certificates when applicable'.[59] According to Arrol's Directors' minutes of 22 January 1918, Alloa staff received £357 worth of bonuses. The Directors' minutes for 17 December 1918 show that Arrol's employees got the same bonus again at the end of that year.

SHIPYARDS

Shipbuilding had been an early industry on the shores of the River Forth, but it had not grown or prospered very much until the start of the war. In fact, in March 1914 the *Journal* had reported rather dismally 'What is likely to be the last launch at Alloa for some time at least took place on Tuesday morning... when there was launched a single-decked steel screw steamer...'[60] Its pleasure can be sensed, therefore, when the Industrial Retrospect for January 1915 was able to comment that 'the prospect of re-opening the Kelliebank Shipyard has caused much satisfaction.'[61] It seems clear that the war kick-started Alloa's shipbuilding industry; one of the first war-linked ship-repair activities in Alloa occurred in the period up to February 1915, when a fleet of six steam drifters received a complete overhauling in Alloa's dry dock before being sent off for mine-sweeping duties in the North Sea.[62] The *Scotsman* commented that '1914 has proved a good year for business. Up to August trade proceeded satisfactorily, except for occasional labour difficulties here and there, and after the outbreak of war, shipbuilders have continued to be well employed...with a considerable amount of work in hand...' The *Scotsman* continued by pointing out that the tonnage produced by Jeffrey's Yard in 1914 was double what it had been in 1913 (four vessels were built instead of two).[63]

Forth Shipbuilding and Engineering began in the early part of 1916 and then the industry developed rapidly, with that company trying to take over the other yards. In August 1916, a 2,200 ton cargo ship called *The Countess of Mar* was launched from Kelliebank, the first to be produced by the Forth Shipbuilding Company.[64] This led to much satisfaction in the editorial column of the *Journal*,[65] which saw it as 'a revival of the industry in our midst'. Unfortunately, the ship itself did not last long; being torpedoed in the Bay of Biscay in August 1917 with a loss of twenty lives.[66]

Local Retrospect for 30 December 1916 noted that Jeffrey's Shipyard and Forthbank Shipyard had as much work as they could possibly undertake, with Jeffrey's Yard having launched its fourth steamer of the year, with another four steamers in hand.[67] One of the rare surviving photographs of shipbuilding in wartime Alloa is of three coasters from Jeffrey's Yard waiting to be fitted out in 1916. *Redstone* was successfully launched on 19 June 1916 by the wife of its Glasgow owner.[68] Its sister ship may have been *Blackstone*, which was launched from Jeffrey's Yard by the same lady in December 1914.[69] *Cargan* was launched in July 1916[70] and set sail on time to its Irish owners in December 1916.[71]

During the war, Jeffrey's Yard did very well and formed itself into a private limited company in July 1916 with four shareholder/directors.[72] It took on a number of

Three ships built by Jeffreys Yard 1915–1916 (*Clackmannanshire Archives and Local History Service*)

government contracts, including the construction of fenders, booms and boom mountings for Rosyth dockyards.[73] The company also made compound and triple expansion marine engines during the war years and the owners ploughed back profits into the company. During that time they employed about 400 male workers[74] and around

Notice of the launch of Portus Herculis (*Alloa Advertiser*)

fifty female workers.[75] Alloa's shipyards did not make warships as such, unlike in World War II when they produced tank landing craft. Their output was generally cargo ships which could have had a wartime use. This is supported by reminiscence; 'They were cargo ships. We never built any passenger ships. Some were 3 to 5 thousand tons so they were quite big ships.'[76] In another reminiscence, Dan [born 1905] recalled that 'They built some big ships. They used to come into the docks and get partly fitted out. I think the biggest was the *War Cherry*, I don't remember if it was the *War Plum* or the *War Plume*, but the crane was not big enough to put the boilers in.'[77]

When ships were launched they generally received an announcement in the local press. The launching of the *Portus Herculis* in April 1917 attracted 3,000 spectators and was well covered in the press, since it was the biggest ship launched so far.[78]

Both the *Advertiser* and *Journal* were, however, sadly lacking in photographs of the ships, the shipyards or the workers. They often had full page spreads of what they considered to be interesting pictures of the recent events at Kelliebank, but the photographs were usually of various local celebrities who had been invited to the launch of the ship.

However, at the launch of the *Portus Herculis*, the Director of Forth Shipbuilding Company, T.G. Owens Thurston went out of his way in his speech to praise the women workers in the shipyard. He said 'I am astonished at the good work these women are doing... the way the women workers are carrying out their duties is admirable...'[79] His generosity of spirit was matched by the generosity of his pocket, since he awarded a bonus of £1 to all skilled workers and 10 shillings to all women and labourers.[80]

As a further sign of the increasing recognition of the importance of Alloa's working women, the last ship to be launched by Forth Shipbuilding during the war, on Monday 4 November 1918, was launched by Miss Christina Ferguson, female worker from the yard. The *Advertiser* referred to her rather patronisingly as 'a humble employee', but the *Journal* noted proudly that 'Alloa can now boast of the first lady war worker to christen a vessel' and ran a big spread with several photographs.[81]

There was still a role for a couple of men as the foremen.[82] (*Alloa Journal*)

Reminiscence evidence from 1917 commented that 'the shipyards were very busy at that time, during World War I. You were deafened by the noise of the riveting machines, the hammering and the clanging, so it was a very busy place down there at that time.'[83] Another interviewee noted that 'There was a lot of women worked in the shipyards and they were there when the boats came to be fitted out. They did everything the women; it wouldn't have been a trade. Some of them married the men that worked with them. They would be a sort of plater's mate.'[84]

In August 1918, Alloa shipyards had a visit from a senior French officer, Capt. G Barbey, who gave a rousing speech about how important their work was.[85] His speech on France's war aims was reported at length in the local press.[86] The Admiralty clearly thought that it was well worth building up Alloa's shipbuilding industry, because in the last months of the war there were serious discussions with the Burgh Council about procuring buildings in Kelliebank to create a hostel for up to 250 shipyard workers.[87] The Admiralty was prepared to pay the refurbishment costs of £2,000. The Council seemed to drag its feet over this, however, and lost the chance when the Admiralty backed down on the urgency of this plan in October 1918 and merely requested that the Council should try to make available some good billets for the workers.[88]

(*Alloa Advertiser*)

The Industrial Retrospect noted on 28 December 1918 that the shipyards showed most evidence of the abnormal wartime prosperity.[89]

In 1918 Jeffrey's Yard launched:

Falavee	359 tons (wrecked in Carlingford Loch January 1942)
Calgorm	500 tons
Gracehill	500 tons (ran aground 1957)
War Colne	900 tons (launched in January 1919[90], scrapped in Holland 1956)

Forth Shipbuilding took over the Kelliebank Yard and made huge additions to the plant and machinery. It also took over Jeffrey's Yard in 1918 and now had 808 employees.[91] The *Journal*'s Retrospect then went on to proudly list the boats that Forth Shipbuilding had launched that year:

Orleans	2,475 tons	
War Pibroch	3,000 tons	(scrapped in France 1959)
War Clarion	3,000 tons	(torpedoed August 1944 on way to Juno Beach, Normandy)
War Platoon	3,000 tons	(scrapped in Greece 1960)
War Cherry	3,900 tons	(sunk after hitting a mine in Thames Estuary, November 1939)[92]

Forth Shipbuilding launched more vessels in 1919 which had been ordered and laid down in 1918. These included *War Melon*, *War Darenth* and *War Prune*.[93] These were the last of the H-type 'Standard ships' that had been ordered by the Government's Shipping Controller, but were now just sold to private shipping companies or allocated to different British shipping companies through Lord Inchcape's scheme. The last ship ordered by the Shipping Controller to be made in Alloa was *Allie*; it was launched in July 1919[94] and was the largest steamer out of the twenty-six ships built by Jeffrey's Yard since 1912.

There is evidence of a fairly long running dispute, starting in October 1918 and going on right through 1919, between the Forth Shipbuilding Company and the North British Railway Company. Forth Shipbuilding wanted extra rights for mooring vessels and fitting them out in the Wet Dock and the wharfs next to it. They also wanted

The *War Prune*, later re-named *SS Sunpath*, almost ready to be launched from Jeffrey's Yard [by then part of Forth Shipbuilding] in late 1918 or early 1919.[95] (*Clackmannanshire Archives and Local History Service*)

to put up a 100-ton crane. North British Railway Company either owned this land or had the rights to it and they must have had bad previous experiences with Forth Shipbuilding. Their lawyers told them in early June 1919 that 'There is a tendency on the part of this firm to take liberties with the Company's property in Alloa'. They were fitting out vessels and 'causing a good deal of work to be done on the dockside... A careful watch will have to be kept or the whole dockside will be converted into a yard by this firm'. This is what concerned the North British Railway Company: that if the Wet Dock was being used as a fitting out basin, this would deter normal traders from using it. They noted that Forth Shipbuilding had three ships there at one time, which 'was quite contrary to the spirit of the agreement.' They also disliked the somewhat brusque tone of a note from Forth Shipbuilding to the harbourmaster in mid-June 1919, which said 'We herewith intimate that our No. 36 SS *War Darenth* will be in the wet dock on Saturday first'. The North British Railway Company offered, quite generously, the use of the wharf with no charges beyond normal harbour dues, but on condition that only one boat was to be fitted out at a time. However, after much correspondence, by November 1919 Forth Shipbuilding decided to take no more action over the matter.[96]

AIRCRAFT PRODUCTION

Caudron was a French company and it opened its Alloa factory and airfield in 1916 on a 52-acre site between Forthbank and Bowhouse, right alongside the River Forth.[97] It became part of the British Caudron Company and operated for six years.[98] It made a plane of its own; the G3 seems to be the one in most of the photographs. It can be recognised because there was very little airframe behind the pilot's seat. The company also assembled Sopwith Camels, Sopwith Comets and the de Havilland-designed Royal Aircraft Factory BE2s. Adrian Ure has argued that Caudron <u>did</u> assemble Sopwiths, but is not convinced that this was done in the Alloa factory; he does offer evidence, however, that at least 50 BE2cs [numbers B6151-6200] were made in Alloa.[99]

There were quite a few reminiscences in Alloa Docks Oral History Project about the Caudron factory and the airfield; indeed, that is the chief source of information. One interviewee remembered that 'It was just a metal structure, with corrugated iron. It was quite a big place. They took so many planes away each week, maybe three or four. The same pilot came for them and flew them round and about to give them a trial and he went away west.'[100]

Another interviewee remembered the very happy atmosphere in the works with people singing away and that '...mostly the women were with the fabrics, sewing. We

(*Alloa Advertiser*)

all took our turn in what I told you was doping (*This means putting a very intoxicating and inflammable liquid onto the fabric covering the aircraft, which then dried and helped to shrink it into the right shape round the wooden airframe.* We had a special big shed for the dope, not to begin with but the men complained for some could not stand the fumes...the girls did the doping there; they would put it on with a brush. I think it was three coats and then varnished.'[101] She continued with the observation that the wages were just over £2 a week which included three nights' overtime, and 'that was considered a good job'.[102]

Some of the Caudron girls[103] (*Clackmannanshire Archives and Local History Service*)

A Caudron G3 plane over Alloa during the war, being flown by Rene Desoutter.[104]

In the middle of July 1917 there was a big fund raising week in Alloa for the Red Cross, with all sorts of activities; one of these was a fete in Alloa Park. Before this fete, Caudron had two aeroplanes flying low over Alloa dropping handbills reminding the public of it.[105] At the fete itself, they offered joyrides at half a guinea (10/6) a time; there were 16 flights and they raised £70 for the Red Cross. The *Advertiser* asserted that these flights were largely taken up by ladies,[106] although the lady in the photograph below was the daughter of the managing director of Caudron, so she was possibly already an experienced flyer showing how it was done, rather than a paying customer.

Girl in Caudron plane (*Advertiser*)

Caudron tried to expand but did not have much success. One interviewee remembered that 'They were intending to build sea-planes because they had a big jetty down by the river and there was three rails and a platform on it and they could haul it up and down... [but] they never built them.'[107] A female worker who was interviewed recalled 'the big exodus when the aeroplane works stopped'[108] but, talking more tersely of the company's demise, a male interviewee said '...and then the war finished, it collapsed'.[109]

ENDNOTES

1. *Alloa Journal* 2 Jan 1915 p. 3 col. 1
2. *Alloa Advertiser* 30 Dec 1916 p. 2 col. 5
3. *Alloa Journal* 6 Jan 1917 p. 3 col. 3
4. *Alloa Advertiser* 29 Dec 1917 p. 3 col. 3
5. *Alloa Advertiser* 28 Dec 1918 p. 3 col. 3
6. *Alloa Journal* 29 May 1915 p. 2 col. 7
7. *Alloa Advertiser* Retrospect 30 Dec 1916 p. 2 col. 5
8. All this is found in one of the boxes of Alloa Coal Company's documents in the National Archives. BT2/3972
9. This pit is near Cowie, Stirlingshire.
10. J.L. Carvel *One Hundred Years in Coal* (1944) pp. 104-109
11. *Alloa Journal* 22 May 1915 p. 2 col. 7
12. *Alloa Journal* 23 Oct 1915 p. 2 col. 7
13. *Alloa Journal* 22 May 1915 p. 2 col. 7
14. J.L. Carvel p. 106
15. *Alloa Advertiser* 19 Aug 1916 p. 2 col. 4
16. *Alloa Journal* 17 Feb 1917 p. 3 col. 1
17. *Alloa Advertiser* 21st June 1919 p. 3 col. 3
18. John L Carvel *Alloa Glass Works* (1953) Chapter 6 p. 52
19. *Alloa Journal* 2 June 1917 p. 2 col. 5
20. John L Carvel *Alloa Glass Works* (1953) Chapter 6 p. 51
21. *Alloa Journal* 2 Jan 1915 p. 3 col. 2
22. *Alloa Advertiser* 30 Dec 1916 Local Retrospect
23. Meeting of Directors of John Paton and Sons Ltd minute book 27 April 1916
24. *Alloa Journal* 25 Aug 1917 p. 2 col. 3, *Alloa Advertiser* 1 Sept 1917 p. 3 col. 1
25. Isobel Stewart *The Romance of Paton's Yarns 1813-1920* (1982)
26. Meeting of Directors of John Paton and Sons Ltd minute book 27 Sept 1918 reveals that the vast majority of the shares were held by about 20 people.
27. Meeting of Directors of John Paton and Sons Ltd minute book 25 Feb 1915
28. Meeting of Directors of John Paton and Sons Ltd minute book 31 May 1916
29. Meeting of Directors of John Paton and Sons Ltd minute book 20 July 1916
30. Meeting of Directors of John Paton and Sons Ltd minute book December 1916
31. Scotsman article 21 July 1917
32. The problem was that companies who kept money in their 'contingency fund' were entitled to transfer it into shares, but Paton's Mills kept theirs in a 'reserve fund'; the question was, were these the same thing? H.P. Macmillan obviously thought they were.

33 This is all to be found in box GD 457/180 of Paton's Mills documents in the National Archives of Scotland.
34 Meeting of Directors of John Paton and Sons Ltd minute book 17 May 1916
35 The Hillfoots Textiles Oral Project, Nellie born 1901
36 The Hillfoots Textiles Oral Project, Bessie born 1903
37 The Hillfoots Textiles Oral Project, James born 1901
38 The Hillfoots Textiles Oral Project, Isabell born 1895
39 *A Short History of George Younger*, Alloa (1925) p. 23
40 Photograph reproduced courtesy of The Scottish Brewing Archive
41 Box GD 457/173, George Younger's documents, National Archives of Scotland.. C. McMaster in *Alloa Ale* (p. 62) states that Younger's acquired the rest of George White in 1919, but my reading of the evidence suggests that Younger's effectively owned George White's from 1915, since there were now no other shareholders. Three directors of Younger's Brewery, George and his two sons, Charles and James, bought 1,850 £10 shares for about £3 15s each.
42 *Alloa Journal* 27 Feb 1915 shows the bottleworks had been declared 'non-union'
43 *Alloa Circular* 3 March 1915 p. 3 col. 5
44 Box GD 457/172, George Younger's documents in the National Archives of Scotland
45 *National Guardian* 19 Sept 1914
46 Photograph reproduced courtesy of The Scottish Brewing Archive
47 Directors of Arrol's Brewery Ltd minutes 12 Jan 1916
48 Directors of Arrol's Brewery Ltd minutes 10 May 1916
49 Charles McMaster *Alloa Ale* (1984)
50 Ian Dunnachie *History of Brewing Industry in Scotland*
51 Extract from the letter referred to in footnote.[55] National Archives of Scotland GD 457/173
52 Which led to the second of the four head brewers losing his job
53 Letter in The Scottish Brewing Archive
54 Directors of Arrol's Brewery Ltd minutes 26 Feb 1918
55 *Alloa Advertiser* 23 Aug 1919 p. 3 col.1
56 National Guardian 28 Nov 1914 p. 25
57 All this is found in one of the boxes of George Younger's documents in the National Archives. GD 457/173
58 Box GD 457/173 Younger's documents in the National Archives of Scotland
59 Directors of Arrol's Brewery Ltd minutes 20 Dec 1917
60 *Alloa Journal* 21 March 1914 p. 2 col.6
61 *Alloa Journal* 2 Jan 1915 Industrial Retrospect
62 *Alloa Journal* 6 Feb 1915 p. 2 col.7
63 Scotsman 21 Dec 1914 p. 3
64 *Alloa Journal* 2 Sept 1916 p. 3 col.2 A group of wounded soldiers from Arnsbrae Hospital received an invitation to the launch and were 'accommodated on a special platform near the bow of the vessel.'

65 *Alloa Journal* 2 Sept 1916 p. 1 col.4
66 http://www.wrecksite.eu/wreck.aspx?37428 ???
67 *Alloa Advertiser* 30 Dec 1916 Local Retrospect
68 *Alloa Advertiser* 24 June 1916 p. 2 col.3
69 *Alloa Journal* 19 Dec 1914 p. 2 col.6
70 *Alloa Advertiser* 22 July 1916 p. 2 col.4
71 *Alloa Journal* 16 Dec 1916 p. 4 col.3
72 *Alloa Advertiser* 1 July 1916 p. 2 col.4
73 *Alloa Advertiser*. An article originally taken from the Glasgow Herald, written in early 1919.
74 *A Short History of Jeffrey's Shipyard in Alloa*, written by David Jeffrey's son, published by Alloa Library in 1984
75 *Alloa Journal* 21 April 1917 p. 3 col.1
76 Alloa Docks Oral History Project, William born in 1904
77 Alloa Docks Oral History Project 1983–85
78 *Alloa Advertiser* 28 April 1917 p. 3 col.3
79 *Alloa Journal* 28 April 1917 p. 3 col.4
80 *Alloa Advertiser* 28 April 1917 p. 3 col.4. The women workers at Forth Shipbuilding could be generous too; at the end of March 1917 they paid for and organised a social entertainment and dance at the Co-operative Hall for 50 wounded soldiers from Arnsbrae Hospital. See *Alloa Journal* 7 April 1917 p. 3 col.1
81 *Alloa Journal* 9 November 1918 p. 3 col.1-2, *Alloa Advertiser* 9 November 1918 p. 2 col.5 and p. 3 col.1. She stood in for two 'celebrity' guests who were indisposed due to influenza. In their reports of the launching, neither newspaper actually noted what the ship was called! It was probably 'War Cherry' [see footnote [92]]
82 *Alloa Journal* 17 May 1917
83 Alloa Docks Oral History Project, Mr E born in 1907
84 Alloa Docks Oral History Project, Sarah born 1907
85 *Alloa Journal* 10 Aug 1918 p. 3 col.1
86 *Alloa Advertiser* 10 Aug 1918 p. 2 col.4-5
87 Alloa Burgh Council minute book Sept 1918
88 Alloa Burgh Council minute book 14 Oct 1918
89 *Alloa Advertiser* 28 Dec 1918 p. 3 col.3
90 *Alloa Journal* 18 Jan 1919 p. 3 col. 1. The ship was launched by Miss Gifford Moir.
91 *Alloa Advertiser* 28 Dec 1918 p. 3 col.3
92 *Alloa Journal* 8 Feb 1919 'War Cherry' was launched on 4 November 1918 and was still being fitted out in 1919 when an accident led to three workers being seriously injured.
93 *War Melon* was launched in March 1919, *Alloa Journal* 3 May 1919 p. 3 col.3. *War Melon* was later renamed SS *Macgregor* and was sunk by gunfire from a German U-boat off Puerto Rico in 1942. *War Prune* was launched on 1 May 1919 and left Alloa docks in October 1919 as SS *Sunpath*, but

was eventually bought by a Japanese company and renamed *Taikai Maru*. It was sunk in 1944 by American carrier-based aircraft near Okinawa. *War Darenth* was launched on 3 May 1919, *Alloa Advertiser* 10 May 1919 p. 3 col.2. It was renamed several times during its working life and was eventually scrapped in 1968.

94 *Alloa Advertiser* 2 Aug 1919 p. 3 cols.2-3 By 1941 the British government had requisitioned this ship (now sailing under the name of SS *Trsat*) from its Yugoslavian owners; it was bombed and sunk by German aircraft on 7 Sept 1941, 7 miles off Kinnaird Head, whilst travelling from Reykjavik to Hull, with the loss of three crew.

95 Photograph reproduced courtesy of Clackmannanshire Archives and Local History Service

96 Box BR/HRP.S/8 Alloa Harbour documents in the National Archives of Scotland

97 *Alloa Advertiser* 31 July 1915

98 See *Alloa Advertiser* article on 16 April 1998 for interview with Alloa centenarian who worked in this factory. Photo reference also

99 Adrian Ure *Flight From the Forth* (1986)

100 Alloa Docks Oral History Project, David born in 1905

101 Alloa Docks Oral History Project, Mary born 1899

102 You can see that she was earning not a lot less than the wage that a coal miner [on 9s 6d a day] was getting at the same time!

103 Photograph reproduced courtesy of Clackmannanshire Archives and Local History Service

104 It appears that Caudron aeroplanes were not really very good. Some were sent out to serve on the Eastern Front over Romania and Galicia, where they were not up against very strong opposition. The Australian Air Force also used them in Mesopotamia.

105 *Alloa Advertiser* 14 July 1917 p. 3 col.2

106 *Alloa Journal* 14 July 1917 p. 2 col.5 Caudron also put on aviation displays in the county during War Weapons Week in April 1918. See *Alloa Journal* [6] April 1918 p. 3 col. 3

107 Alloa Docks Oral History Project, David born 1905

108 Alloa Docks Oral History Project, Mary born 1899

109 Alloa Docks Oral History Project, David born 1905

CHAPTER 3

THE LANDOWNERS AND INDUSTRIALISTS

People always seem to be interested in the wartime lives of the 'toffs' and the families from the 'big hoose'. In the case of Alloa's prominent families, the landowners and industrialists, did they do better or worse than the common folk during the war...did they suffer especially or have greater losses? Generally it was expected that this upper class would be the leaders and officers; that they would somehow be more heroic, being made of 'the right stuff'. This chapter will show that across the local 'big families' there was a bit of that; no generals, but plenty of officers, bravery and medals, then wounds and deaths in due proportion.

BRUCE

This family has always had local connections although it was more to Clackmannan than Alloa. However, since they came first alphabetically as well as first in order of heroism, I broke my opening rule of not allowing my gaze to fall more than a mile from the centre of Alloa, to include their story, although, for obvious reasons, they are not recorded in the Burgh of Alloa Roll of Honour. There are two tales of war in the Bruce family... both concerning the Master of Burleigh...though not the same person!

In 1868 Alexander Hugh Bruce, eldest son of one branch of the family, Bruce of Kennet, became 6th Lord Balfour of Burleigh. He had two sons, Robert and George; the eldest, and heir, was given the title of the Master of Burleigh.

The Hon. Robert Bruce, Master of Burleigh, was a professional soldier; he had joined the 2 Battalion Argyll & Sutherland Highlanders in 1898 and served in the Boer War in 1900. He had also served in India and Egypt (1910-13), gaining various

Robert and George Bruce of Balfour as children
(*National Portrait Gallery*)

Master of Burleigh, killed 1914
(*Alloa Advertiser*)

medals and commendations for his work[1] and rising to the rank of Captain by 1910. His fine career was cut short, to the shock of everyone, when he was killed only twenty-two days after the outbreak of war. He embarked from Britain with the 2nd Argylls as part of the British Expeditionary Force on 10 August 1914[2] and was shot at Le Cateau on 26 August 1914; he was killed only four days after his engagement had been announced in the local press.[3] The War Diary of the 2nd Battalion recorded that 'At 1.30pm Major Maclean led an advance of 2 platoons of 'C' Company (Capt Bruce and Lieut Gilikson) through shellfire against German infantry'[4] and at some time during the afternoon Capt. Bruce was wounded, before being killed.[5]

A soldier in the Argylls, Private Reid, witnessed some of the action concerning Captain Bruce's last moments, and a typically heroic account appeared in the *Journal* in September,[6] describing how he '... saw the officer take command of thirty men but sometime later they were cut off from the regiment and captured. In the course of the fighting Captain Bruce flung away his sword and seized a service rifle which had belonged to a soldier who had been killed, and fought side by side with his men.'[7] In a different issue, the *Journal* reported Private Reid's views on Captain Bruce again, that 'He was too brave if anything, he simply wanted to be at them...'[8] Capt. Bruce was reported missing, and it was hoped he had been taken prisoner. The confirmation of his death was not made generally known until early November 1914.[9] He was one of the first casualties to be announced in the local press and, as such a prominent person, it created a shock wave.[10]

The death of the heir meant that the Hon. George Bruce now became Master of Burleigh (from 1914-1921).[11] He had a very different and more successful war than that of his brother, surviving it and ultimately becoming 7th Lord Balfour of Burleigh himself in 1921. He joined the Argylls in August 1914 and served with them until he was wounded in the head by shrapnel at Neuve Chapelle in early 1915. He was not allowed to return to the front and instead was found other duties.[12]

The picture of Captain Bruce was drawn by the war artist Muirhead Bone in November 1916.
(*The Secrets of Rue St Roch*, Janet Morgan)

He became a Captain in the Intelligence Corps from May 1916, based at Amiens.[13] His work there earned him the first of his four 'mentioned in despatches', before he was transferred to Paris in January 1917.

The local press did not get to hear much about his activities during the war, but the *Advertiser* reported him coming home in January 1917 and that he was, at that time, Chief of the Intelligence Dept. at Amiens.[14] The *Journal* noted that he was awarded the Belgian *Croix de Chevalier* medal in October 1917.[15] He rose to become a Brevet Major in the 7th Argylls.

The most interesting account of his wartime actions was written by his daughter-in-law in *The Secrets of Rue St Roch*, which tells the story of Captain Bruce and the underground espionage mission which he set up behind enemy lines. In 1917, based at 41, Rue St Roch in Paris, he organised a spy ring of intrepid men and women, including housewife turned code expert Madame Lise Rischard and Belgian adventurer and balloonist Baschwitz Meau, all of whom risked their lives by infiltrating German-held territory to gather intelligence. Captain Bruce kept a set of files from his Paris office and these were only rediscovered in 1995. Official War Office records were destroyed both in 1919 and during World War II, so the documents kept by Captain Bruce are very important and enabled Janet Morgan to reconstruct a complete account of her late father-in-law's espionage mission.

ERSKINE

This family was Alloa's aristocracy, their titles going back centuries. The only member of the family who was involved in the war was John Francis Ashley, Lord Erskine, heir to his father, the 12th Earl of Mar and Kellie.

Lord Erskine was born in April 1895 so he was old enough to join up in 1914. What followed was a somewhat underwhelming military career, where the local press did not get much information about what he was doing or where he was doing it. He had joined the 3rd Argylls as a probationary 2nd Lieutenant in February 1914,[16] so when war was declared in August 1914 he was able to report for

Lord Erskine (*Alloa Advertiser*)

duty within three days.[17] He then went to France with the 2nd Battalion of the Argylls in the British Expeditionary Force and fought with them during the Battle of the Aisne, serving until the end of the first Battle of Ypres, when he was invalided home.[18] There were clearly difficulties in sending any of this information back to Alloa, because on 1 October his mother was still writing to him in France, saying 'I hope you got the baccy from Edinburgh and the chocolates etc. from Harrods – if you want socks and shirts I can send these to you also…'[19], but three days later she realised he must have actually been in action, because she wrote 'I just got your letter of 24th today. I saw one casualty among A + S hrs. – but didn't know you were there until I got your letter …I am thankful those shells around you did so little damage. The situation on the Aisne is very nearly finished, for all accounts the Germans must retreat. I hope it will be a crushing and decisive defeat and that they will be in an absolute rout.'

She went on to tell him that the Prince of Wales[20] had written to her to say that 'he has always kept every letter you have ever written to him… Poor little soul – he does so long to be where you are, away fighting, and I hope he will be allowed to go out on French's staff sometime soon.' In what appears to be an unsubtle plea to get him to write more often, she ended by saying that 'It is a cruel time for wives and mothers this war. One is simply always longing for news'. She obviously had not realised that he had been injured, but in early November the local press reported that Lord Erskine had been 'invalided home from the Expeditionary Force on two months leave',[21] without being more specific about any of the details. By November 1914 he was fit enough to give a talk to the local Territorials in Sauchie, where it was revealed by one of the other speakers that 'He has got an accident by a piece of shrapnel'.[22] Lord Erskine was there to drum up support for the war and gave a typical 'recruiting speech' in which he underplayed the ability of the navy to defend Britain's shores from invasion and overplayed the desolation a German invasion would cause.

A few more precise details on Lord Erskine's early military career can be found in two sources in the archives of the Argyll & Sutherland Highlanders Museum in Stirling Castle. They have the War Diary of the 2nd Battalion and also the Battalion's 1914 Reinforcement Book showing which officers arrived, when and from where, and then what happened to them. Lord Erskine arrived for his duties with the 2nd Battalion on 19 September 1914, when the War Diary reported that 'Captains Ure and Moorhouse, 2nd Lieutenants Liddell, Lothian and Lord Erskine (3rd A&SH) and Lieut. Blacklock (1st A&SH) joined from base and were taken on strength.'[23] Interestingly, of these six men, two were killed within two months, one was awarded

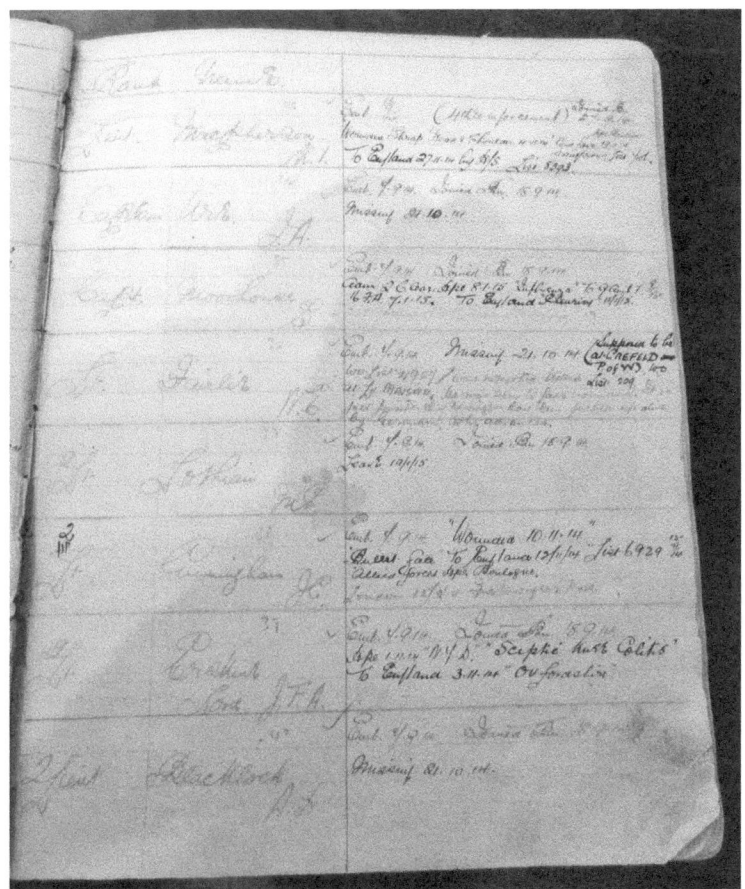

A list of Lord Erskine's injuries
(Argylls Reinforcement Book, Argyll and Sutherland Highlanders Museum, Stirling)

a VC but died later of wounds, while Lord Erskine and two others survived. Lord Erskine certainly landed in the thick of it by joining the 2nd Battalion; they were in action right through the end of September and into October at Bailleul, Vlamertinge and Fromelles, but an especially tough time was in late October. On 21 October for instance, the battalion was at Le Maisnil; the War Diary reported that at 6.15 am 'A' Company was brought up to extend their line sideways to link with the Royal Welsh Fusiliers because the Germans were attacking from the direction of Radighem. There was heavy fighting all day, with some companies surrounded and being lost, which led to two Captains, two Lieutenants and 200 men being counted as missing.[24] At 6.15 pm the War Diary recorded that '1st Platoon, 'A' Coy (Lord Erskine 2/Lieut.) still to come in.' and finally recorded at 12 midnight; '2nd Lieut. Lord Erskine's platoon marched in'.[25] That had been a very long day for him and his men and not one that could really have been called a success. He may also have been involved in the heavy fighting which continued for the rest of October.

There were no more references to Lord Erskine in the Battalion's War Diary, but what happened next was recorded in entries in the 2nd Battalion's 1914 Reinforcement Book. This shows that Lord Erskine was hospitalised on 1 November 1914 with 'NYD'.[26] There then followed a (bizarrely mis-spelt) diagnosis that he had 'Sceptic Knee Colitis', which led to him being invalided home to England on board the hospital ship 'SS *Oxfordshire*'[27] on 3 November 1914. There may be a missing comma between 'Knee' and 'Colitis' in the account, which would make more sense of the report of Lord Erskine's 'accident with a piece of shrapnel', probably the cause of his septic knee.

It looks, therefore, as if Lord Erskine had an heroic and difficult two months of combat on the Western Front, and after that served on home duties. After two months' leave he transferred to the 3rd [Reserve] Battalion of the Scots Guards as a 2nd Lieutenant in early February[28] and served with them, based in Wellington Barracks, London.[29] He was confirmed as a Lieutenant in the Scots Guards on 15 May 1915.[30] He took his military training duties seriously and had attended the Machine Gun Course and the Lewis Gun (special class) course by December 1915. Army Form B199A shows that he was appointed to be ADC to the Earl of Errol on 8 January 1916, but in fact this only lasted until 16 March 1916,[31] when he relinquished the appointment. He then continued on home service in the Scots Guards for the rest of the war.

He was rarely mentioned in the local press, until it was suddenly full of his 'coming of age', or 'reaching his majority' as the phrase went, in April 1916, but his military career to date was not mentioned. He had got his commission in the Scots Guards and was now also a Commander in the Royal Naval Volunteer Reserve.[32] The *Journal*, in reporting Alloa Burgh Council's messages of congratulation to him at the end of April, mentioned that he was 'on active service' without specifying where.[33] He came home to celebrate his 21st birthday and the photograph in the *Journal* showed him sitting with his family and distinguished guests[34] in front of Alloa House.[35]

He was home again in September 1916[36] to help launch the first ship from Forth Shipbuilding's Kelliebank yard (the ship was named after his mother) and that was all there was in terms of public knowledge of his wartime military career; for the remaining two years of the war there is almost a complete blank about Lord Erskine in the local press. A reference to him attending 'a small dinner party given by the King

(Alloa Advertiser)

and Queen' at Windsor Castle in May 1918 [37] was followed by another in the *Advertiser* or *Journal* in 1919, when he was engaged then married.[38] He resigned his commission as from 21 January 1920.[39]

Several peerage websites indicate that he had risen to the rank of Major by the end of the war,[40] although the Burgh of Alloa Roll of Honour listed him only as a Lieutenant in the Scots Guards and Army Form B199A showed the same rank at his demobilisation in 1921. There was no reference to this 'promotion' in the local press or about the start of his career in politics (MP for Weston-Super-Mare in the 1920s and 1930s). He died in 1953, having never succeeded to the Earldom himself, as his father outlived him. The eldest of Lord Erskine's four sons became 13th Earl of Mar and Kellie in 1955.[41]

It appears that, through no fault of his own, Lord Erskine did not distinguish himself particularly during the war. He was a junior officer who, perhaps less than fully fit after his heroic first two months in 1914, was assigned to home duties rather than returning to the Front. His younger brother, Francis Walter Erskine, was born in 1899 and was old enough to serve as a Lieutenant in the Scots Guards in the last months of the war. He is also listed in the Burgh of Alloa Roll of Honour.

It is only fair to note that whilst the Alloa folk may have heard little about the activities of Lord Erskine, they heard and read plenty about his parents, the Earl and Countess of Mar & Kellie. They were both prominent and indefatigable throughout the war in organising fundraising, chairing war committees and in providing local leadership. Barely a week went by without a report in the local press of their activities within the community, or their exhortations to it, in their attempt to keep up enthusiasm for the fight.

The Countess of Mar & Kellie prepares to hand over the bullock which was the prize in the July 1917 auction to raise money for Red Cross funds. It raised £56[42] (*Alloa Journal*)

The Burgh Council recognised in 1919 that it had not really given due honour to Lord Erskine when he attained his majority in April 1916, due to the war being in progress. It therefore organised a public subscription which raised £155 [43] and with this money commissioned a portrait of Lord Erskine which it planned to give him at the end of March or early April 1921.[44]

FORRESTER-PATON

The Forrester-Paton family were the major shareholders in John Paton, Son & Co. Ltd, who produced textiles. They were the biggest local employer and probably the main benefactors to the town of Alloa. In 1914 the head of the family and Managing Director was Alexander P Forrester-Paton,[45] who had three sons and a daughter. The sons were Alexander, John and Ernest and they were all old enough to serve in the armed forces during World War I, yet there are **no** references in the local press to any active military service of these three men; indeed, one is hard pressed to find any reference at all to two of the sons. The likely explanation was that they were exempt, since they would have held senior positions in the business, an important war industry; this was indeed *partly* the case.

There are two clues to a hidden story behind the Forrester-Paton family's war contribution. One appears in the Directors' minutes for September 1918, which stated that they had received 'A telegram and letter dated 23 July from Mr Forrester-Paton at Malta[46]... resigning his position as a director... his decision was dictated by the desire to free the Company from the disability it laboured under owing to his being technically a director though out of the country for over two years and having taken no part in the affairs of the Company. As a consequence the Company was faced with the prospect of his brother Mr A. Forrester-Paton, Director, being refused exemption from military service. This would reduce the number of acting directors to two and throw on them the very onerous and indeed impossible burden...'[47] This letter reveals that the only war-eligible member of the Forrester-Paton family still in the UK did indeed have to appear before a tribunal to be exempted from military service and that there was a risk of him losing that exemption because of a non-active director, John Forrester-Paton, who was living in Malta.

The second clue is a very interesting fragment of a letter, only pages 2–3 of which exist. It has no precise date and no addressee or signature, but it appears to be a letter (of appeal) in the middle of 1918, to the Burgh Tribunal explaining why, in the case of the previous conditional exemption of Alexander Forrester-Paton, he should be granted exemption again. The letter explains the difficulties the Company would have in being properly run: '... Some directors have died (one an elderly gentleman partly as a consequence of his efforts to carry on in war conditions). Another director is a staff officer in France, having been engaged continuously there almost since the outset. Another of the Directors unfortunately is a conscientious objector. He was in a minority of one on the board and resigned office. He is now abroad in connection with work for YMCA. It is quite impossible to get any assistance from him. That left:

Mr Procter
Mr J. Graeme Thomson
Mr Alex. Forrester-Paton – the gentleman whose case is now in question.

What the Company, that is really Mr Procter, submits is that business cannot be carried on by himself alone. Increasing burdens on himself and his remaining colleagues are aggravated by the growing demands from the naval and military authorities and the difficulty of carrying on in war conditions.'[48]

The letter went on to say that on 12 June 1917 'conditional exemption was granted by the local tribunal to various persons in employment of the company (13 employees) including Mr Alexander Forrester-Paton',[49] but on 11 June 1918 'this case had been considered again by the tribunal and Alex. Forrester-Paton's exemption was withdrawn'. The letter ends here – there is no page 4.

It appears that, until the middle of 1918, John Paton, Son & Co. Ltd. was essentially being run by the three directors listed above (with a fourth in Malta) and in June 1918 the Burgh Tribunal refused to exempt Mr Alex. Forrester-Paton. The letter quoted above[50] seems to have been addressed to the tribunal, explaining that the Malta director had now resigned, leaving just three to carry the workload and pleading for the continued exemption of Alex. Forrester-Paton.[51] Nothing of this appeared in the local press.

We have already noted that a common response of the Burgh Tribunal to requests for exemption was to grant it on condition that the person claiming exemption then joined the local volunteer regiment. This had clearly been the case for Alex. Forrester-Paton following his June 1917 exemption, because the *Advertiser* in March 1918 noted that he had been promoted from a temporary 2nd Lieutenant to a temporary Lieutenant in the Clackmannanshire Regiment.[52] One suspects that there may have been a happy outcome to the June 1918 withdrawal of exemption, because the *Journal* of 28 August 1918 announced that Alex. Forrester-Paton had been appointed as a Lieutenant in the County Volunteers.[53] It seems that the Burgh Tribunal had granted his further exemption after all, and he had been given a promotion to a permanent rank as well.

YOUNGER

This was a commercial family who were ennobled, a family with two main branches, the senior branch based in Gargunnock and the other at Arnsbrae House.[54] They were all closely connected to Alloa by their brewing empire, which was still run from offices based in the town, as well as by the fact that the second surviving son married into the Paton family.[55]

By 1914 the head of the family was Sir George Younger, Baronet (1911) who became 1st Viscount Younger of Leckie in 1923. He had already lost one son, Edward, killed aged nineteen in the Boer War in 1901 and he had two more sons, James and Charles, who had marked the loss of their elder brother by commissioning a chancel screen in Alloa' St John's Church, and an ornate silver plaque, decorated with a fine enamel by Phoebe Anna Traquair, describing his death.

By 1914, as the *National Guardian* expressed it, these two brothers were '...at the front with their regiments'.[56]

Like so many sons of the upper classes, Charles Frearson Younger seemed to have a glittering career ahead of him; he had what the *Journal* neatly called 'gilt-lined prospects...'[57] He had been educated at Winchester and New College, Oxford;[58] he was a skilful cricketer who had played regularly for Clackmannan County, Grange and I Zingari, a travelling side.[59] He played for Scotland against the South African touring team in 1912. He married in June 1913 and was a director in the family brewing firm,[60] but he lost little time in joining up when war was declared, enlisting in the Lothians and Borders Horse on 29 August 1914.[61] He was thirty-one when he died of wounds sustained in action on 21 March 1917 on

Charles Frearson Younger
(*Winchester College*)

the Somme, and was buried at Aveluy Communal Extension cemetery, near Albert. The *Journal* bemoaned his loss in the slightly flowery language of the time; 'He died the death of a young patriot, with his face to his country's enemy; and a soldier's death and a hero's grave are his'.[62] Seven years later his widow Marjory was among the special guests at the unveiling of Alloa's war memorial in 1924.[63]

The other and now sole surviving son James[64] had been serving with the Fife and Forfar Yeomanry in Gallipoli, Salonika and Egypt for most of the war, being invalided from Gallipoli through frostbite.[65] By 1916 there were already signs of what would become an illustrious military career when he was mentioned in despatches in September.[66] The rest of his story can be found in Chapter 14 on Alloa's bravest soldiers.

Captain James Paton Younger was the son of James Younger, previously resident at Arnsbrae (the family also lived at Mount Melville, near St Andrews, built in 1905, so they were not resident at Arnsbrae all the time by then) before lending it as a soldiers' convalescent home from April 1915 to February 1919.[67] J.P. Younger was the cousin of James and Charles; their fathers were brothers. He, like them, joined up quickly; 'When he enlisted at the outbreak of the war he was finishing his education at Oxford.' He joined the 3rd Argylls but served in the 2nd battalion and was wounded in September 1917.[68] Somewhat curiously, Alloa did not seem to want to take much credit for his military service and his name does not appear in the Burgh of Alloa Roll of Honour. This is strange, since there must have been a very strong local connection; after all, he later lived at Arnsbrae himself, became Managing Director of Younger's Brewery in 1930, following his cousin James; was Alloa's Provost between 1932-1938,[69] served as Lord Lieutenant of Clackmannanshire between 1955-1966 and was knighted.

J.P. Younger's name is in the 1914 Reinforcement Book of the 2nd Argylls, indicating that he joined the battalion in January 1915,[70] having travelled to France from Southampton on the *Normannia*.[71] Coincidentally, higher up on the same page is the reference to the arrival in the battalion of Robert Gifford Moir, whose story features in Chapter 14.

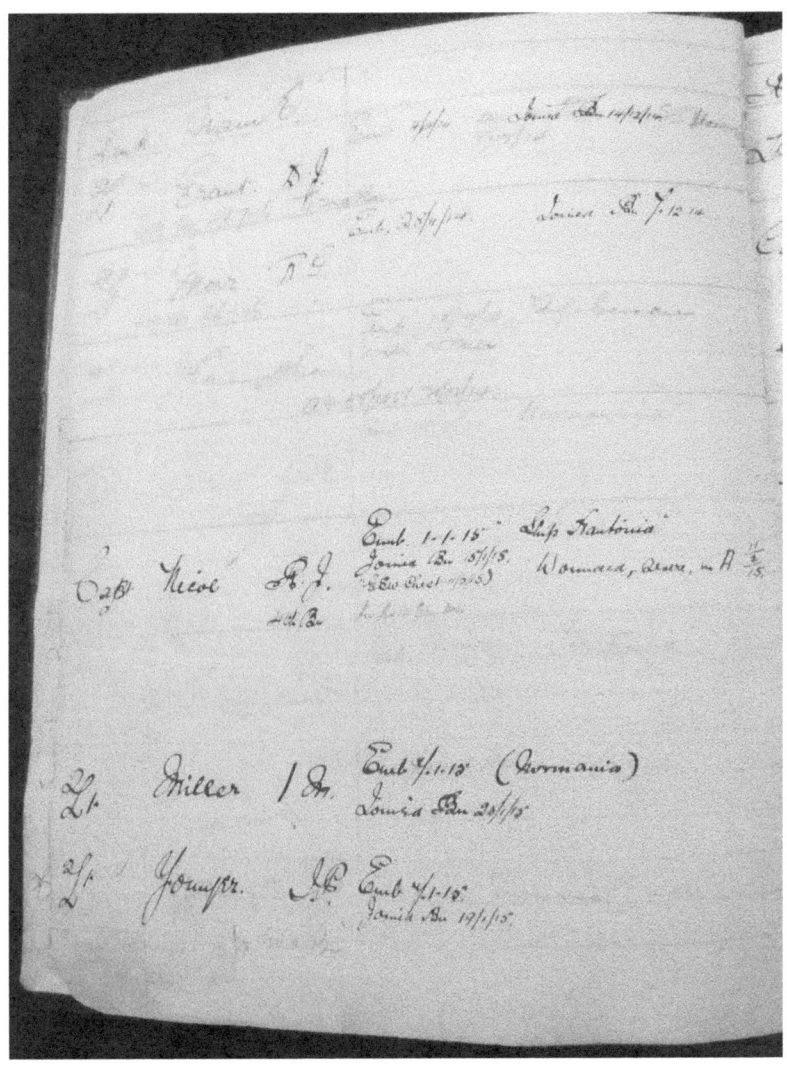

J.P. Younger in the 1914 Reinforcement Book of the 2nd Argylls
(*Argyll and Sutherland Highlanders Museum, Stirling*)

ENDNOTES

1. *Alloa Advertiser* 7 Nov 1914 p. 3 col. 3 and *Alloa Journal* 7 Nov 1914 p. 3 col. 3 reported 'his death was instantaneous'
2. 2nd Battalion Argylls 1914 Reinforcement Book.
3. *Alloa Journal* 22 Aug 1914 p. 2 col. 7
4. War Diary of 2nd Argyll and Sutherland Highlanders 26 Aug 1914
5. *Scotsman* 17 Sept 1914 Private Reid said that Capt. Bruce had been wounded, apparently in the legs. Colonel Hyslop [Battalion CO of the 2nd Argylls] in his personal diary said 'Robert Bruce got a slight wound in his leg as he stood by me but he made nothing of it.'
6. *Alloa Journal* 19 Sept 1914 p. 3 col. 6. This story also appeared in the *Scotsman* on 17 Sept 1914. Private Reid was from Dundee
7. *Alloa Journal* 17 Oct 1914 p. 3 col. 7 gave an obsequious account of Capt. Bruce's nobility of behaviour by referring to his refusal to take different size portions of food than the other ranks, whilst on a march.
8. *Alloa Journal* 10 Oct 1914 p. 2 col. 7
9. The Army must have had an identifiable body to bury because he has a CWGC grave at Le Cateau Military Cemetery [plot III C2]. The three month gap between being marked as missing and confirmed as dead could be explained by him falling in what then became enemy-occupied ground until November, but his body was later found and identified. He was buried, probably more or less where he died, by the Germans, who made a wooden cross to place over his grave. His brother managed to locate the grave and brought back the wooden cross. It was placed beneath the fine marble memorial to Captain Bruce, erected by his family, in Clackmannan Parish Church, where it remains today.
10. There were many eulogies from the local pulpits reported in *Alloa Journal* 14 Nov 1914 p. 3 cols. 1–3. Robert Bruce's name is first on the list of the fallen on Clackmannan's war memorial.
11. *Alloa Journal* 14 June 1919 p. 3 col. 2 was at pains to point out that 'The Hon George Bruce has not assumed the designation of Master of Burleigh, used by his elder brother, who fell in 1914...' yet most other sources imply he did.
12. *The Secrets of Rue St Roch*, Janet Morgan (Penguin, 2005) p. 19
13. He was a fluent French and German speaker and writer. See *The Secrets of Rue St Roch*, p. 19
14. *Alloa Advertiser* 17 Jan 1917 p. 3 col. 2
15. *Alloa Advertiser* 29 Sept 1917 p. 3 col. 4, *Alloa Journal* 6 Oct 1917 p. 3 col. 2
16. From records provided by the Regimental Archivist of the Scots Guards at Wellington Barracks.
17. *Alloa Journal* 10 Aug 1914 p. 2 col. 3
18. Army Form B.199 giving Lord Erskine's record of service shows that he was with the BEF from 6 September 1914 to 11 November 1914.
19. National Archives Mar and Kellie Muniments GD 124/15/1852. There are only four letters from Violet, Countess of Mar to Lord Erskine in France. The immediacy of her comments, the depth of her understanding of the way the war was going, and the compassion of her views makes you wish there were far more of them.

20 The Prince of Wales referred to was, of course, the man who became King Edward VIII and abdicated in 1936.
21 *Alloa Journal* 7 Nov 1914 p. 2 col. 4
22 *Alloa Journal* 21 Nov 1914 p. 3 col. 1
23 War Diary of 2nd Argyll and Sutherland Highlanders 19 Sept 1914. The Commander of the 2nd Argylls, Lieut. Col. Hyslop DSO, wrote his own diary in which he recorded the arrival of five officers from 3rd Special Reserve battalion on 18 Sept, but does not mention Lord Erskine by name, although he does mention Ure and Blacklock. There apparently were special problems with losses in B Company which was where these two officers were to be assigned.
24 Lieut. Blacklock was among those killed; Lieut Lothian was slightly wounded. See War Diary of 2nd Argyll and Sutherland Highlanders 21 Oct 1914
25 War Diary of 2nd Argyll and Sutherland Highlanders 21 Oct 1914
26 NYD stood for 'Not Yet Diagnosed' but was sometimes used as a euphemism for an early type of shellshock shown by a general debility, being run down, lassitude, not eating, disinterest in life etc... all of which could be explained by the Colitis.
27 2nd Battalion Argylls 1914 Reinforcement Book. SS *Oxfordshire* was built by Harland and Wolff in 1912, and was the first ship to be requisitioned for war service, two days before the war started. She was converted at Tilbury into 'Naval Hospital Ship No 1' with 562 beds, and worked in the English Channel in 1914, then Gallipoli in 1915. See http://www.roll-of-honour.com/Ships
28 *London Gazette* 23 Feb 1915 [p. 1834] noted his transfer to the Scots Guards as from 12 Feb 1915
29 *Alloa Journal* 30 Jan 1915 p. 2 col. 5, *Alloa Circular* 3 Feb 1915 p. 2 col. 5
30 Found in the letter referred to in footnote[18]
31 *London Gazette* 14 March 1916 announced the appointment, but two days later he had given it up!
32 *Alloa Journal* 15 April 1916 p. 3 col. 1
33 *Alloa Journal* 29 April 1916 p. 3 col. 2
34 Very little royalty came to Alloa during World War I, but this picture shows one of them; HSH Prince George of Battenberg; his mother was a granddaughter of Queen Victoria. He was a brother of Louis Mountbatten, later Lord Mountbatten of Burma, and his sister was Princess Alice, mother of the Duke of Edinburgh. See Chapt.7 for the visit of HRH Princess Christian in September 1916.
35 *Alloa Journal* 29 April 1916 p. 3 col. 5
36 *Alloa Journal* 6 Sept 1916 p. 3 col. 2
37 *Alloa Journal* 25 May 1918 p. 3 col. 2
38 *Alloa Advertiser* 6 Sept 1919 p. 3 col. 1, 6 Dec 1919 p. 3 col. 1
39 *London Gazette* 20 Jan 1920
40 Perhaps they were confused about the end of which war. He was given the rank of Honorary Major in 1945 at the end of World War II, when he 'had exceeded the age limit of liability to recall' See Lord Erskine's Army Form B199A
41 thePeerage.com website The second of his four sons was killed in action in 1945
42 *Alloa Advertiser* 28 July 1917 p. 3 col. 1. A year later, in the June 1918 fete, the Red Cross committee tried the different fund-raising strategy of raffling the bullock rather than auctioning it. This time

they sold 4,000 tickets in advance at half a crown each; it raised over £500 and was won by a man from Kilmarnock who happened to be the brother of the President of the SFU [*Alloa Advertiser* 29 June 1918 p. 3 col. 2]

43 Alloa Burgh Council minute book 8 Nov 1919
44 Alloa Burgh Council minute book 14 Feb 1921
45 *Alloa Journal* 27 Feb 1915 p. 3 col. 1 Alexander P. Forrester-Paton Esq died in 1915, aged 62. His three sons were among the eight pall bearers at his funeral. A fourth pall bearer was his son-in-law, Mr J. Duncan Millar.
46 The reference to Malta shows that they were writing about John Forrester-Paton, who had been in the YMCA since his youth and became a member of the Scottish National Council in 1913. The YMCA biographical website states that 'During World War I he served with the British YMCA on Malta'. He later became World President of the YMCA. The youngest brother, Ernest, was a final year medical student in London in 1915 and then went straight out to India as a medical missionary. He had no war service but the Alloa Advertiser 13 Jan 1917 p. 2 col. 5 did report on his medical assistance during an outbreak of plague in Jalna. Ernest was a Former Pupil of Alloa Academy [Secondary Admission Register no. 80]
47 Meeting of Directors of John Paton and Sons Ltd (John Paton, Son & Co. Ltd) minute book 24 Sept 1918
48 Given the enormous financial rewards that the board of directors were receiving as a result of their wartime efforts [see Chapter 3], some may find this plaintive cry of being overworked a little hard to swallow
49 *Alloa Journal* 30 June 1917 p. 3 col. 4 refers to that meeting of the tribunal, but not in enough detail to record names
50 This letter was possibly written by the Company Secretary, J.S. Reid of 1, Grange Road, Alloa.
51 Box GD 457/180, Patons & Baldwins documents in the National Archives of Scotland
52 *Alloa Advertiser* 30 March 1918 p. 3 col. 1
53 *Alloa Journal* 24 Aug 1918 p. 3 col. 3
54 James Younger, the brewer, married Janet McEwan in 1850. They had five sons and a daughter. The sons were George, John [died age 14] James, William and Robert. The two sons most connected with Alloa's history during the Great War were George and James; it was their sons who served in the Army. Robert Younger, the youngest of the five sons, was a high court judge during the war and was joint chair of the Advisory Committee as to Internment and Repatriation. His interest in this area led him to generously offer to fund 50 visits to Switzerland at £12 each for wives and relatives of any British prisoners interned there. See *Alloa Advertiser* 19 Sept 1916 p. 2 col. 5. After the war, now elevated to the peerage as Lord Blanesburgh, he was Principal British Delegate on the Reparations Commission at Paris from 1923 to 1930, which tried to supervise Germany's obedience to the financial clauses of the Treaty of Versailles.
55 James Younger married Annie Thomson Paton in 1886 and their only son was James Paton Younger
56 *National Guardian* 12 Sept 1914 p. 17. This was the publication of the brewing and licensed trades association and they would have been well aware of the Younger family's importance in the brewing industry.

57 *Alloa Journal* 17 March 1917 p. 3 col. 2
58 He gained a 3rd class degree in Natural Sciences (Chemistry) in 1908.
59 *Alloa Advertiser* 31 March 1917 p. 3 col. 2
60 *National Guardian* 7 April 1917 p12 contained a fairly full obituary of C. F. Younger
61 From Grange Cricket Club Roll of Honour, found online.
62 *Alloa Journal* 17 March 1917 p. 3 col. 2
63 Just to demonstrate how everyone seemed to want to claim a share of a war hero, C.F. Younger's name was inscribed on Alloa's War Memorial, the memorials in St John's Episcopal Church, Clackmannan County Cricket Club and Grange Cricket Club in Edinburgh. It was also inscribed on Gargunnock Parish Church's war memorial (that was the location of his father's home) and on the Roll of Honour in Holy Trinity Scottish Episcopal Church, in Stirling. It was also recorded in the Roll of Honour at the Scottish National War Memorial in Edinburgh Castle (where it is spelled incorrectly) and on the Roll of Honour of the Lothians and Border Horse Yeomanry Regiment in Dunbar Parish Church (which is itself, an abbreviated version of the full roll held at Redford Barracks, Edinburgh) At Winchester School his name was commemorated in their War Memorial Cloister, on a memorial in his boarding house, in their handwritten Roll of Honour and also in a set of volumes called *Wykehamists who died in the War*. At New College, Oxford his name is on Eric Gill's memorial in their antechapel. Additionally, Lord Blanesburgh commissioned a series of stained glass windows and an organ as a memorial to his two brothers, and also his two nephews who were killed in action (ie Edward in the Boer War and Charles in World War I). This was placed in St Thomas the Martyr Church, Winchelsea, East Sussex and was unveiled by the Archbishop of Canterbury on 9 May 1931. See *Glasgow Herald* 23 April 1931 p. 8 col. 4 and *Times* 11 May 1931 p. 11. That is a total of 15 commemorative inscriptions in all, 17 counting his name on the Younger family gravestone in Alloa's Greenside Cemetery and his own CWGC gravestone in Aveluy Communal Extension Cemetery [Grave M8].
64 He inherited the title from his father and became 2nd Viscount Younger of Leckie
65 *Alloa Advertiser* 30 Sept 1916 p. 3 col. 4
66 *Alloa Journal* 30 Sept 1916 p. 3 col. 4
67 He and his wife lived at Mount Melville, just outside St Andrews, and became great benefactors to that town and the Kingdom of Fife. He was granted an honorary LLD by St Andrews University in June 1917, and thereafter was generally styled as Dr James Younger. See *Alloa Journal* 27 June 1917 p. 3 col. 3
68 *Alloa Journal* 15 Sept 1917 p. 3 col. 5
69 *Alloa Advertiser* 20 Sept 1974 p. 1 col. 6 for an article on the front page a week after his death
70 Capt Younger's medal card in the National Archives [WO372/22/130681] confirms 7 January 1915 as the day his European military service started and therefore his entitlement to the 1914-15 Star
71 *Normannia* was built by Fairfields Yard, Govan in 1912 and served as a troopship. She was lost in an air raid in 1940

CHAPTER 4

THE IMPACT ON SCHOOLS AND EDUCATION

When considering the range of sources available for investigating schools and education in Alloa during the war, it might be thought that the school log books kept by the Head Teacher or Rector would be the best. After all, this was a weekly diary about school life which the Rector/Head Teacher wrote up every Friday (and on other occasions if he felt like it). However, the Heads' chief worry, especially in primary schools, was whether staff or pupils were ill; they did not spend a lot of time analysing the impact of world events on their schools. Log books, therefore, build up only a very indistinct picture of the impact of outside events on everyday school life. The only other school-based source for Alloa Academy are the minutes from the school's Literary and Debating Society, but it had very few wartime meetings. Certain aspects of school life are quite well dealt with in the letter books of the Alloa Burgh School Board and the minutes of the School Board and the Burgh Council – after all, both of these dealt with the business of running schools and obtaining or releasing staff and are therefore sound on the impact of staff going off to war. However, there are only incomplete sets still extant for both of these sources for the wartime years.

The Alloa newspapers did tend to report some school events, so hints in the log books about social events like fundraising for soldiers, Belgians or Serbs can be fleshed out with more detail by checking the press.

This chapter will first look at the secondary schools, Alloa Academy and the Grange School/Burgh School, then the four primary schools. There is reasonable evidence from log books for St John's Primary and Sunnyside, but very little for the Primary Department of Alloa Academy or St Mungo's Roman Catholic Primary School. Each section covers, according to available evidence, the impact on staff and pupils, including former pupils, and the social-everyday life of the pupils in the school.

ALLOA ACADEMY

Alloa Academy c.1900, viewed from the West End Park. This is gives the best
view of what the school looked like during the war.
The Academy looked out over the West End Park and the bandstand
(*Clackmannanshire Archives and Local History Service*)

The impact on the staff was very much split into two phases; there was the early release of a few male staff in the first rush to join up, though only a few went. The School Board claimed that almost all the rest of the male staff were exempt from military service because, as Principal teachers, they were 'protected'.

Then, from 1916 onwards, there was an attempt by the recruiting authorities, by constantly changing the rules of exemption, the qualifying medical standard needed and the age limits, to call up the rest of the male staff. Sometimes this was resisted successfully and in many cases recruitment was so late in the war that when the training time was added in these teachers never actually had to serve abroad.

One impact that the war had was on Matthew Goldie Blair, the Rector. No one knows if he planned to retire in 1914 but, after twenty-five years' service as the Rector, he was already 62.[1] The issue was perhaps not raised, however, until early 1917 when the School Board noted that 'Mr Matthew Blair, in ordinary circumstances should retire from service under the age limit in April of this year, but the Board desires that Mr Blair be allowed to continue his service until the termination of this war. Mr Blair has written that in this present national emergency, he is willing to...'[2] He therefore worked on until April 1919 and became the oldest (at sixty-seven) and, at thirty years, the longest serving Rector in Alloa Academy's history.

STAFF, 1910-1911

BACK ROW.—Mr P. Christie, Mr Bert Murray, Mr J. F. Duffin.
SECOND.—Miss A. T. Mayes, Mr J. Atkinson, Miss M. Dow, Mr C. H. Watts, Miss M. Aikman, Mr R. Macfarlane, Mr W. H. Andrew, Miss J. D. Hunter, Miss E. McDougal, Mr W. Bremner.
FRONT.—Mr W. Campsie, Miss M. D. Cock, Miss M. Blackwood, Mr P. J. Moodie, Mr M. Blair, Miss J. Maitland, Miss E. I. Mill, Mr P. Walker.

Alloa Academy staff photograph from the 1935 *Alloa Academy Magazine*.
Every single man in this picture features in our story. Only two more male teachers were appointed before 1914 (Mr Doull and Mr Douglas).

Within five weeks of the start of the war, the first teacher left Alloa Academy for war service. Joe Duffin (science and maths) volunteered for the 9th Highland Light Infantry in Sept 1914[3], although on 10 September 1915 he returned to duty at the school, having been discharged on health grounds.[4] Mr Duffin's classes were shared out between other staff, including the Rector and it was the end of November before a new teacher was in place.[5] The letter of appointment, offering Mr Duffin's position to Mr Ironside, rather poignantly commented that 'The Assistant has joined the Army. It is hoped that he may not be absent beyond the present session, but one cannot say how long his absence might continue.'[6] Indeed, one could not.

Mr Peter T. Moodie, head of the Primary Dept. in Alloa Academy, was a Captain in the Territorials (H Company 7th Argylls) and he was called up immediately.[7] In these early days there was an agreement that posts should be kept open (Dept. circular No 463) and that 'the balance of pay' should be offered if the Army pay was less than the teaching salary. On 30 September 1914 Joe Duffin in fact received a rather quaint offer from James Cuthbert, Secretary of the School Board, who wrote that 'I can quite understand that army pay at the moment is a minus quantity and therefore, for this month at all events, I shall take responsibility for paying full salary'.[8] Captain Moodie received a letter on the same date saying that was going to be paid half his salary.[9] In due course Captain Moodie was promoted to Major and the School Board noted that 'his salary was then equivalent to what he was paid by the Board. No allowance was accordingly granted.'[10]

There was concern by February 1916 that more teachers might be called up and indeed this became the case as the second phase of enlistment began. On 17 March 1916 Mr Douglas was to be called up, but by the end of April he had been placed on reserve and returned to his teaching duties.[11] Mr Macfarlane and Mr Watts both had their appeals to the local tribunal rejected, but meanwhile the War Office deferred their enlistment.[12] On 31 March 1916, despite his earlier setbacks, Mr Duffin was determined to do his bit and went off to join the Government Meteorological Service in London[13] (though in the end he went to Falmouth).[14]

There is some evidence that the role and importance of women in schools was increasing. For instance, on 28 April 1916 Miss Nellie Cairns was transferred into the school from the Grange School 'for the period of the war'.[15] There seemed to be a recognition that the comings and goings of male staff, as they were called up or sent back, would have a bad effect on pupils' learning and that it would be better to recruit women for the duration. However, this was not always the case. In October 1918 the School Board wrote to Miss Troup offering to transfer her as an art teacher to Alloa Academy, rather than actually appoint her to what would have been considered as a promoted post. They planned to transfer her <u>at her existing salary</u> and offered the bribe of a guaranteed job at the end of the war.[16] At the end of 1916, recognising the extra contribution that all the remaining teachers had made, the School Board offered a War bonus of £15 to married teachers and £10 to unmarried teachers 'without distinction of service or sex, including the Headmaster.'[17]

No male teacher serving in the Academy was killed during the war; the only one who almost came into that category was Mr Bert Murray, who had been on the Academy teaching staff before the war but was promoted out of the county. However, he went on to become Captain Murray MC of the Gordon Highlanders and was killed in July 1918. Mr Murray is in the 1910-11 staff photograph. The school did, however, lose one serving member of staff, Andrew Ross. He had become School Janitor by 20 February 1915,[18] but reported for military service on 8 June 1916[19] and was killed on 13 November 1916. It took a while for the death to be confirmed, but then the local press featured a longish article about him.[20]

The letter of condolence that the School Board sent to his wife actually went missing and they recognised this in a second letter, which was finally sent to her on 27 March 1917. That letter ended by saying that 'We engross in our minutes an expression of deep sympathy for Mrs Ross and her family, as Mr Ross was the first one in the service of the Board who has fallen…' That last sentence was what his widow would already have read almost two months earlier in the *Journal* on 3 February 1917.

Considering that the war had now lasted for two and a half years one cannot help thinking that the men from Alloa who worked in the Education Service had escaped fairly lightly. However, later in 1917 a note in the letter book[21] records that in fact there were only six staff employed by the Alloa School Board (including two women) on some sort of war service and only three of them were serving abroad, so perhaps it was not so fortuitous. The Alloa average of one death for every six that served seems to be close to the mark here as well.[22]

From September 1916 onwards there was a rush to get Alloa Academy's male teachers into uniform. Mr Charles Watts the Art teacher was called up.[23] He served, was wounded (broken arm) in November 1917, became a prisoner of war (notified in February 1918) [24] and returned home with a group of other POWs on 14 December 1918.[25] His wife had been employed as his temporary replacement in November.[26] He was fit enough to offer outdoor sketching classes in April 1919[27] but he had apparently suffered from his poor conditions in captivity and died in December 1920. A week after Mr Watts' call up, Peter Walker, William Andrew and William Bremner were all called up for **re**-examination.[28] Of the three, Mr Andrew and Mr Bremner were classified as Fit B2, but this in fact meant UNFIT for General Service.[29] Peter Walker never went off to fight himself, but in August 1918 he lost his nineteen-year-old son, an Academy FP, who died of wounds in Rouen Hospital.[30] On 7 September 1917 Mr Campsie and Mr Douglas went off to the war,[31] but the Recruiting Office, still desperately short of men, did not give up on the other male teachers at the Academy… Mr Andrew, Mr Doull and Mr Bremner were called up again to the National Service

Medical Board for examination.[32] Mr Andrew was now re-classified as Grade 1[33] but it was later discovered that he was (temporarily) 'protected', and Mr Bremner was over-age but, was called up anyway in September 1918 when the rules were changed again. He went off to join the RAF and started his training at RAF Blandford in Dorset.[34]

Incredibly, in the last three weeks of the war the School Board was still fighting to retain the teaching services of Mr Christie, the technical teacher at the Academy. Apart from the Rector, he was the only male member of staff who was already OVER forty-five at the start of the war, and by the time he received his call up papers in October 1918 he was over fifty. No wonder the letter from the School Board to the Recruiting Office stated rather abruptly that 'He is not liable to be called up either for service or a medical examination'.[35]

The male staff of the Academy were therefore pretty hard hit by the war. Mr Douglas and Mr Doull were the only additional men who arrived after those in the 1911 photo, and **every single male teacher** was considered for service, often rejected then considered again... and again. Only the Rector, Mr Walker and Mr Christie did not actually serve; every other man on the staff did, at least as far as going off for training.

The impact of the war on the pupils of the Academy can firstly be seen in the commemorative Roll of Honour that recognised the military contribution of **former** pupils. However, although 'former', many of them were so young and had left the Academy so recently that the majority of the staff would have known the names and taught many of them, recognised the younger siblings in the school and felt the loss as the school's itself.

The first reference to a Roll of Honour is in a message from the School Board to all Rectors/Head Teachers at the end of September 1914, stating that 'It was suggested... that a Roll of Honour should be prepared and kept in the school containing the names of all former pupils who have volunteered for service in any branch of His Majesty's Forces during the present war...'.[36] It must have taken a while to prepare this, because it was only by the end of February 1915 that the School Board recorded the details of the fine piece of work that was now on display.[37] The School Board was shown 'an ornate and chaste design of a coloured illuminated heading for the roll on which it was proposed to engrave the names of the pupils of the school who had joined the colours or were on active service, which had been executed by Mr Watts, Art Master. The design embodied the Union Jack, the French, Belgian and Russian flags. The centrepiece included the Scottish lion, surmounted by the thistle, the rose and

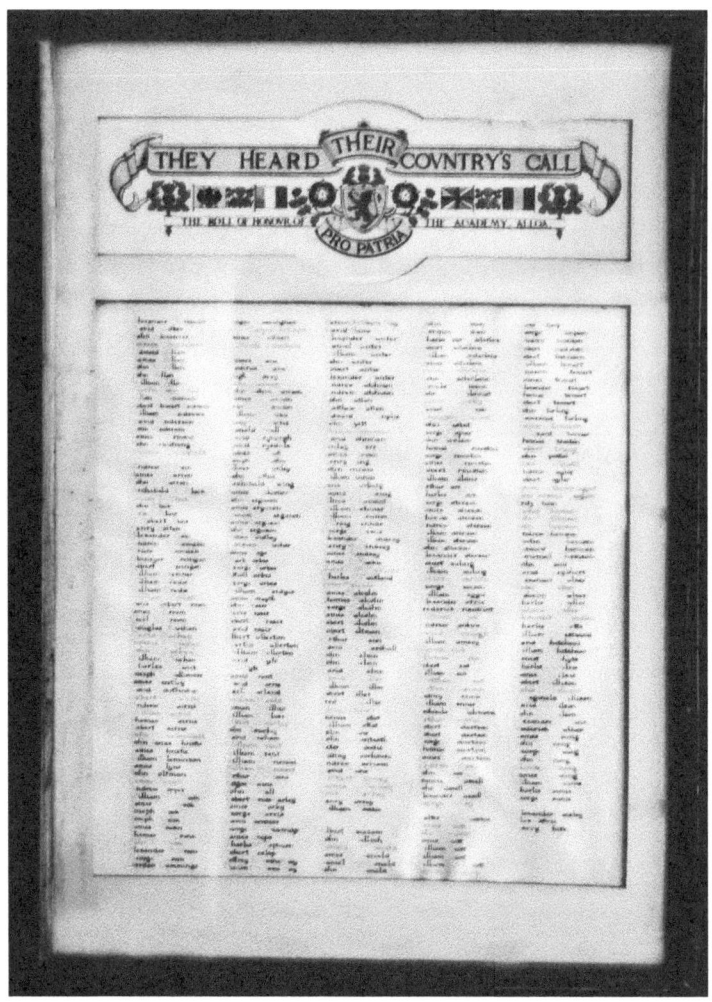
School Roll of Honour (*Photo by Anthony Cervi*)

the shamrock, with the inscription at the top: 'THEY HEARD THEIR COUNTRY'S CALL'. The design of the heading was much admired and gratefully accepted by the members of the board.[38] This Roll of Honour was first mentioned in the log book on 16 July 1915 when the Rector, in his comments at the end-of-term service, wrote that it '...is now exhibited in the school hall. The beautiful headpiece was designed and wrought by Mr Watts, Art Master'.[39]

This framed Roll of Honour can still be seen in the new Alloa Academy building, although there is nowhere public to display it so it is stored in the archive room. The heading is the original and is exactly as the Rector and *Alloa Journal* described it in 1915. At the end of the War someone must have drawn up the full list of names that had been added each month during the War, put them in alphabetical order and neatly inscribed the new list on the sheet of paper which was then added below the heading. The former pupils who were killed were written in gold; those who served but survived were written in black. In spite, however, of all the thought that had been given to it, three names omitted from the alphabetical list still had to be added at the bottom right; it should not be assumed to be infallibly accurate; quite a few names were probably missed out.[40]

The Roll of Honour records that 349 former pupils/teachers/staff from the school served in the war in some capacity; of those, fifty-nine died. The Roll does **not**, however, include Bessie Coltman, the only woman from Alloa to serve and die, and a former pupil of the school in the Primary Dept. She died of pneumonia in November 1918. Her name **is** on the Alloa War Memorial in Bedford Place, but she is not recorded as an official 'war dead' by the Commonwealth War Graves Commission. The Roll of Honour does include Charles Watts, Art teacher, who died of his wounds in 1920 (though not written in gold) and also Bert Murray, teacher until 1912, as well as Andrew K. Ross, the Janitor.

The roll also records one set of twins, three brothers, several pairs of brothers, two former duxes and two cousins of the same name who lived in the same house.

It has been noted already that the Rector's log book, is hardly the best source for additional information on the honours list of former pupils in the war, since only **four** former pupils are mentioned by name during the entire war.

The first was in June 1915, when Alfred B. Lamont had been given permission to leave school after sitting the Intermediate exam, because he was going to 'work in munitions'.[41]

The next was about James Lennox Dawson in December 1915, when the Rector wrote that 'The crowning event this week has been the receipt of news that James L. Dawson, a former pupil and Junior student of this school, now acting Company Sergeant Major of 187th Company of Royal Engineers, has been awarded the most distinguished honour of the Victoria Cross for valour on the field of battle. The hero himself being home on furlough visited the school today [Friday] and received a wildly enthusiastic ovation from pupils and staff, to whom he afterwards addressed a word of thanks.'[42] He had some friendly company on that day, since four of his classmates who were also officers happened to be home on furlough and they made up an informal

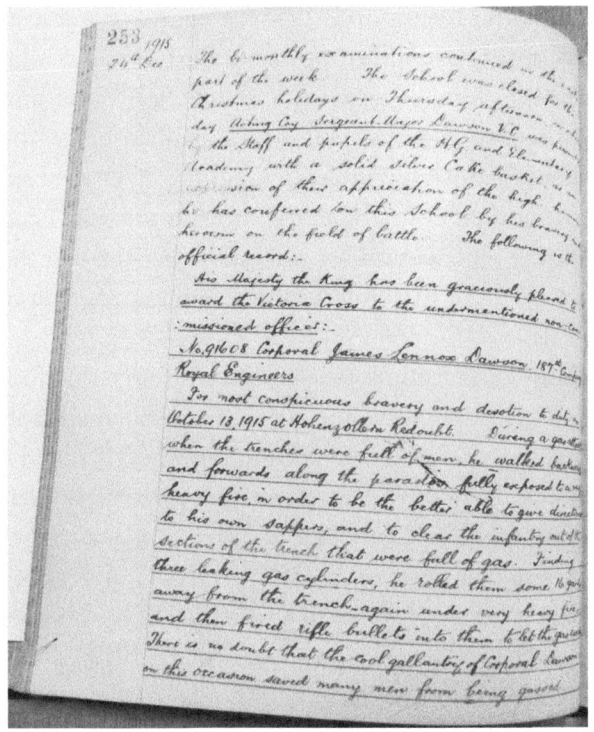

'guard of honour' for him in the school.[43]

On 24 December the Rector copied out the entire VC citation into the log book and underlined it in red ink; and mentioned that the hero visited the school again to be presented 'with a solid silver cake basket as an expression of their appreciation of the high honour he has conferred on this school by his heroism and bravery on the field of battle.'[44] One wonders what the hero was supposed to have done with this wonderful confectionery holder in the trenches and its present whereabouts remain a mystery.[45]

The third reference to a former pupil was in October 1917, concerning the death on the field of battle of John S. Thomson, a Dux medallist of 1909 who had gone on to be a Classics master in Mackie Academy, Stonehaven, before joining up. The school flag flew at half-mast during the day.[46]

The fourth reference to a former pupil echoed the third. By now the war was over, but on 6 December 1918 'The school flag flew at half-mast in honourable sympathy and regret on account of the death of a former pupil, Private William Cairns, who died from pneumonia following upon influenza while home on leave.'[47] The Rector perhaps wanted to mention this FP's name because he had two sisters who were both serving as teachers in the school.

Given that fifty-nine former pupils died during the war, one wonders how often the school flew the flag at half-mast and in which different ways the school or staff were informed of the continuing losses of FPs. Although the Rector recorded the loss of only two in the log book, it seems unlikely that the school did not show similar signs of respect when notifications came in of all the other deaths. Indeed, other evidence supports this view, because in May 1915 the local press recorded that the

Alloa Academy flag flew at half-mast in memory of five (named) former pupils who had fallen in the war.[48] The *Advertiser* also reported that the school flew the flag at half-mast on Monday 27 May 1918 in recognition of the FP, John Buchan being reported missing but still being awarded the Victoria Cross.[49] This was not reported in the log book either. Perhaps it became so routine that the Rector simply did not bother to write up something like this in his log book each week. The lack of references to FPs as casualties in the log book does suggest that its purpose was genuinely to be a record of the day to day educational (usually routinely humdrum) activities of the school, rather than a commemorative tribute.

How great was the impact of the war on the social and everyday life of the pupils? The log books indicate clearly that educational life for the pupils, as we would know it, did progress largely as normal during the war. The log book is full of information on visits by inspectors, discipline issues, deployment of staff for best results, the school sports and who would be Dux etc; all the normal activities of school life. Where there *were* changes it was clearly in a focus on fund raising for war-related charities and a growing recognition, as the years passed, that war service was the likely inevitable consequence of reaching the age of eighteen, for boys **and** girls in their different ways and preparations should be made for that.

The Academy pupils were keen fund raisers: in October 1914 it was Belgian Flower and Fruit day and the pupils brought in contributions, chiefly chrysanthemums, to be sent to Edinburgh.[50] Then in June 1916 the Rector recorded the holding of Kossova Day in support of the Serbians… a lecture sent down to schools by the Serbian Committee was read out by the Rector and contributions were taken, adding up to just over £1.[51] That somewhat measly total was surpassed the following week, when the Rector reported that Mr Watts and his committee organised a Cake and Candy Sale for the starving children of Belgium. This was much better supported, raising £73 for the Belgian Committee.[52]

Empire Day was always dutifully observed at the end of May each year by all schools, as pupils gathered round the flag in the West End Park, sang the National Anthem and listened to an uplifting address, usually given by the local minister or members of the School Board. This was not only marked during wartime; the local press gave detailed reports of this patriotic event in many of the pre-war years.[53]

It was not mentioned in the log book, but another fund raising project, organised within the school from June 1916, was for the collection of salvage; chiefly lead, zinc, silver foil etc. Charles Watts put a letter in the *Journal*, asking for these items 'to be given to any of the school children' and he 'would send off the first parcel by the middle of July'.[54] It is not known what happened to this initiative, since Mr Watts was called up in September of that year.

Another initiative that the Rector did not report in his log book was how Mr Christie of the Technical Department helped the war effort. As early as November 1915 he and the pupils were producing trench periscopes for Major Abercrombie of the 1st/7th Argylls.[55] By April 1916 he had developed this into something he called a 'sniperscope', which the local Territorial officers inspected to great acclaim.[56] He was asked to present it to the War Office for further study. Once again, what became of this idea received no further coverage in the local press. Perhaps the school should have pressed for more publicity, to match that gained by pupils in the Technical Dept. of Stirling High School, who appeared in a photograph in their local paper showing their efforts in producing trench periscopes.[57]

In his log book entry on 16 July 1915 the Rector mentioned that 'The 3rd number (War Number) of the *Academy Magazine* was ready for sale on the closing day.'[58] These war issues would probably be invaluable as sources of evidence on how the school was affected by the war, from the point of view of the pupils; none however seem to have survived.

This magazine, produced within the Academy by the Literary and Debating Society, was extensively reported upon in the *Circular*,[59] which mentioned that it opened with an address from the Society to all serving FPs. The heartfelt message below, taken from the minute book of that society, is likely to be that very address. It made the following resolution which was 'passed with great applause':

'That we, as present and former pupils of Alloa Academy, in the annual reunion of the Literary and Debating Society now assembled, desire to express our sense of loss in the absence from our midst of those who have gone forth to defend us; our pride in their courage and self-sacrifice; our confidence that none of them shall be put to shame, whatever may betide. If a message from the old school can cheer some hour of hardship or danger, we would further assure them how anxiously our hearts follow them with sympathy, honour and affection, desiring for all of them, all comfort and success, with a speedy, glorious return.'[60]

The *Circular*'s article on this magazine referred to an art supplement which not only included a copy of the illuminated heading of the Roll of Honour but also the names 'now standing at 115' and some portraits; and ran to thirty-six pages. For these reasons, the price of the magazine was as high as 6d.

The war had an impact on normal school life in a variety of other ways. On more than one occasion, often near the start of the new session, the Rector observed that the school could not get deliveries of books and materials due to 'Railway traffic being rather disorganised on account of the war.'[61]

Leith was not bombed by German Zeppelins until 2 April 1916 (eight people were killed, including three children), but from January 1915 onwards the government was sufficiently alarmed by attacks in England that they issued The Lights (Scotland) Number 1 Order in February 1916, in effect introducing a local blackout. The Town Clerk's office reported that suitable arrangements could be made for schools 'without much difficulty'.[62] There was little reference elsewhere to this blackout, and one wonders how much school life was affected by it.

Following circulars from central government, War Savings schemes were introduced across all the schools in the burgh, from October 1916. In the weeks following, the Rector addressed various classes about the importance of 'saving their pennies'[63] but he did not mention it much in the log book (perhaps on only two or three occasions), unlike the Heads in the primary schools, who commented fairly regularly on how much their schools had saved each week.

1916 saw the implementation of the Summer Time Act which brought the clocks forward an hour, and the School Board commented very favourably 'in every respect' on its working, and recommended that it be renewed for 1917. As with other things, this seems to have passed the Rector by and he did not record whether it had any impact on the education of Alloa Academy pupils.

As mentioned earlier, as the war years passed, it became clear to the Rector that school was not just a preparation for life; it was a preparation for war service. At the beginning of 1917 the Rector expressed his concerns about the hardship that would be imposed upon senior boys who were either already eighteen or approaching the age of eighteen and might be liable to be called up.[64] He was concerned that some of the best pupils simply might not stay on for more education if they knew that, whatever their results and ambitions, their only destination was military training once they reached the age of eighteen. He expressed his concerns to the Education Dept. but their response was that the pupils concerned might be able to claim exemption.[65] This was a somewhat unhelpful and unbelievable response. At the very time when we have already noted that exemption and medical rules for teachers were being amended to draw more of them into the recruitment net, it is hard to imagine that the military authorities would voluntarily forgo calling up intelligent eighteen-year-olds just because they fancied going to university instead. That said, however, the 1915 Dux of Alloa Academy was allowed to start his medical studies at Edinburgh University rather than be called up.

To help the preparation of its pupils for a military life the Academy set up its own Cadet corps.[66] The School Board was worried about how to organise this and what it might cost so it wrote to Dollar Institution to enquire how theirs worked.[67] The reply was obviously encouraging because the Cadet corps was in fact set up in the Autumn term of the 1917–1918 session and sixty-four of a possible eighty-nine eligible boys volunteered. Mr Walker and Mr Doull agreed to run it.[68] Other local schools also had cadet forces. The School Board letter books noted that Sunnyside had forty-one cadets, Grange School had sixty-four and the Burgh School had twenty-four.[69] The Burgh Council was very concerned about how the Alloa public might see this militarisation of their young people. The *Advertiser* devoted over two columns to reporting on the Councillors' discussion of 'British versus Prussian militarism', in an attempt to calm any possible fears.[70]

As with all the schools in the burgh, from October until late November 1918, the Influenza outbreak (Spanish Flu) had a major impact on school life. The County Medical Officer closed all schools. In his log book entry of Friday 15 November, the Rector wrote that 'School was reopened on Monday morning and closed at midday, the Sanitary authority of the Burgh having again extended their [closing] order.'[71] This meant that the school <u>was in fact open</u> for a morning session on Armistice Day, but the Rector did not think to enter such a momentous event in the Academy's log book, despite news of the Armistice having clearly reached Alloa before midday.

The impact of the war on the school did not finish on Armistice Day. The pupils were still avidly raising money for War Savings certificates into 1919; they collected over £196 in January.[72] Then there was the continuing impact on the pupils of the slow return of demobilised staff. Mr Doull returned to his science teaching duties by mid-February 1919,[73] but the real problem was that a new modern languages teacher, Mr William Fortune, had been appointed and the Army was very slow to release him,[74] so that 'the conduct of the classes in French has fallen entirely on the shoulders of Miss Mary Cairns, a very unsatisfactory state of affairs'.[75] A temporary extra teacher was eventually employed and she was finally released on 28 November 1919, when the school was assured that Mr Fortune would indeed take up his duties on 1 December 1919. That seemed a long time to wait for his arrival.

GRANGE SCHOOL AND THE BURGH SCHOOL

This is complicated: there was a third secondary 'school' in Alloa in 1914 called the Burgh School, in Ludgate, but it was not really a school. It was 'a centre for domestic instruction,'[76] offering 'supplementary classes' in needlework and cooking, art and technical subjects. Despite the School Board's opposition, the Territorials requisitioned the Burgh School's Ludgate building for their own training purposes.[77] On the bright side, the Council was able to collect 14s 6d per day rent from the army for its use and occupation of the building.[78] The Burgh School therefore gave up its premises and merged with the Grange School almost as soon as the war started (from 5 October 1914). The Headmaster of the Grange School was Mr Alexander Wilson, but when he died suddenly in September 1915[79] the Headmaster of the Burgh School, William Roy almost automatically took over as the Head of the combined school.

However, the two schools still kept a distinct existence throughout the war, although they were sharing the same building and the same Headmaster, who continued to keep records in separate log books The schools are covered separately in the following section, therefore, to give the Burgh School its due credit.

GRANGE SCHOOL

The war-related comments in the log book were very sparse, generally being concerned with two areas only; the release of staff on different occasions and raising money for charitable organisations.

There were few references to the impact of the war on staff. In September 1916 Miss Laidlaw was granted leave of absence to train as a supervisor of munitions workers,[80] then in November 1917 Miss Ferguson was allowed leave from School for a month's training as a VAD at Arnsbrae House.[81] Miss Urquhart was allowed time off to bid farewell to her brother, who had been home on leave from Greece in February 1918[82] and Miss Waller was allowed time off in May 1918 following the death of her brother in a flying accident whilst training in Montrose.[83] This was in fact the third son in the Waller family to be killed in the War.

School fund-raising efforts for the war started early on; in October 1914, along with the local churches and other schools, the pupils had collections for the Belgian Relief Fund and two visiting ladies handed out miniatures of the Belgian flag.[84] Fund-raising was something that the Grange School implemented quite successfully with its pupils.

On 30 May 1916 the headmaster recorded that the school would provide financial assistance 'to the destitute children of Belgium' as well as having a collection 'in aid of the Scottish Women's Hospitals in Serbia'.[85] The school seems to have put some effort into these activities, because 'drafts' for £15 10s were sent off to the two named charities.[86] Along with other schools under the Alloa School Board's direction, Grange School also set up a war savings scheme for pupils. The Headmaster reported that The War Savings Association 'has been quite satisfactory' when a total of just under £2 was collected for the week in early October 1916.[87] By February 1917 the Headmaster reported that the month's total was over £42, so the rate of savings must have picked up quite a bit. In fact, by the end of the war he proudly wrote that they had saved over £1,000 and in honour of that the pupils were given a short day.[88]

Other charitable groups that attracted the attention of the pupils were collections for the Russian Red Cross flag day (May 1917), the Limbless Soldiers and Sailors flag day (May 1917) and the Queen Alexandra Rose Day Fund (July 1917).[89] The School also organised a pageant in June 1918 which raised £44 on the first night of showing and over £30 on the second.[90]

There were few other war-related references in the school's log book. In May 1915 Empire Day was celebrated at a meeting in the public park [91] and in December 1915 James Lennox Dawson VC visited the school,[92] even though he himself had not been a pupil there. Having come home to Alloa on leave, he patriotically did the rounds of all the local schools. The only other war-related activity in the Grange School was that it did participate in the School Board's initiative and briefly set up a Cadet Corps.[93]

BURGH SCHOOL

The school's roll was 138 in September 1914 and it had about six staff, but also got the use of Academy staff such as Mr Watts for art lessons and Mr Christie for technical instruction.

The first wartime staffing issue in the log book was that the school took on Mr James Laing from September 1914, at the very moment when most other men were joining the army.[94] How could this be? The clue that this man may have been either unfit or too old for active service appeared in the log book in June 1918, when it was noted that there was discussion concerning 'an application by Mr Laing that he be allowed off duty on 28th inst. so as to take up his two-months course of military service with volunteers'.[95] The local volunteers (more properly called the Clackmannanshire

Volunteer Regiment) was the preferred destination for men exempted by the local tribunal on medical, age or 'protected' grounds.

The log book also indicates that there was a fair amount of uncertainty in the Burgh School staff in the early months of the war. They knew, for instance, of Mr Moodie's absence from the Primary Dept of the Academy and that attempts had been made to recruit a part-time substitute from the Burgh School. That plan progressed as far as the offer of a teacher for three periods of two hours per week.[96] Then, from late September, the staff heard 'a rumour that the school building was to be used for military purposes'. That was when Mr Roy visited the Grange School and discovered that four rooms were able to be made available to him.[97] In early October the news was confirmed that 'Notice has been received from the Clerk that the use of the school premises has been granted to the military authorities, and that arrangements for transferring the work of the school to the Grange should be made'.[98]

Apart from the early staffing issues, there was very little else that was war-related except for the two references to Miss Herald. In February 1917 'Miss Herald was off duty today, word having been received from the War Office that her brother had been killed in action in Mesopotamia'[99] and it seems likely that it was not unconnected that a year later Miss Herald also wanted leave of absence to do a VAD training course in July 1918.[100] This permission was granted, although it was in school time.

As with the Grange School, the main impact on the pupils of the Burgh School was in raising money for war-related charities. They collected £2 10s 2d in October 1914 for the Belgian Relief Fund[101] and a month later £1 15s 4d for the Scottish Red Cross.[102] There were collections in aid of Belgium again in May 1916,[103] Serbia in June 1916,[104] and the Scottish Women's Hospitals got £15 in July 1916.[105]

Two occasions of charitable giving were more unique to the Burgh School. The first was in April 1916, when there was 'a collection to purchase croquet mallets for Convalescent soldiers at Arns Brae Hospital.'[106] This inspired idea raised almost £2 10s. The other was that the Headmaster's log book twice referred to the school making collections for specific gifts to former pupils in the forces. In December 1914 he noted that 'Christmas gifts were dispatched to the fifty former pupils of the school who are under arms'[107] and in April 1916 he wrote 'Last week, pupils collected £3 17s to send gifts to old pupils who have joined HM Forces'.[108] As with all the schools in the burgh, it was agreed in 1916 to form a War Savings Association,[109] and the Headmaster was instructed to explain the scheme to the pupils.[110]

Another war-related event which concerned the pupils was the return to Alloa of

Corporal Dawson VC in December 1915. They were given a half day on the 20th and when he actually visited the school on 22 December he received 'a rousing welcome'.[111]

The pupils showed their patriotism every May as usual on Empire Day and the log book recorded that for its celebration in May 1916 'The children sang a verse of *Songs of Motherland* and two verses of *God Save the King*.[112] Yet more patriotic, though, was that some of the senior pupils who had been the winners of an RSPCA essay-writing competition agreed to forgo their trip to the presentation in Edinburgh, 'In view of the fact that the Country is at war and as an exercise in practical thrift...'[113]

The only other war-related references in the log book were the meetings in September 1916 to discuss '...arrangements for darkening the school to meet the darkening regulations',[114] and the recognition of the impact of the Spanish Flu in 1918, when the log book recorded that 'The attendance at the schools in town has been very low, and is rapidly falling owing to an epidemic of Influenza...'[115]

The last reference to the war, as with almost every local school, was in July 1919, when it was noted that 'A holiday was given today in celebration of the signing of peace'.[116]

ALLOA SCIENCE AND ART SCHOOL

In 1885 Alloa Burgh Council set up and supported financially the Alloa Science and Art School. This was a smart name for the Continuation (evening) classes which met mainly in the Town Hall, where there was a suite of classrooms and laboratories on the upper floors, but were taught by teachers from all the local schools. It was accountable to the Council and supervised by a sub-committee from it so there were well-kept minutes which dealt largely with details of finance and appointments. The varied programme of subjects for men and women included cooking, ambulance, millinery and needlework, as well as engineering, mining, art, chemistry, commercial, building construction and even naval architecture. These Continuation classes were well supported throughout the war, with 792 students in October 1917. They had a small problem in September 1917, when it was decided to cancel the Confectionery class due to lack of sugar. They also had trouble with getting the shipyard workers into the classes because they were doing so much overtime and general problems with staffing as the war progressed and teachers had to join up. There was no real shortage of replacement teachers though, possibly partly due to patriotism and also it because they were quite well paid, at 4 shillings per hour. The accounts showed that Peter Christie, the Academy Technical teacher, gained an additional £85 on his normal salary for

1917–1918, Peter Walker gained £67 and Joe Atkinson, the Acting Headmaster of the Academy Primary Dept. gained £35. That did not, however, stop many of them asking the Council for an increase for the 1918-1919 session, which was flatly rejected.[117]

ST JOHNS PRIMARY SCHOOL

The usual sources – log book, School Board minutes etc – are available for St John's Primary School, but a former pupil of the school, Charles Palmer, also wrote a history of the school back in the 1990s when he was still a pupil at Alloa Academy, and some of his research have been incorporated into this chapter. The Headmaster for the war years was Mr Sidney Perry. As with the other Alloa primary schools, references to the impact of the war were few – there was, for instance, only one war-related reference during the whole of 1916.

In December 1915 the Headmaster attested under the Derby scheme,[118] (an early attempt to organise recruiting, but not going as far as conscription) but as the only man in the school and probably 'protected' he would hardly have thought he was ever likely to be sent off to war.

St John's was a type of voluntary–funded school linked to the Episcopal Church and was therefore on a slightly different financial footing from Sunnyside and the other primary schools, which were controlled by the Alloa Burgh School Board. Staff were concerned, therefore, in December 1916 about whether they would receive the War Bonus that was being distributed by the Alloa School Board; £15 extra on an average salary of about £75 pa was, after all, not something to be ignored.[119] In September 1917 the staff petitioned the managers for an increase in salaries. This request was put on hold for the teaching staff, but the female caretaker was given a rise to 11 shillings a week.[120]

In July 1918 Miss Pearson was given leave of absence to visit her brother, who had been injured in a flying accident, presumably war-related, in Grantham.[121]

The first reference to the impact of the war on pupils was as early as September 1914, when the Headmaster noted that 'he had forwarded a list of the names of pupils whose fathers are serving in the Imperial Forces, with his opinion as to whether or not they are properly clothed and fed'.[122]

Like all the other local schools, there was plenty of charitable giving by the pupils. There was a collection in October 1914 for Belgian relief, then in October 1917 the headmaster noted 'The lessons were interrupted for a short time this afternoon to allow two ladies to take a collection from the pupils for the relief of desolated villages in

France on the Somme'[123] and in May 1918 they contributed towards Alexandra Rose Day.[124] They also started their War Savings Association,[125] but, apart from that, there were NO other log book references to the war's impact on St John's Primary School.

In November 1918, like all the other local schools, St John's was closed due to the Spanish Flu epidemic. However, the Headmaster, Mr Perry **did** open the school on Monday 11 November 1918, when he at least knew that the Armistice had happened. He noted proudly on that day[126] that 'School met, percentage of absentees thirty... before dismissal of pupils, the surrendering of Germany was notified to them and a few patriotic melodies were sung, including the National Anthem'. So the school was opened just long enough for him to record the important news, then the pupils were sent home again, as per the instructions of the School Medical Officer. The last war-related entry in the log book was on 1 July 1919, when the Rector recorded that 'A whole holiday given today, because the terms of peace were signed by the German delegates on Saturday June 28th'.[127]

The school was losing money during the war and Charles Palmer's view is that the strains of the war on its funds (a loss year-on-year right through the war)[128] were sufficient to push the school into a position of surrendering its autonomy willingly by 1919, when it was transferred by sale to the local authority.[129]

ALLOA ACADEMY PRIMARY DEPARTMENT

There is very little documentation at all for this primary school. The Headmaster, Mr Peter Moodie, left for war service very early on, because by 27 August 1914 (only the third week of the war) the School Board was already making alternative arrangements for paying him.[130] Indeed, a cheque for £16 was sent to him on 2 September to make up for his missed August salary.[131] The log book also implied that he must have had some input into the teaching in the Academy itself, because it recorded that 'Mr Brooke, organist in Moncrieff Church has been temporarily appointed to teach the Music to Intermediate pupils and Junior students during Mr Moodie's absence at the war'.[132] Mr Moodie himself had a fairly successful war, getting a musketry certificate in August 1915,[133] being promoted to Major in May 1916,[134] being mentioned in dispatches[135] and being awarded the Territorial Decoration by 1919 for his long service as a Territorial officer. That allowed him to put the letters TD after his name.

In Mr Moodie's absence, Mr Atkinson was quite quickly appointed as Acting Headmaster of the Primary Department (with Mr Blair as advisor).[136] The Council recognised Mr Atkinson's efforts in 1916 by granting him an honorarium of £30 (his senior assistant Miss Moyes got £20) due to 'the additional duties laid upon them during the past two years due to the absence of Mr Moodie on military service'.[137] In May 1919 Mr Moodie declined the Council's request to resume his position as head of the Primary Department. (he had done the job since 1891),[138] and Mr Atkinson was offered the job, since he had done it so capably during the war.[139]

Two lady members of staff left the school during the war; Miss E. MacDougall went to the 4th Scottish General Hospital at Stobhill and Miss A.T. Moyes went to Gretna as a welfare supervisor, presumably in the munitions industry.[140] The School Board also wondered if Miss Janet Laidlaw was serving in war work somewhere.

SUNNYSIDE SCHOOL

It is worth noting that at the time of World War I, primary schools in Alloa were big, with large class-sizes. In 1914, Sunnyside had 743 pupils and seventeen staff, including the Headmaster. By comparison, Alloa Academy had only around just over 200 pupils, with a new first-year intake of between fifty-eight to seventy each year and a staff of about twenty, including the Rector. Grange School, the 'junior' secondary, had 448 pupils in September 1914.

Sunnyside had to manage without two of its three male teachers from fairly early on. Mr James Younie and Mr Ronald Christie both joined up and served in Mesopotamia and France respectively.[141] Mr Younie had attested under the Derby Scheme in 1915 and then joined the Royal Garrison Artillery in June 1916,[142] rising to become a Sergeant by the war's end.[143] He only returned to his teaching duties in November 1919.[144] The only mention of Mr Christie's war service in the log book was a reference on 25 January 1918[145] and an entry once the war was over which welcomed him back to duty in the school.[146] He served as a Sergeant in the RAMC.[147] One other male teacher at Sunnyside was involved in military duties; Mr R.G. Duff had been transferred from the Grange School in October 1916[148] and was sent off to attend Volunteer Officers Drill classes. However, it was only in April 1918 that he had his military medical examination which he passed Grade 3,[149] meaning that he was not actually fit for active service. He was appointed to be Assistant Adjutant to the 1st Clackmannanshire Volunteer Regiment[150] and, following his letters to the School Board, had his salary made up on the same terms as other serving teachers.[151] This Volunteer Regiment was a sort of World War I version of the Home Guard, where the men who were interested but too old, in reserved occupations or granted conditional exemption by the tribunal were expected to show their willingness to do a bit of military training.

As elsewhere, the impact of the war on female staff was often that they needed time off to mourn loved ones who had been killed in action. In October 1918, Miss Keith was granted most of the week off, having just had news of 'the death of her brother in action in France.'[152] On 6 December 1918 Miss M.A.J. Cairns was given the same sad privilege on account of the death of her brother.[153] His death was one of the four wartime references to former pupils found in the Alloa Academy Rector's log book.

Sunnyside's log book recorded what must have been an unusual and progressive event for Alloa in 1915; the school was visited by the new Burgh Medical Officer, Dr Ethel Cassie.[154] Not many women were given that sort of job in those days, but the previous Burgh Medical Officer Dr C.C. Finlator was engaged in RAMC duties in Egypt. He in fact returned to duty in April 1919.[155] Alloa seemed to be a pioneer in this respect, though it should be pointed out that the Burgh Council only managed to retain Dr Cassie's services in mid-1917 by giving her a £50 per year pay rise, which encouraged her to withdraw her resignation.[156] Even though she served as Medical Officer for over three years of the war, she was **never** given a permanent appointment. In September 1918 she left the burgh for a permanent position in Leith.[157] She was replaced as interim Medical Officer by Dr Josephine Cairns, before Dr Finlator resumed his duties. It was Dr Cairns whose signature was on all the certificates authorising the closure of schools in late 1918, during the Spanish Flu epidemic.

Empire Day was also observed every May throughout the war, when 'patriotic addresses were delivered' to the pupils.[158] Alloa's first VC winner, James Lennox Dawson, visited the school on 22 December 1915. He may have had a rousing reception at the Grange School, but Sunnyside's log book, in a little bit of one-upmanship, was able to announce possessively that Sunnyside School was 'where he received his early training'.[159] The *Scotsman* recorded Dawson's 'common touch' at his old school, where 'he greatly delighted the children by allowing them individually to inspect the medal.'[160] War savings activities also received several mentions in the log book from 1916 onwards. By the end of March 1918, the pupils of Sunnyside had saved almost £800.[161]

ST MUNGO'S PRIMARY SCHOOL

Very little has been discovered about this school during the war years. It was a church voluntary school, like St John's, but served the Roman Catholic community of Alloa, and its premises were on the north side of the Clackmannan Road. Its roll was 200 pupils in early 1915.[162] The school's log book for the war years does exist, but it was very sparse on detail about almost everything. It was a four-teacher school led by Miss S. Sharkey, with three certificated assistants. There seems to have been great pressures on the school, with 'several children unable to attend on account of extreme poverty'[163] in September 1914. Its 1915 Report from the inspectors further added that there were sixty-three infant children but only fifty-six desks; 'so impossible for a single teacher effectively to supervise all the children at once, [leading to] a considerable degree of restlessness and inattention'.[164]

The first (indirect) reference in the log book to the war was in October 1915, when 'Ladies of Red Cross Organisation visited school ... to distribute flags'.[165] The only specific reference to the war was in May 1917 when 'The War Savings Association was begun in this school this week'. Subscriptions to the fund were to be collected on Monday and Friday each week.[166] The school did open on 11 November 1918 but the headmistress wrote nothing about the Armistice and merely recorded 'School re-opened today but as percentage of absentees was 22 per cent the school was re-closed by the Medical Officer.'[167] The head teacher Miss Sharkey, could, of course, have opened and closed the school before news came through of the Armistice. She did write one more war-related entry in July 1919, noting that 'The Education Authority granted a whole holiday today in honour of Peace'.[168]

ENDNOTES

1. The national census of April 1901 has the Rector's age as 49
2. Alloa Burgh School Board letter book. Letter to Scotch Education Dept. 1 Feb 1917
3. Alloa Academy Rector's Log Book 11 Sept 1914
4. Alloa Academy Rector's Log Book 10 Sept 1915
5. Alloa Academy Rector's Log Book 27 Nov 1914
6. Alloa Burgh School Board letter book. Letter to Mr Thomas Ironside 13 Nov 1914
7. Alloa Burgh School Board letter book. Letter to Mr P.T. Moodie 27 Aug 1914
8. Alloa Burgh School Board letter book. Letter to Private J.F. Duffin 30 Sept 1914 James Cuthbert was later to become the Town Clerk
9. Alloa Burgh School Board letter book. Letter to Captain Moodie 30 Sept 1914
10. Alloa Burgh School Board letter book. Letter to Captain Moodie 2 Sept 1917

11 Alloa Academy Rector's Log Book 17 March 1916
12 Alloa Academy Rector's Log Book 17 March 1916 [Mr Macfarlane was promoted out of the county during the war]
13 Alloa Academy Rector's Log Book 31 March 1916
14 Alloa Burgh School Board letter book. Letter from Mr Duffin 27 March 1916
15 Alloa Academy Rector's Log Book 28 April 1916
16 Alloa Burgh School Board letter book. Letter to Miss Troup 1 Oct 1918
17 Alloa Burgh School Board letter book. Letter to Scotch Education Dept. 28 Nov 1916
18 Alloa Burgh School Board letter book. Letter on school business 20 Feb 1915
19 Alloa Academy Rector's Log Book 9 June 1916
20 *Alloa Advertiser* 20 Jan 1917 p. 3 col. 2
21 Alloa Burgh School Board letter book. Letter concerning war service late 1917
22 Alloa Burgh Roll of Honour. Add up the figures and divide the number of those killed into the number that served.
23 Alloa Academy Rector's Log Book 8 Sept 1916
24 *Alloa Journal* 9 Feb 1918 p. 3 col. 5
25 *Alloa Advertiser* 14 Dec 1918 p. 3 col. 5
26 Alloa Academy Rector's Log Book 22 Nov 1918
27 *Alloa Journal* 19 April 1919 p. 2 col. 1
28 Alloa Burgh School Board letter book. Letter to Recruiting officer 23 Sept 1916
29 Alloa Burgh School Board letter book. Letter to recruiting Board 4 Oct 1916
30 *Alloa Journal* 31 Aug 1918 p. 3 col. 3, 7 Sept 1918 p. 3 col. 3
31 Alloa Academy Rector's Log Book 7 Sept 1917
32 Alloa Academy Rector's Log Book 24 May 1918
33 Alloa Burgh School Board letter book. Letter Scotch Education Dept. 24 May 1918
34 Alloa Burgh School Board letter book. Letter dated 4 Sept 1918
35 Alloa Burgh School Board letter book. Letter to Assistant Recruiting Director, Stirling 20 Oct 1918
36 Alloa Burgh School Board letter book. Letter to Matthew Blair 30 Sept 1914
37 *Alloa Journal* 27 February 1915 p. 3 col. 7
38 *Alloa Journal* 27 February 1915 p. 3 col. 7
39 Alloa Academy Rector's Log Book 16 July 1915
40 The following names of former pupils **do** have names and addresses in the Alloa Academy Secondary Admissions Register which match those in the Burgh of Alloa Roll of Honour but are **not listed** on the Alloa Academy Roll of Honour: George Manson, James Arnott, James McInnes, Norman Wright, Albert Chisholm, Carel Watt Fidler and James Lawson Cairns
41 Alloa Academy Rector's Log Book 25 June 1915. This boy was born in April 1898 [Alloa Academy Secondary Admission Register No. 919] so he was already over seventeen years old when he applied to leave
42 Alloa Academy Rector's Log Book 10 Dec 1915
43 *Scotsman* 24 Dec 1915

44 Alloa Academy Rector's Log Book 24 Dec 1915
45 He probably gave it to his mother, along with a set of knives and forks from Sunnyside School, since she had received a 'handsome silver tea service' from the Council at her son's civic reception in the Town Hall, reported in *Alloa Circular* 29 Dec 1915 p. 3 col. 3. With all these gifts added together she must have had a full dining set!
46 Alloa Academy Rector's Log Book 19 Oct 1917. The Dux is the prize for and the title of the cleverest pupil in the school; see Chapter 11
47 Alloa Academy Rector's Log Book 6 Dec 1918. The Rector got this slightly wrong; William Cairns' rank was now a Cadet in the Royal Engineers [ie a trainee officer]; he had been a Sergeant in a signal company and had served in Italy. He certainly was not a Private. See *Alloa Journal* 7 Dec 1918 p. 2 col. 3
48 *Alloa Journal* 29 May 1915 p. 3 col. 7
49 *Alloa Advertiser* 1 June 1918 p. 3 col. 1
50 Alloa Academy Rector's Log Book 23 Oct 1914
51 Alloa Academy Rector's Log Book 30 June 1916
52 Alloa Academy Rector's Log Book 7 July 1916
53 *Alloa Advertiser* 27 May 1916 p. 4 col. 3 had a whole column reporting it
54 *Alloa Journal* 24 June 1916 p. 3 col. 5
55 *Alloa Journal* 20 Nov 1915 p. 3 col. 5
56 *Alloa Journal* 15 April 1916 p. 3 col. 1
57 *Stirling Observer* 6 June 1916 p. 3 col. 1
58 Alloa Academy Rector's Log Book 15 July 1915
59 *Alloa Circular* 21 July 1915 p. 2 col. 4
60 Minute book of Alloa Academy Literary and Debating Society
61 Alloa Academy Rector's Log Book 18 Sept 1915
62 Alloa Burgh School Board minute book 23 Feb 1916
63 Alloa Academy Rector's Log Book 8 Dec 1915
64 Alloa Academy Rector's Log Book 26 Jan 1917, 2 Feb 1917
65 Alloa Burgh School Board letter book 20 March 1918
66 Alloa Academy Rector's Log Book 25 May 1917
67 Alloa Burgh School Board letter book, letter to C.S. Dougall 1 June 1917
68 Alloa Academy Rector's Log Book 14 Sept 1917, 21 Sept 1917
69 Alloa Burgh School Board letter book 20 March 1918
70 *Alloa Advertiser* 1 Dec 1917 p. 3 cols. 2-4
71 Alloa Academy Rector's Log Book 15 Nov 1918
72 Alloa Academy Rector's Log Book 17 Jan 1919
73 Alloa Academy Rector's Log Book 14 Feb 1919
74 Alloa Academy Rector's Log Book 25 April 1919 refers to him 'being retained by the Army in Germany' so it is possible he was serving with the Allied occupation forces in the Rhineland

75   Alloa Academy Rector's Log Book 23 May 1919. Mary Cairns was the sister of Nellie Cairns [see p. 35], and both became long-serving Academy staff. They were the only teachers where pupils were allowed to refer to them by their Christian names [ie Miss Mary or Miss Nellie] in order to distinguish which one they meant
76   Alloa Burgh School Board letter book. Letter to Staff Captain J.R. Turner 14 Oct 1914
77   Alloa Burgh School Board letter book. Letter to A.P. Moir, Territorial Association 23 Sept 1914
78   Alloa Burgh School Board letter book 3 Oct 1914
79   Grange School Headmaster's Log Book 7 Sept 1915. *Alloa Circular* 8 Sept 1915 p. 3 col. 3 for detailed obituary
80   Grange School Headmaster's Log Book 5 Sept 1916
81   Grange School Headmaster's Log Book 7 Nov 1916
82   Grange School Headmaster's Log Book 11 Feb 1918
83   Grange School Headmaster's Log Book 23 May 1918
84   Grange School Headmaster's Log Book 23 Oct 1914
85   Grange School Headmaster's Log Book 30 May 1916
86   Grange School Headmaster's Log Book 14 July 1916
87   Grange School Headmaster's Log Book 13 Oct 1916
88   Grange School Headmaster's Log Book 28 Feb 1919
89   Grange School Headmaster's Log Book 13 June 1918
90   Grange School Headmaster's Log Book 18 June 1918
91   Grange School Headmaster's Log Book 26 May 1915
92   Grange School Headmaster's Log Book 22 Dec 1915
93   Grange School Headmaster's Log Book 8 March 1918
94   Alloa Burgh School Headmaster's Log Book 3 Sept 1914
95   Alloa Burgh School Headmaster's Log Book 21 June 1918
96   Alloa Burgh School Headmaster's Log Book 10 Sept 1914
97   Alloa Burgh School Headmaster's Log Book 22 Sept 1914
98   Alloa Burgh School Headmaster's Log Book 2 Oct 1914
99   Alloa Burgh School Headmaster's Log Book 19 Feb 1917
100 Alloa Burgh School Headmaster's Log Book 21 June 1918
101 Alloa Burgh School Headmaster's Log Book 30 Oct 1914
102 Alloa Burgh School Headmaster's Log Book 20 Nov 1914
103 Alloa Burgh School Headmaster's Log Book 30 May 1916
104 Alloa Burgh School Headmaster's Log Book 29 June 1916
105 Alloa Burgh School Headmaster's Log book 14 July 1916
106 Alloa Burgh School Headmaster's Log book 27 April 1916
107 Alloa Burgh School Headmaster's Log Book 16 Dec 1914
108 Alloa Burgh School Headmaster's Log Book 7 April 1916
109 Alloa Burgh School Headmaster's Log Book 10 July 1916
110 Alloa Burgh School Headmaster's Log Book 26 Sept 1916

111 Alloa Burgh School Headmaster's Log Book 22 Dec 1915
112 Alloa Burgh School Headmaster's Log Book 24 May 1916
113 Alloa Burgh School Headmaster's Log Book 12 May 1916
114 Alloa Burgh School Headmaster's Log Book 15 Sept 1916
115 Alloa Burgh School Headmaster's Log Book 18 Oct 1918
116 Alloa Burgh School Headmaster's Log Book 1 July 1919
117 Alloa Science and Art School Management Committee minute book
118 St John's School Headmaster's Log Book 9 Dec 1915
119 St John's School Management Committee minute book 18 Sept 1917
120 St John's School Managers minute book 20 Sept 1917
121 St John's School Headmaster's Log Book 1 July 1918
122 St John's School Headmaster's Log Book 18 Sept 1914
123 St John's School Headmaster's Log Book 19 Oct 1917
124 St John's School Headmaster's Log Book 26 Oct 1914
125 St John's School Headmaster's Log Book 11 may 1917
126 St John's School Headmaster's Log Book 11 Nov 1918
127 St John's School Headmaster's Log Book 1 July 1919
128 St John's School Managers minute book. The debt in September 1916 was £328; by December 1917 it was £564
129 *History of St John's School* by Charles Palmer p. 56
130 Alloa Burgh School Board letter book 27 Aug 1914
131 Alloa Burgh School Board letter book 2 Sept 1914
132 Alloa Burgh School Board letter book 2 Oct 1914
133 *Alloa Circular* 4 Aug 1915 p. 3 col. 2
134 *Alloa Journal* 20 May 1916 p. 2 cols. 4-5
135 7th Battalion Argylls Regimental History p. 69 [plus photograph]
136 Alloa Burgh School Board letter book 2 Sept 1914
137 Alloa Burgh School Board minute book 14 April 1916
138 *Alloa Journal* 11 July 1914 p. 3 col. 2
139 *Alloa Advertiser* 3 May 1919 p. 4 col. 1. Mr Atkinson later became headmaster of Sunnyside, until 1941
140 Alloa Burgh School Board letter book late 1917
141 Alloa Burgh School Board letter book late 1917
142 Sunnyside School Headmaster's Log Book 16 June 1916
143 Burgh of Alloa Roll of Honour
144 Sunnyside School Headmaster's Log Book 21 Nov 1919
145 Sunnyside School Headmaster's Log Book 25 Jan 1918
146 Sunnyside School Headmaster's Log Book 21 March 1919
147 Burgh of Alloa Roll of Honour. Alloa Advertiser 15 July 1916 p. 2 col. 5 refers to him getting appendicitis while on active service in Salonica

148 Grange School Headmaster's Log Book 5 Oct 1916
149 Sunnyside School Headmaster's Log Book 24 May 1918
150 Alloa Burgh School Board minute book 29 April 1918
151 Alloa Burgh School Board minute book 24 June 1918
152 Sunnyside School Headmaster's Log Book 4 Oct 1918
153 Sunnyside School Headmaster's Log Book 6 Dec 1918
154 Sunnyside School Headmaster's Log Book 30 April 1915
155 Sunnyside School Headmaster's Log Book 10 April 1919
156 *Alloa Journal* 28 July 1917 p. 3 col. 2
157 *Alloa Advertiser* 27 July 1918 p. 2 col. 5
158 Sunnyside School Headmaster's Log Book 28 May 1914
159 Sunnyside School Headmaster's Log Book 23 Dec 1915
160 *Scotsman* 24 Dec 1915
161 Sunnyside School Headmaster's Log Book 28 March 1918. Using the Retail Price Index, that figure of £800 would be equivalent to over £30,000 in today's [2013] money. However, Sunnyside's World War I total was not a patch on what its pupils raised in World War II. In one week alone in April 1943 the pupils banked over £1,000. On 18 Sept 1944, the Director of Education visited the school to congratulate them on having their success in War Savings announced on the radio. See Sunnyside School Headmaster's Log Book
162 *Alloa Journal* 30 Jan 1915 p. 3 col. 7
163 St Mungo's Primary School Log Book 18 Sept 1914
164 St Mungo's Primary School Log Book 20 May 1915
165 St Mungo's Primary School Log Book 22 Oct 1915
166 St Mungo's Primary School Log Book 4 May 1917
167 St Mungo's Primary School Log Book 11 Nov 1918
168 St Mungo's Primary School Log Book 1 July 1919

CHAPTER 5

SPORT AND THE WAR

This is quite a mixed bag of topics, some small and only interesting to a few. If a generalisation can be made about sport in Alloa and World War I it is that the larger team sports, often watched by crowds and taking part in national leagues, went into a deep decline during the war years, but not as quickly as might have been expected in the case of football. However, the smaller individual sports, perhaps not needing necessarily to be played by fit young men of fighting age, carried on more or less as normal, making some adjustments for wartime circumstances.

FOOTBALL

The war started in football's off-season so there was not really a season to interrupt; it was more a question of what the wider public thought should be allowed to go on, given the new war circumstances. After all, the *Circular*'s view was that 'Football while our country is at war savours of sacrilege, and a good deal of criticism has been levelled against the Football Association for allowing the game to proceed'.[1] However, it did go on to say that in times such as these, 'for a respite from the realities of warfare', it could be that there was nothing better than the 'people's game'. It might be pointed out that, after only two weeks of being at war, the *Circular* could hardly argue that it was particularly well-informed on what it called 'the realities of warfare'.

Alloa Athletic FC was not in the top flight; it was a semi-professional team playing in the Central League and many of the clubs it played would be recognised as playing at the Junior level today, although in the 1913–14 season it had played Glasgow Rangers in the Cup, had been outclassed and lost 5–0. There was a meeting in Edinburgh in early August 1914 to consider postponing opening matches, since 'several teams have been seriously affected by the embodiment of the territorials',[2] however, nothing seemed to happen and Alloa Athletic played **all** its 1914–15 season's fixtures. The *Journal* generally included a couple of columns on its back page, giving details of the football, golf and bowls matches being played. Alloa Athletic took on the likes of Bo'ness, Clackmannan, King's Park, Broxburn, Forfar and Stenhousemuir.

Alloa had another team, Alloa Seafield Thistle, which played in a lower league, and they also completed a full season of fixtures in 1914–15.

After that first wartime season, though, things were clearly not going well in the Central League and in August 1915 the *Journal* published an article called 'Alloa Athletic's policy for coming season'. This noted that 'Were it left to the Athletic's officials to decide, there would be no football of any kind played by the local club next season'.[3] However, it was recognised that there were standing charges like ground rent, rates and so forth that the club had to meet whether they played or not, so they were looking for some sort of income. This lack of support for playing must have been widespread, because the Central League was suspended from August 1915 onwards and Alloa could not get a place in the Eastern League,[4] so there was no senior football for Alloa Athletic from then on, and the club gradually fell into debt. They were invited to take part in the reconstituted East League for the 1917–18 season but declined, owing to difficulties with their ground.[5]

Alloa Seafield Thistle carried on the Stirlingshire Junior League for the 1915–16 season, but the *Journal* became less interested in giving match reports on what was clearly a lower standard team. In fact, on 25 March 1916 it did not mention the local team but reported in glowing terms on the 2/7th Argylls football team, which was having a run of success.[6] By the 1916–17 season there was no regular match reporting of Alloa Seafield at all in the *Journal*. Instead, it reported quite fully on a series of big war-charity football matches between groups of local military or local workers,[7] which sometimes failed to raise the amount of money expected, partly due to poor weather hitting attendances:

Paton's Mills versus RAMC (Tillicoultry) which took place at the Recreation Park on 2 Dec 1916[8]
Jeffrey's ship workers versus Kelliebank bottling plant workers on 6 January 1917.[9]
Shipyard workers versus Paton's Mills on 27 January 1917.[10]
Blairhall Colliery versus Melvin's Foundry on 3 February 1917.[11]
Shipyard workers versus Younger's glass workers on 24 February 1917.[12]
Queen's Park Strollers versus RAMC (Tillicoultry) on 3 March 1917.[13]

Such scratch local military or works teams carried on playing matches against each other in a mini-league for the rest of the war years, often getting a decent report in the local press. However, there was no serious professional football and in fact Alloa Athletic FC wound itself up as a business in February 1919. They had assets of about £6 10s- and debts of about £105 (chiefly rent). The members immediately set up a new limited liability company worth £3,000 (divided into 3,000 shares at £1 each)[14] to keep a senior football club going,[15] and it still called itself Alloa Athletic. The directors of the new team managed to assemble a decent collection of players – curiously, three of them were ex-soldiers from the 7th Argylls – and they played their first match of the 1919–20 season in the Central League against Bathgate on 16 August 1919[16] and won 2–1. The popularity of football in that immediate post-war period should not be underestimated; when Alloa Athletic played East Stirling in the Qualifying Cup in 1919 there were 8,000 spectators.

CRICKET

Clackmannan County Cricket Club was the local team, playing at the Arns, and they played sixteen matches in their rather unsuccessful 1914 season, which started on Saturday 2 May; they only won one county match and one friendly. Their professional and new junior professional (Arthur West and Mark Wilson) generally played well and the other outstanding player was Charles Frearson Younger, who scored 184 runs and took 14 wickets.

The last match they played in the 1914 season was against Stirling County at Williamfield on Saturday 1 August, the weekend before the declaration of war (Stirling County made 99 and Clackmannan County made 94 all out). Their next match should have been against Stewartonians (Edinburgh) but was postponed, as were the remaining two county matches. Less than a week after the start of the war, the local press noted that four players of the Alloa XI were on active service and reported the view of Clackmannan County CC that 'Irrespective of the depletion of club strength, the Committee thought they would be respecting the general trend of popular feeling in departing from the fixture'.[17]

The minutes of the last wartime AGM of Clackmannan County CC, held in the Royal Oak Hotel on Friday 16 April 1915, reveals a lot about the way it planned to organise itself.[18] At that meeting the President, Thomas S. Knox, noted that cricket had been more or less cancelled, so Clackmannan CCC's ground, the Arns, was placed at the disposal of the Army. It was agreed that any club members in the armed forces should not have to pay their subscriptions for the duration of the war. The club made an offer of all its pavilion garden seats for the use of wounded soldiers at Arnsbrae House, which had just recently been fitted out as a convalescent hospital. It was also agreed to start a Roll of Honour. The President said 'it would afford him much pleasure if the club would allow him to prepare the Roll and have it done up in suitable style so that it might stand as a permanent record of the club's connection with the war'. The Secretary reported that there were at least forty names of serving soldiers ready for inclusion on the roll. They probably did not appreciate then just how many of the club's members and sons of members would actually perish, then feature on the war memorial which Thomas S. Knox would end up paying for.

The Arns did not, however, remain totally silent to the sound of leather on willow during the war years. The club scorebook shows that one match was played in 1915 and the local press recorded details of another match in 1917. Both matches were against teams from battalions of soldiers in training camps nearby and for the first match Clackmannan County put out a scratch team composed of the two professionals (one of whom, Mark Wilson, was home on leave from the Navy[19]), a few veteran members and a club member home on leave from the Army.

This match was against a team from the 2nd/5th King's Own Scottish Borderers training battalion stationed at Rumbling Bridge and took place on 17 July 1915, raising funds for Arnsbrae Red Cross Hospital. Clackmannan County scored 136 runs in their 29 overs but the KOSBs only made 106 runs despite a promising start. Perhaps they missed the batting skills of Lieut. Henery, who had to retire from the crease early, on account of having to leave for the Dardanelles.[20] The weather was favourable, there was a fair crowd, they were entertained by a band from the 3rd/7th Argylls, and the *Circular* commented that the 'Old Lights' of the Alloa XI 'showed they had not forgotten how to wield the willow'.[21]

The second match was against a team from the Cameron Highlanders and took place on 7 July 1917 in aid of Red Cross Week.[22] The Alloa XI was under the charge of veteran club member T.A. Bowie, who had played six pre-war internationals for Scotland, and in his scratch team were West, the professional, and Sidney Perry, the headmaster of St John's Primary School. There was a good attendance and the weather was ideal.[23] The Cameron Highlanders batted first, making 122 runs. In response, although the Alloa XI made a good start – their first three batsmen got half the required total – the rest fell away and they were all out for 110. They could not really cope with the bowling skills of Lieut. B.L. Peel who took 6 for 38.[24] The match raised £16 for the Red Cross.[25] After that, there was no more cricket at the Arns for the rest of the war.

It was also the case that not every Clackmannan County cricketer forgot their interest in the sport entirely during the war. Lieut. J.C. Brown, who had played three times for the club in 1914 season and scored 19 runs, joined the Royal Engineers and became captain of their cricket team. In one match in 1917, for REs against the Cygnets, he 'had the splendid analysis of 7 wickets for 16 runs'.[26]

There were no more AGMs until 3 April 1919,[27] when the same President, T.S. Knox, was in the chair.

At this meeting, before proceeding with routine business, the chairman 'made feeling reference to the severe loss sustained by the Club by the death on service in the war of no fewer than 12 members, the majority of them active participants in the game...'[28]

He went on to explain that 'It had not been found possible to compile the Roll of Honour referred to [*in the last 1915 minutes*]. No-one foresaw in 1915 that the war would last for years...' He suggested that it be delayed until a complete record could be obtained. That took another three years; and Clackmannan County Cricket Club's war memorial was finally unveiled in May 1922.[29] It contained the names of thirteen members who had played actively for the club, and a further sixteen who were the sons of members. Four of the team who had actually played in the 1914 season were killed. By now T.S. Knox had resigned as President, but he sent a note to accompany the memorial he had paid for once it was ready. He asked that Clackmannan County CC 'accept this from one... who desires to pay tribute to those, as the tablet says, who "Played the game". As a club, we were called on to pay a heavy toll, no club of our size in Scotland being harder hit, but we have the great and grand consolation of knowing that when our boys fell they died the death of heroes.'[30]

(*Photo by Walter Crowe*)

Besides Clackmannan County, Alloa did have another cricket club; St John's Cricket Club, attached to one of the local churches. It had been in existence since 1900 and played on a pitch in a field in the Mar Policies which had been loaned by the Earl of Mar. Its Committee kept good records in a minute book which also included all batting and bowling averages. It was a small but thriving club; it played eighteen matches in 1914 and won nine of them.[31]

The first wartime meeting recorded in their minute book was two months into the war, for their half-yearly general meeting.[32] It was noted that they had given three guineas to the Prince of Wales' National Relief Fund. The Chairman then '...drew attention to the great loss that Lady Mildred Allsopp has sustained by the death of her son Tony through the sinking of the *Aboukir* in the North Sea on 22 September 1914.[33] Both Lady Allsopp and her son had rendered the club effective assistance at the recent concert...' This reference, mentioned only in the St John's Cricket Club minutes and Lady Mar's personal letters to her son, shows just how diverse were the ways that the impact of war extended into different parts of Alloa's population.[34] The private letters of Lady Mar, reveal something of the passion and outrage which she felt and which she would never have expressed in her public life. For example, on 1 October 1914 she wrote that Lady Allsopp '...will never get over Tony's loss. He was just the light of her eyes. She said he looked so thin and... strained at Chatham and he was 6 foot tall at fourteen. Evidently they had all been very seasick the day before they were torpedoed and he may have strained his heart and the fearful cold of the water may have numbed him at once and exhausted him – poor child. It is wicked to have sent those children in that fearful strain... those slow old boats are absolutely defenceless.'[35]

St John's Cricket Club held a meeting in early 1915 to discuss the chances of playing cricket in the forthcoming season. The minutes sounded optimistic when they noted that 'The general position of the club in the current year in view of the war was discussed. It was unanimously resolved that cricket should continue to be played but no fixture list should be compiled, it being left to the discretion of the Committee to arrange fixtures if found practicable.'[36] However, the reality was that no more cricket was played by the club in the war years, the next meeting of the Committee was over four years later in April 1919 and at that meeting the club almost ceased to exist.

In April 1919 the Committee met; their first act was to agree the minutes of the meeting on 23 February 1915. The Chairman said that there had been no meetings 'owing to the war'...and made 'sympathetic reference to the loss the club had sustained in the deaths of James Asquith, Arnold Asquith, Robert Stobbie and Harry Hall...'

This led to debate about whether there were enough players left to form an effective team, and the question was then put to the meeting by the Chairman as to whether the club should continue. Mr Perry said 'he did not think that the war should be the means of putting a stop to the national game of cricket', and the vote for his motion was carried. St John's cricket team played on in 1919, but only just. The club folded in 1924 due to lack of members, and it seems likely that the impact of the war was what started its decline and fall.

SWIMMING

Alloa had an Amateur Boating and Swimming Club, with ladies' and men's sections and boating and swimming sections. Its boating section held its 1914 Regatta on the River Forth on the last Saturday of July;[37] there would be no more of those for a few years. In respect of its swimming sections; while there is not much evidence for its week-by-week wartime activities, it did run very successful annual swimming galas right through the war. The first of these was held on 16 October 1914, and under a heading of 'Gala at the Baths', the *Journal* noted that Alloa Baths 'were crowded to the utmost capacity'.[38] The programme included a demonstration of ornamental swimming, an exhibition on the trapeze, and races between some of the local territorial soldiers. It raised £14 for war relief funds, some of which was clearly spent on comforts sent to the soldiers in the 7th Argylls. In May 1915 the Club President announced in the local press that he had just recently received a belated 'thank you' note from Captain Ramsay Tullis in that battalion. The letter appeared, unfortunately, in the same issue of the *Journal* as the announcement that Captain Tullis had sustained a serious injury in the fighting around Ypres.[39] In fact, Captain Tullis had died of wounds four days earlier,[40] but the *Journal* could not have known that at the time.

By 1915 it seems that the ladies' section of the swimming club was now running the gala. It was held on 4 November 1915: a big attendance was again reported in the local press[41] and it raised £29.

The 1916 gala was held on 17 November 1916. In his opening remarks the Chairman criticised those who said that this sort of thing should be stopped because of the war. He agreed that horse-racing should be stopped, but argued in the gala's defence that it 'developed the muscles and kept its members more fit... and the entire proceeds were to be devoted to war purposes'.[42] Musical entertainment was provided by the RAMC orchestra, which was stationed in Tillicoultry,[43] and the *Advertiser* thought that 'altogether the gala was an unqualified success'.[44] It raised £25 for Scottish Women's Hospitals for Foreign Service.

The 1917 gala was held on 1 December 1917 and contained a programme which was 'of exceptional merit...and embraced no fewer than seventeen distinct events'.[45] There was no reference in the local press to the club running a 1918 gala. The end of the war and the local elections of December dominated the town and it may have been postponed.[46] In February 1919 there was a meeting 'to consider the question of the resuscitation of the Club after its wartime dormancy'[47] when it was noted that this was the first meeting to be held since 18 February 1914.[48] It evidently revived, because they held another gala in July 1919,[49] which raised £41 for YMCA funds,[50] and in August 1919 started building a new club house next to the ferry pier.[51]

Besides the Amateur Swimming Club, Alloa also had the Ladies' Norwood Swimming Club which met at Alloa Baths right through the war. It offered recreational swimming, organised swimming certificates for local pupils, held competitions and galas and encouraged an interest in life saving. Its committee meetings were normally held in the Ladies' cloakroom of the Baths.

On 25 June 1914 (three days before the Archduke's assassination) the club decided to hold its annual gala in September.[52] This might have looked like a bad decision, and by early September '...owing to the war, the Gala Committee had delayed making any arrangements...'[53] However, it was agreed that the gala should take place and 'proceeds should be given to the local Relief Funds'. The gala was held on 28 September and it made over £13. It received a good review in the *Journal*,[54] which commented that 'the pond hall was beautifully decorated with flags and bunting. There was a large attendance of ladies'.

The club may have continued with the gala, but they did agree to cancel their 1914 Annual Dance on account of the war.[55] The evidence in the Committee minutes and the fact of there being regular Committee meetings right through to the end of October 1917 suggest that this club had a nucleus of enthusiastic members who made some effort to sustain a limited programme of events. In the middle of 1915 they reported on a good attendance (eleven members) at lifesaving classes,[56] and they were confident enough to hold their [14th] gala on 18 October 1915.[57] This raised just over £19 for Arnsbrae VAD Hospital.[58] The *Circular* reported at length on the evening's programme.[59]

In the main, things progressed well over 1916. It was agreed to hold a whist drive on 16 March which raised £11 for the Soldiers' and Sailors' Families Association.[60] Then it was agreed to hold an illustrated lecture on lifesaving, diving and swimming.[61]

Attendances must have held up; there were still regular weekly practices on a Monday evening.[62] However, the club decided not to hold a swimming gala at the end of 1916; the *Journal* reported instead on its 'Open Night' on 4 December, where there were swimming races for the club championships.[63] This idea of an Open Night was repeated in 1917.[64] The club seems to have gone into a bit of a decline in the later years of the war; the first committee meeting of 1918 was not until 27 November. As with the 'resuscitation' of Alloa Amateur Boating and Swimming Club, Norwood Ladies Swimming Club also revived itself in 1919; enough to have an excursion for fifty of its members to Pittencrieff Glen, Dunfermline in July 1919[65] and its first post-war gala on the evening of 22 September 1919.[66] This function was chaired by Mrs A. Forrester-Paton, who admitted that 'it induced a certain amount of shame that she could hardly swim', but the *Journal* called it 'a distinct success' and it raised money towards the YMCA Red Triangle Club, though the exact amount was not specified in the local press.

GOLF

The Alloa Golf Club kept going right through the war, playing at the Arnsbrae course, and there was regular reporting in the local press of monthly medals and special tournaments. In early September 1914 the minute book noted that 'In consequence of the European war the Secretary had received a circular in connection with a proposed Athletes Volunteer Force. The matter was discussed...'[67] However, nothing further came of this; possibly because Capt. A.P. Moir was a senior Committee member and he was opposed to this rival of his beloved Territorials.[68]

Right from the start of the war and continuing steadily through it, the club was generous in its contributions to war charities. In the first week of September 'The Committee unanimously agreed to give a donation £2 2s from the club to each of the following funds: Prince of Wales' National Relief Fund, Soldiers' and Sailors' Families Association and the Red Cross Fund. The Secretary also reported that he had received Bronze medals for competition from *Golf Illustrated* – the entry fee to go to '...the Golfers' section of the Prince of Wales' Fund. The Committee accepted the medals and authorised a singles and doubles competition...'[69] The two competitions actually raised £7 towards the Fund.

In readiness for the new 1915 season, the Committee passed several resolutions at its February meeting:

Firstly they '...resolved that the sum of £100 should be invested in the Government War Loan...',[70] then they 'further resolved that:

(a) That there be no club matches this season,
(b) That in consequence of the number of club members in the Army, the Greenfield Trophy be not played for this season,
(c) That there be no prizes other than the first in any competitions,
(d) That an entry fee of 1s be charged [*in several named competitions*] and 6d in the Spring and Autumn medals, the amount received to be applied to the various war funds.
(e) That no subscription be asked from Service members.'[71]

The Committee also agreed in 1915 that '...in the present national crisis it is not desirable that changes should be made and that the present officials should continue in office...'[72]

Alloa Golf Club started its Roll of Honour in February 1915[73] by inscribing in their minute book the twenty-nine names of club members serving in the armed forces. There was no further reference to this Roll in the minutes and it is very difficult to know how many of them died (at least three or four) because the members would have come from all over the Hillfoots, not just Alloa. There was also never a hint in the minute book that Alloa Golf Club should have a war memorial to its fallen members, although two members who fell in action received a particular mention in the minutes; one of them in the rather quaint language so typical of those days. The minute book noted that on 9 March 1916 'The Chairman referred in sympathetic terms to the loss which the club had sustained through the death of Capt. R.R. Tullis 1st/7th Argyll and Sutherland Highlanders who has been killed in action in France. It was agreed to minute the loss to the club of a gentleman who was a true sportsman, a keen golfer and a dutiful and respected citizen.'[74]

By March 1916 the club had invested £200 in Exchequer bonds and war stock.[75] For some reason they had received £150 from Clyde Navigation in November 1915[76] and £100 of this was put towards a War Loan.

Over the following years a lot of the club tournaments had a war charity focus; a big one was during Red Cross Week in July 1917, when the club organised a golf gymkhana,[77] raising just over £22 for Red Cross funds.[78] The club was a little short of active members by mid-1918, when they received the same request to participate

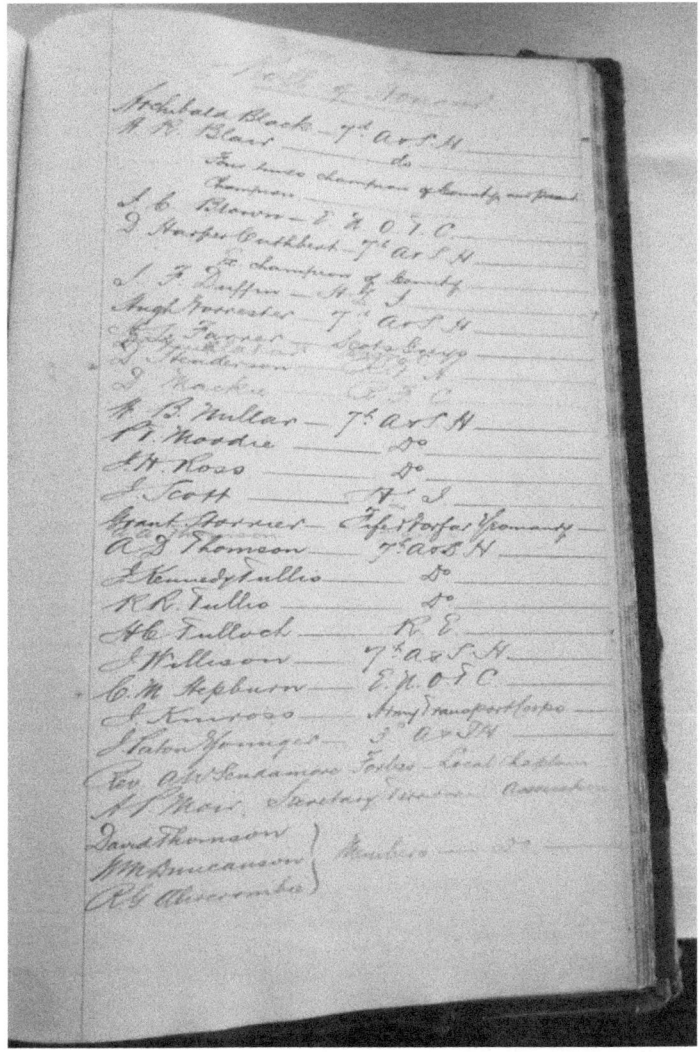

Alloa Golf Club Roll of Honour February 1915
Two names, written in paler ink, may have been added to the Roll at a later date

in Red Cross fundraising between 17-22 June, but the Committee sent a note to the fete's organiser, Mrs Graham Paton, saying that they '...received the request with every degree of favour and resolved... to give a donation of £15 from the funds and that members run a clock golf and other attractions on the Fete day in Alloa Park.'[79]

The Arnsbrae VAD Hospital was right next to the golf course and the club had an attachment to making contributions to it. The minute book had regular entries such as '£8 14s 6d had been collected from Sweepstakes for Arnsbrae...'[80] or '...during last season £2 11s had been collected at mixed foursomes for Arnsbrae Hospital'.[81] However, the minute book was honest enough to admit that relations with the hospital were not always good. In June 1916 it was noted that 'The matter of soldiers in the Arnsbrae VAD Hospital abusing the Golf Course was considered and it was resolved to warn the Authorities at Arnsbrae of the matter.'[82] Later minutes indicate that this was little more than leaving gates open and possibly letting in sheep from neighbouring fields, but in May 1918 the club threatened the hospital with a warning that 'the privilege of allowing the inmates to walk over the course may be withdrawn'.[83]

Before the war, the club employed a full-time green-keeper but they realised they could not hang onto him without a pay rise. In early 1915, therefore, 'It was agreed to recommend that in view of the increased cost of living in consequence of the War, the wages of Gemmell the green-keeper be increased from 25s to 27s a week until the close of the playing season'.[84] In 1916 the club lost Gemmell's services altogether when he was called up to the army, but the club paid a sort of pension to his wife of 5s a week as long as 'she attended to the pavilion, towels etc.'[85] By March 1919 Gemmell had been demobilised and resumed his green-keeping duties, this time at a wage of £2 10s a week, twice his pre-war wage, an indication of the inflation caused by the war.

One last war-related reference is that, at its first post-war AGM in March 1919, the Captain of Alloa Golf Club, Mr John Graeme Thomson of Norwood,[86] sent the club a letter which was read out. In this letter he stated that 'He thought it only right that the Golf Club should have a trophy which in years to come would remind them of the great victory of the Allies over the Central Powers, and of those good friends and members of the club who had died in the field of battle'.[87] He then presented the club with the Victory Trophy, and added 'One condition only would I make; namely that the trophy cannot be won outright... I wish our sons and grandsons to compete for this trophy in years to come and in that way the memory of our Victory and the memory of our friends who died will be a lasting one.'[88] The first competition for this trophy was held on 31 May and 7 June 1919; it is still competed for annually.[89]

BOWLS

This sport continued almost uninterrupted during the war years, with plenty of reports in the local press about different competitions in the different bowling clubs in the burgh. However, many of the local clubs cancelled some of their matches. In

September 1914, Alloa (West End) Bowling Club's committee minutes noted that 'In consequence of the unsettled state of the Country (through the Great War) it had been deemed advisable that the proposed Handicap Comp. should be departed from...',[90] patriotically, they also cancelled subscriptions for members on military service and it was agreed to write to the local Territorials 'Inviting the officers of the Battalion to accept Hon membership during their sojourn in Alloa'.[91]

In March 1915 the Alloa Bowling Club wrote to other local clubs that they 'did not deem it advisable to arrange for the usual fixtures, in consequence of the Great War', and cancelled inter-club tournaments. They pursued this idea further in April 1915, when at their AGM 'The Chairman at the outset made reference to the present European conflict and said that they as a sporting combination could not be expected to enter with the same enthusiasm into their games now as in time of peace. The members would always have in their minds, thoughts regarding their fellows who were fighting the battles of the nation in Flanders.'[92] This idea that competitive play should be abandoned was widely shared, not just by bowlers. The *Journal*'s 'Jottings' column commented that in many local sports 'they were taking the element of serious play out of the game, leaving them entirely recreative, or played, in some cases, with the penalty attached of subscription to a war fund. That is an entirely reasonable attitude.'[93]

At the AGM of the Clackmannan and Kinross Bowls Association in May 1915, Councillor Alexander Wilson of Alloa Bowling Club hit the nail on the head when he explained why bowling should continue during the war, but inter-club games should be scrapped: 'It is true that the majority of men engaged in the game of bowling were beyond military age, but the main objection to the playing of tournaments at such a time was that reports of these things get into the papers which were sent to the front and read by men on active service, and he did not think that was desirable.'[94] Alloa Bowling Club's view on why there were to be no inter-club tournaments was actually written onto the membership card for the 1915 season – the original card can be seen in the club's minute book in the National Archives.

Like all other local sporting bodies, war-related fundraising underpinned most club matches. The highlight for the Alloa Bowling Club was the special Red Cross bowling tournament in July 1917 which took place every afternoon and evening for the whole week.[95] In a nice gesture towards military-community links 'it was resolved to obtain the services of wounded soldiers from Arnsbrae Hospital as markers'.[96] The tournament had an average attendance of about 300 people per day; they played 1,160 rounds[97] and it all raised £20 for Red Cross funds.[98] Not to be outdone, Alloa (East

End) Bowling Club organised its own charity tournament and raised £10, which it sent to the Red Cross.⁹⁹

The May opening of the 1917 season at Alloa Bowling Club; a photograph which proves the point that Alexander Wilson was making; there are only two or three younger faces amongst Alloa's bowlers (*Alloa Advertiser*)

CURLING

This must surely be considered a minority sport, but there were various artificial ponds in the burgh and around the county; Italy Pond, Lornshill Pond, The Delph, etc. and curling started as soon as the season was cold enough. There was a big report in the local press in November 1915, of 'perfect ice' on Italy Pond and Tulliallan Pond, when the Hon. George Bruce, Master of Burleigh was back home on leave to skip the Kennet rink.[100] Lord Mar himself went out and skipped a rink on Alloa Pond in January 1917.[101] The *Circular* reported in October 1915, that Alloa Curling Club had produced its own Roll of Honour of those serving in the armed forces; possibly noteworthy, if only for the fact that it contained fifteen names, all of whom were officers.[102] Like several of these rolls of honour;[103] where is it now?

FISHING

This sport also continued uninterrupted by the war. The *Advertiser* had a weekly section called 'Angling Notes', which gave the conditions and the catches at Loch Leven, Glenquey Loch and other favoured spots.

In 1915 the Devon Angling Association agreed to offer free permits to fish the Devon to any officers and men who were billeted in the district.[104] In 1915 there were still various competitions being run (four on Loch Leven), but at their AGM in April 1917 the members of the Clackmannanshire Fishing Club agreed to suspend fishing competitions for the season, 'owing to the war'.[105]

In the name of equality it must be pointed out that there were other sporting clubs in Alloa during the war years, but there were only very occasional references in the press, or in their own records if they exist, of any of their wartime activities. They included billiards in the Alloa Baths billiards room, badminton in the Alloa Baths gymnasium, and tennis at the Grange Road tennis courts.

Lastly, the local press in 1914 also reported the news of the demise of the Glorious 12th; 'As a result of the war there will be little or no grouse shooting this year. The sportsmen have mostly been called up for service while many of the country houses are being prepared for Red Cross or other benevolent work.'[106] That must have been a blow for those used to taking part.

ENDNOTES

1. *Alloa Circular* 19 Aug 1914 p. 3 col. 5
2. *Alloa Journal* 8 Aug 1914 p. 4 col. 3
3. *Alloa Journal* 7 Aug 1915 p. 4 col. 3
4. *Alloa Journal* 21 Aug 1915 p. 2 col. 6
5. *Alloa Journal* 4 Aug 1917 p. 3 col. 1
6. *Alloa Journal* 27 March 1916 p. 4 col. 4
7. These matches were all played at 'The Recs' even though Alloa Athletic FC itself was not playing any more
8. *Alloa Journal* 9 Dec 1916 p. 4 col. 3
9. *Alloa Journal* 13 Jan 1917 p. 4 col. 4
10. *Alloa Journal* 3 Feb 1917 p. 4 col. 5
11. *Alloa Journal* 10 Feb 1917 p. 4 col. 4
12. *Alloa Journal* 3 March 1917 p. 4 col. 2
13. *Alloa Journal* 10 March 1917 p. 4 col. 5
14. *Alloa Journal* 19 April 1919 p. 2 col. 1
15. *Alloa Journal* 15 Feb 1919 p. 2 col. 5, p. 3 cols. 3-4
16. *Alloa Advertiser* 2 Aug 1919 p. 4 col. 5
17. *Alloa Journal* 8 Aug 1914 p. 3 col. 1
18. Clackmannan County Cricket Club Annual General Meeting minute book 16 April 1915 in Royal Oak Hotel at 8.15 pm
19. Mark Wilson did not forget to play the game in the war; he was noticed getting 78 not out for a Naval XI versus a London select in May 1917. See *Alloa Journal* 7 June 1917 p. 3 col. 2
20. *Alloa Journal* 24 July 1915 p. 3 col. 4. CWGC records show that Lieut. Henery was killed almost two years later and is buried in Gaza War Cemetery
21. *Alloa Circular* 21 July 1915 p. 3 col. 5
22. *Alloa Advertiser* 7 July 1917 p. 4 col. 3
23. *Alloa Journal* 7 July 1917 p. 4 col. 3
24. *Alloa Journal* 30 June 1917 p. 3 col. 2. It turns out that Lieut. Peel was a regular player for the Grange Cricket Club in Edinburgh; he survived the war.
25. *Alloa Advertiser* 7 July 1917 p. 3 col. 1
26. *Alloa Journal* 8 Sept 1917 p. 2 col. 5. He was also Alloa Academy's Dux in 1908. *Alloa Advertiser* 4 August 1917 p. 2 col. 4 also records details of a cricket match held in France between the Argylls and the Cameron Highlanders in which the local lad, Lieut. S. Andrews (Victoria Street) top scored with 27 runs in what was a 44 run victory for the Argylls
27. *Alloa Journal* 29 March 1919 p. 2 col. 4. The meeting was held in Kilncraigs Hall, a part of Paton's Mills.
28. Clackmannan County Cricket Club Annual General Meeting minute book 3 April 1919
29. *Alloa Advertiser* 6 May 1922 p. 3
30. Letter from T.S. Knox to James Younger, President of CCCC, 31 March 1922

31 St John's Cricket Club minute book 1 Oct 1914
32 St John's Cricket Club minute book 1 Oct 1914
33 Tony Allsopp was the fifteen-year-old nephew of Lady Mar, and in the letters she wrote to her son Lord Erskine, serving in France, she expressed her sense of loss. National Archives Mar and Kellie Muniments GD 124/15/1852/1-2 St John's Cricket Club minute book 23 Feb 1915
34 In what became known as Broad Fourteens, three British cruisers were torpedoed one after the other by a German U-boat, as some of the ships stopped to try to rescue the survivors from the others! The sinking of *Aboukir*, *Hogue* and *Crecy* led to 1,459 sailors losing their lives
35 National Archives of Scotland Mar and Kellie Muniments GD 124/15/1852/1-2
36 St John's Cricket Club minute book 23 Feb 1915
37 *Alloa Journal* 1 Aug 1914 p. 3 col. 7
38 *Alloa Journal* 17 Oct 1914 p. 2 col. 6
39 *Alloa Journal* 29 May 1915 p.3 cols. 5+6
40 7th Battalion Argylls Regimental History p. 69
41 *Alloa Journal* 6 Nov 1915 p. 4 col. 5
42 *Alloa Journal* 18 Nov 1916 p. 3 col. 3
43 *Alloa Journal* 11 Nov 1916 p. 3 col. 1
44 *Alloa Advertiser* 18 Nov 1916 p. 3 col. 1
45 *Alloa Journal* 1 Dec 1917 p. 4 col. 1
46 Although the club members would have been involved in the earlier Red Cross swimming gala on 14 June 1918. See *Alloa Journal* 15 June 1918 p. 3 col. 1, 22 June 1918 p. 3 col. 1. Another gala was held in August 1918 under the auspices of the Gordon Highlanders, so Alloa's swimmers were probably kept fairly busy through 1918 without actually organising their own gala. See *Alloa Journal* 31 Aug 1918 p. 3 col. 3
47 *Alloa Journal* 1 March 1919 p. 3 col. 1 when it was noted that the last AGM had been held in February 1914
48 *Alloa Journal* 1 March 1919 p. 3 col. 1
49 *Alloa Journal* 19 July 1919 p. 1 col. 3
50 *Alloa Advertiser* 30 Aug 1919 p. 2 col. 5
51 *Alloa Journal* 23 Aug 1919 p. 3 col. 2
52 Alloa Ladies Norwood Swimming Club Committee minute book 25 June 1914
53 Alloa Ladies Norwood Swimming Club Committee minute book 3 Sept 1914
54 *Alloa Journal* 3 Oct 1914 p. 3 col. 6
55 Alloa Ladies Norwood Swimming Club Committee minute book 24 Oct 1914
56 Alloa Ladies Norwood Swimming Club Committee minute book 8 July 1915
57 Alloa Ladies Norwood Swimming Club Committee minute book 9 Sept 1915
58 Alloa Ladies Norwood Swimming Club Committee minute book 25 Oct 1915, *Alloa Circular* 17 Nov 1915 p. 3 col. 3
59 *Alloa Circular* 20 Oct 1915 p. 3 col. 5
60 Alloa Ladies Norwood Swimming Club Committee minute book 16 March 1916
61 Alloa Ladies Norwood Swimming Club Committee minute book 22 March 1916

62 Alloa Ladies Norwood Swimming Club Committee minute book 26 Oct 1916
63 Alloa Ladies Norwood Swimming Club Committee minute book 1 Oct 1917
64 Alloa Ladies Norwood Swimming Club Committee minute book 1 Oct 1917
65 *Alloa Advertiser* 12 July 1919 p. 3 col. 1
66 *Alloa Journal* 20 Sept 1919 p. 3 col. 2
67 Alloa Golf Club minute book 3 Sept 1914
68 See Chapter 1 and footnote[27]
69 Alloa Golf Club minute book 3 Sept 1914
70 *Alloa Journal* 6 March 1915 p. 3 col. 1
71 Alloa Golf Club minute book 19 Feb 1915
72 *Alloa Journal* 10 March 1915 p. 3 col. 5
73 *Alloa Circular* 6 Feb 1915 p. 3 col. 5, *Alloa Journal* 6 Feb 1915 p. 3 col. 3
74 Alloa Golf Club minute book 9 March 1916 The other golfer who was killed in action and who received a minuted tribute was Lieut. David Harper Cuthbert, the son of Alloa's Town Clerk. It was minuted that he was 'one of the outstanding players of the club'
75 *Alloa Journal* 11 March 1916 p. 3 col. 3
76 Alloa Golf Club minute book 26 Nov 1915
77 *Alloa Advertiser* 7 July 1917 p. 2 col. 1
78 *Alloa Advertiser* 14 July 1917 p. 3 col. 3 but there was no reference to this in the minute book
79 Alloa Golf Club minute book 17 May 1918
80 Alloa Golf Club minute book 26 Feb 1916
81 Alloa Golf Club minute book 1 March 1917
82 Alloa Golf Club minute book 2 June 1916
83 Alloa Golf Club minute book 17 May 1918
84 Alloa Golf Club minute book 19 Feb 1915
85 Alloa Golf Club minute book 2 June 1916
86 John Graeme Thomson was one of the three directors of John Paton, Son & Co. Ltd.
87 *Alloa Journal* 29 March 1919 p. 2 col. 5
88 Alloa Golf Club minute book 27 March 1919
89 *Alloa Golf Club: A Centenary History 1891–1991* p. 13. In the early days of this competition, the competitors had to play two double rounds of golf on consecutive weekends. The trophy had a suitable victory inscription and five shields on it, each with a flag of one of the victorious Allied powers. The trophy could not be awarded to the first person who won it since it had not come back from the silversmiths; it was not returned for another two months. See *Alloa Advertiser* 14 June 1919 p. 3 col. 4 and *Alloa Journal* 14 June 1919 p. 3 col. 5
90 Alloa Bowling Club Committee minute book 16 Sept 1914
91 Alloa Bowling Club Committee minute book 7 April 1915
92 Alloa Bowling Club Committee minute book 7 April 1915
93 *Alloa Journal* 10 April 1915 p. 2 col. 7
94 *Alloa Journal* 22 May 1915 p. 3 col. 8

95 *Alloa Journal* 7 July 1917 p. 3 col. 1
96 Alloa Bowling Club Committee minute book 13 June 1917
97 Alloa Bowling Club Committee minute book 25 July 1917
98 *Alloa Advertiser* 14 July 1917 p. 2 col. 5
99 *Alloa Journal* 14 July 1917 Special Supplement p. 2 col .4
100 *Alloa Journal* 27 Nov 1915 p. 3 col. 5
101 *Alloa Advertiser* 13 Jan 1917 p. 2 col. 5
102 *Alloa Circular* 27 Oct 1915 p. 4 col. 3
103 *Alloa Journal* 17 May 1919 p. 3 col. 1 reported on the first post war AGM of Alloa Tennis Club. The President, Mr GA Rae 'paid a fitting tribute to those who had died, those who were maimed and to their relatives'. He also proposed that a permanent Roll of Honour of the club should be drawn up and placed in the club house, and he offered to pay for it. This roll is also missing
104 *Alloa Journal* 24 April 1915 p. 2 col. 6
105 *Alloa Journal* 7 April 1917 p. 3 col. 1
106 *Alloa Advertiser* 15 Aug 1914 p. 2 col. 8

CHAPTER 6

WOMEN AT WAR

World War I is generally regarded as one of the great watersheds in women's rights, the first occasion when their role in society was recognised as essential for the good of the nation, and their status was given more respect, leading up to 1918, when some women were granted the vote. Are there any signs of this improvement in women's status in Alloa between 1914 and 1918?

There is evidence of only a small political role for Alloa women in the pre-war months. There had, for instance, been lady voters in the Alloa School Board elections in March 1914, when the *Journal* wrote rather patronisingly about an epidemic of nervous lady voters, '… some of whom had to have their hand held by the strong grip of the election officials…' while they marked their cross;[1] but there were no female candidates. Local women had been praised for their role in supporting the local Unionist party,[2] where over 1,000 lady members had helped during electioneering; but there was no evidence that their views had an impact on policy making. The evidence suggests that Alloa women had a somewhat passive and subordinate role in politics in the pre-war years. There were no women councillors on Alloa Burgh Council, although that was not true for all four burghs in Clackmannanshire; Dollar had the redoubtable Mrs Lavinia Malcolm, the first lady Councillor in Scotland and their Provost throughout the war years. There is no evidence either of much activity by the women's suffrage organisations in Alloa, although a local suffrage society did exist; the only political action the local press editorial columns constantly reported on was the Irish Question.

However, within a fortnight of the start of the war, the local suffrage society had made its position clear; 'The National Union of Women's Suffrage Societies wishes it to be known that it has suspended its ordinary political work for the time being and is preparing to use the entire organisation of the Union for the help of those who will be the sufferers of the economic and industrial dislocation caused by the War.'³ In October it became clear who those 'sufferers' might be when, at a meeting of the Society, it was unanimously decided that '...the Society should forgo its usual propaganda, and devote itself to the care of necessitous children in the locality'.⁴ Perhaps necessitous children mattered more; certainly nobody seems to have noticed that they had suspended their normal agenda. There was no sign of concern for women's suffrage in the local press until April 1917 when, in a letter to the *Journal,* a writer expressed his resentment that, in these difficult war circumstances, time in Parliament should need to be spent on the issue.⁵ The following month one unreconstructed male chauvinist wrote to the *Journal* that 'The vast majority of women, whose aptitudes, ambitions and desires are domestic and maternal, shrink from responsibilities and duties of a public or political nature'.⁶ I wonder who W.M. Cheshire felt he was speaking for; certainly not Lavinia Malcolm in Dollar or the citizens of that town who had supported her appointment. Another writer, a fortnight later, felt that the whole issue of women's suffrage should be left to a referendum after the war.⁷

There was, therefore, a flurry of interest in the local press in the middle of 1917, but there was barely any real comment in the ground-breaking days of February 1918, when women over the age of thirty actually received the vote. One exception, in March 1918, was when 'A professional' writing from Alloa told the *Scotsman* that she thought professional women were being hard done by because they were denied the vote if they were living in lodgings.⁸ She advised, in brief, that the answer lay in renting unfurnished rooms then hiring the furniture, which would then turn a woman from a renter into a householder.⁹ I am not convinced that would have worked. Another exception, illustrating the claimed link between women wanting the vote and using it to correct men's evil ways, was the meeting of the British Women's Temperance Association at Alloa's Townhead Institute at the end of February 1918; with a good turn out, they were able to hold a mock election over the issue of how far they should go, once they had the vote, on the route to prohibition.¹⁰ It was probably not surprising at a temperance meeting that eighty-three of the 150 ladies voted for full prohibition.

The local Liberal Association held a special meeting in February 1918 to '...consider what steps would be required to bring the organisation in line with the new order of things that would be brought about by the passing of the Representation of the People bill...'¹¹ A month later they reconstituted the Association so that it 'included both men and women electors'.¹² There was no comment, however, on any policy changes that might be introduced, particularly on prohibition.

By the time of the general election in December 1918 there were at least some statistics in the local press on the size of the local women's vote (11,974 women out of the possible total of 32,003 voters in the new constituency of Clackmannanshire and East Stirlingshire)[13] but, among fairly wide reporting on what the different candidates stood for, there was no reference to any special comment on how the newly enfranchised women might make this a different type of election, or what the three candidates might have thought of offering in order to catch the women's vote.

Women might have been a bit overlooked politically, but on the economic front, no one was in any doubt about their value, and of 'the many directions in which women had willingly and cheerfully come forward in the present national emergency and undertaken work that had previously been undertaken by men'.[14] For instance, the *Journal* commented as early as May 1915 that 'Owing to the effect of the War on the Alloa Post Office... the first postwoman will be sent out on Monday'.[15] The *Circular* by the middle of 1915 took the rosily optimistic view that 'The war... has removed much of the former sex antagonism that existed in relation to industrial employment.'[16]

There was still a big need, even by 1917, for 'substitution'; for women to step into the working shoes of men of military age, and the War Service for Women Movement held public meetings locally to raise more interest in that. By 1917 the government had also accepted more the idea of 'substitution' taking place within the armed forces; the local press in September 1917 gave precise details of the need for women to assume some duties within the military services.[17] The *Advertiser* reported the government's view that the Women's Auxiliary Army Corps needed recruits at the rate of 10,000 a month. They were clearly hoping to extract these from the ranks of domestic workers, hoping that 'cooks, housemaids, waitresses' could be persuaded to enlist; after all, they would be doing the same work as before, but this time they would be doing it for the Army. One assumes, due to their lack of mention in the Burgh of Alloa Roll of Honour, that no women from Alloa actually joined the female military services.[18] There were, however, a few WAACs living locally, because the *Journal* reported in September 1917 that '27 Women's Auxiliary Corps had arrived for duties in Devonvale Billets'.[19] It is difficult to know, however, from reading the rest of the piece, whether it was written by a typical male chauvinist of his time or just with heavy irony, as he continued with the observation that they were 'to take over the culinary and other duties for which the gentler sex are better fitted than 'the lords of creation'.

By September 1918 the government was still hoping for a massive enlistment of 12,000 women during Scottish Women's Recruiting Week, and a big poster appeared in the *Advertiser*.[20] Of course, not every Scottish woman wanted to volunteer to go off somewhere and stay in a hostel or barracks and be a 'skivvy' for the armed forces, so the *Advertiser* also included a lengthy propaganda piece, occupying almost a whole' column, by 'an unbiased observer' (male), which tried to put a better 'spin' on it.[21] The last paragraph of this piece described cosily how 'Happiness, indeed, is the note of all these little communities. The common life and the perfect order, promote an atmosphere of good fellowship and give-and-take, and where there is order there can be no discontent, no worry. Girls, if you want to do well by yourself, join up. No shop, no office, no factory, and no kitchen can give you what army life can give – health abundant, joyous companionship – the free, full life of the army girl.' How much of this would have been believed is debatable, given that earlier he had slipped in the point that the girls were expected to work 8-10 hour shifts, the first one starting at 4.30am. The *Journal* did report that 'Nearly 100 application forms were received, and a very fair proportion of these have been returned filled up'[22] but had little else to say about it.

The Burgh of Alloa paid a public tribute to the wartime role of its women in the speeches from the bandstand in the public park on the Thanksgiving holiday, 12 November 1918. Ex-Baillie Mitchell praised warmly 'home workers...especially the women...tenacity and grit were displayed in the most wonderful way. [They] put their backs into the work, both in munitions and supplies. When this page falls to be written, the womanhood of Great Britain will stand out in bold relief and be remembered for ever. They have created an asset to the British nation that has never before been realised...'[23] I wonder if he would have been so enthusiastic in praising this 'asset' if he had pondered the issue of the continued employment of, say, Alloa's fifty female shipyard workers in the post-war years. Of all the local press, only the *Circular* flagged up any concern about what might happen to all the war-employed women once the war was over. In fact, it raised the issue in the same week as the signing of the Armistice. It commented that there was considerable discussion over what 'thousands of our girls will do after the war. The matter is a serious one...to avoid friction and disappointment. It is certain that many girls will get married of course... but there are thousands who will never return to the comparative slavery of the factory.'[24] Lady Mar echoed these concerns with her comment that '...arising out of the war they had thousands of women employed in all branches of trade and industry... men were now beginning to realise that in many departments of life they could not do without women.'[25] Her pious hopes of women hanging onto their wartime jobs, were, I fear, not to be so easily realised once the men came home and the local press in 1918 had no better suggestions to make than to hope that the delegates in the new parliament would deal with the problem. None of those delegates, of course, in that first post-war parliament, were going to be women.

In terms of other aspects of the way Alloa's women rallied to the war effort, Lady Mar's prominent role as a leader of the community, the importance of Dr Ethel Cassie as the Medical Officer for the burgh from 1915-1918, the two Alloa School Board primary teachers who went off to be a nurse[26] and a welfare supervisor in the munitions factories have been noted already.

Last, the Burgh of Alloa Roll of Honour may not have included any names of local women who joined the female branches of the military services, but it did include the names of six women from Alloa who served as nurses. These were the 'local heroines' and details of the activities of some of them appeared fairly regularly in the local press; five of them survived the war.

(Mary) Evelyn Thomson was in Queen Alexandra's Imperial Military Nursing Service (QAIMNS) and rose to quite a high rank. She was mentioned in despatches by General French in June 1916 for her actions in France, then by General Milne in December 1916 for her actions in Salonika.[27] She became Acting Matron in the hospital in Salonika and was awarded the Royal Red Cross medal (1st class) in 1917. Only 264 RRCs were awarded during World War I.[28] She was a pupil at Alloa Academy Primary Department (Admission No. 333) but her secondary education was at Dollar Academy. She lived in Glebe Terrace. Her brother, Lieut. Edward Thomson, survived the war.[29] Her service records are not available at the National Archives because she served in the nursing wing of the armed forces until after World War II, so they are still confidential. She became Matron of the Infirmary at Chelsea Hospital (where the Chelsea Pensioners live) from 1925-1948, and was awarded the MBE in the 1947 New Year's Honours list.[30]

Janie Cuthbert was trained and employed as a PE teacher, but in June 1916 she went off to France as a Red Cross nurse. She became a masseuse (nowadays known as a physiotherapist) at 11th Stationary Hospital in Rouen, France.[31] She lived at 9, Claremont, and was the daughter of the town clerk. Her younger brother 2nd Lieut. David Harper Cuthbert was killed in action in 1917 and her younger sister died in Edinburgh in 1918 whilst training to be a doctor.

Jean Hall Bayne came from Fenton Street, Alloa, but in July 1915 she left her job in the County Hospital, Motherwell, to join the Scottish Women's Hospital in Valjevo, Serbia, under the command of Dr Alice Hutchison.[32] Some sort of official information was sent to her parents in January 1916 which mentioned that their town was under attack and that they were short of food, but then the Austrians captured the town and things improved. There was no need for concern about the British contingent of nurses because the hospital was partly staffed by captured Austrian troops being used as orderlies, and they had been treated well; once they were actually in charge, the Austrians behaved  well towards the nurses. By 12 January 1916 her parents had received a note from her (posted in November 1915) saying that everything was fine, even though she was effectively a prisoner.[33] She returned to Alloa in February 1916, full of exciting stories about her time in Serbia.[34] She added her 'pennyworth' to the propaganda war with her observation that: 'All along the line we learned to rely on the common Austrian soldier for politeness and on the average German soldier for being as brutal and nasty as he could possibly be.'[35] For her efforts in Serbia she was awarded the Serbian Samaritan Cross.

Bessie Coltman was in QAIMNS. By 1915 she had passed various nursing exams and was sent off to Malta that year.[36] She rose to become a Sister/Staff nurse and was awarded the Royal Red Cross medal (2nd class). There were 919 awards of this medal to nurses during World War I.[37]

The British Journal of Nursing in December 1918[38] claimed that she had been awarded an MBE 'for devotion to duty', but there is no reference to this anywhere else, including

ALLOA NURSE'S DEATH.
The Late Sister Coltman.

her obituary in the *Alloa Journal* on 7 December 1918. She was well travelled, because she also served in East Africa before coming home on leave in May 1918. She was then stationed in Kent, but fell ill and came home to Alloa in August. She died of pneumonia at home on 26 November 1918.[39] Her funeral '…was of a military character… and the Pipe Band of the Gordon Highlanders was present…'[40] She lived in Ochil Street; her brother, Lance Corporal John Coltman, survived the war. She was a former pupil of Alloa Academy Primary Department (Admission No. 522), but her name does not appear on the Alloa Academy Roll of Honour. It does, however, appear on St Mungo's Church war memorial and Alloa war memorial, but there is no mention of her in the official CWGC Register. The Burgh of Alloa Roll of Honour records that she was awarded the 1914-15 Star. This was normally awarded for service in France/Flanders, but it was also awarded 'to those individuals who saw service in any other operational theatre from 5 August 1914 to 31 December 1915'.[41]

Most of the information above has been gleaned from the local newspapers; and one has to admire the tact and discretion of their reporting, because Bessie Coltman's real story, as told in her full military record in the National Archives in Kew, is even more tragic.[42] She had trained from 1909 to 1912 at Ruchill Hospital, Glasgow, then worked at the Aberdeen Royal Infirmary as a charge nurse. She joined QAIMNS in October 1915 and in early 1916 she was sent out, via Port Said, to join the East African Force in what was then known as Tanganyika, and served at 15th Stationary Hospital, Morogoro. She caught malaria in April 1917 and was 'invalided to S. Africa'.[43] She seemed fit enough to resume service following a medical examination in June 1917 at No. 2 Hospital, Maitland (Cape Town), where they just thought she was a little anaemic. However, things could not have been right because she was 'struck off the strength' in East Africa in February 1918 and sent home with four weeks' leave. She was posted to Queen's Hospital, Frognall, Sidcup on 13 June 1918 but served only one day before being invalided. She appeared before a Medical Board at Vincent Square Hospital on 21 June where a margin note in her file referred to her 'neuralgia and debility'; she was granted sick leave on 20 July 1918 but things then went steadily downhill. By 9 September, 'because of her medical condition she was removed to an asylum' and she spent the rest of her life at Woodilee Mental Hospital, Lenzie.

Her file shows that there was a small dispute between the Inspector of the Poor in Alloa, the Glasgow Parish Authorities and the General Board of Control (GBC) in Edinburgh as to who should pay for her care since she had not been discharged from QAIMNS and it was believed that the Military Nursing Authorities should pick up the bill for someone who had been declared insane and sent to an asylum. The GBC inquired rather coldly as to 'whether any arrangements have been made for classifying as "Service Patients" women who become insane as the result of their military service during the present war, or, if they are not entitled to be so classified, whether there is any likelihood of arrangements being made for the treatment of such women on lines similar to male "Service Patients".' This dispute was settled, perhaps, by the note in her file which stated that she was 'Discharged Insane on 15-10-18'. I think we are aware that judgements of insanity in women were very much more gender-biased in those days than they are (hopefully) today; for instance, she could have been clinically depressed and in a state of great debility following malaria, which remains in the body; many women were certified and put in asylums for far less. Be that as it may, her mental and physical condition were unlikely to have made her very resistant to any sort of disease, and she survived for only just over two months in the asylum. Her mother, Jessie, wrote to the War Office on 27 November 1918 saying that 'I am very sorry to inform you that my Daughter Bessie Coltman Died yesterday in Woodilee Hospital, Lenzie with Pneumonia following an attack of Influenza'.

Her mother spent some time writing letters to the War Office asking for a pension (a dependent's allowance) and compensation. She received £9 12s 11d in November 1919 and there is a note of a further single payment of £107 in July 1920. These letters revealed that Bessie Coltman had **two** younger brothers (Pte. W.D. Coltman 9687, RAOC, and Pte. John Coltman 10164, RAOC) whereas the Burgh of Alloa Roll of Honour recorded only one. She also had a younger sister, Jessie, who was unable to work during the war due to illness. There are documents in Bessie Coltman's file which show that the military authorities did regard 'the lady's disability as "in" and "by" her military duties in the service', but that was not enough, apparently, for the CWGC to grant her the status of being a full military casualty entitled to an entry on the War Graves Register and a war grave.

Mary Smith was a nurse in QAIMNS and came from Hill Street. Her brother John Smith, who was in the Royal Engineers, survived the war.[44] There was no other information about her in the local press during all the war years. The Burgh of Alloa

Roll of Honour records that she was awarded the 1914-15 Star, so she must have been on active service somewhere from quite early on. Indeed, her records are available at the National Archives in Kew and they show that she was working at the Royal Infirmary in Glasgow when the war broke out but volunteered for military nursing service on 24 February 1915. She was on the list of 'Nurses Temporarily Employed With QAIMNS' rather than being properly in it (ie she was in the QAIMNS Reserve), so she had to renew her contract five times during the war, for either six- or twelve-month periods. She reached the rank of Acting Sister before she finally resigned from the service in order 'to return to private nursing'.[45] In her Army Form B.103 there is evidence of her wide-ranging nursing service across Northern France; chiefly around Abbeville, Rouen and Wimereux. This included serving at three different Stationary Hospitals, (3rd, 25th and 41st), three General Hospitals (6th, 14th and 83rd) and two Casualty Clearing Stations (64th and 38th), before finishing on 34th Ambulance Train from August to November 1918. With all that service – and only taking a fortnight's leave on four occasions in 1917 and 1918 – it is no wonder that her final confidential reference stated that 'She has always carried out her duties in a satisfactory manner. I have always found her a very efficient nurse, tactful, kindly and reliable.' Major Brown, the Officer Commanding 34th Ambulance Train, wrote 'I concur. Miss Smith's kindly ways have made her an instrument for good while on the train'. Her good service entitled her to a gratuity, which she received on 2 April 1919.

Annie McDonald served in 58th Scottish General Hospital in St Omer, France and came from Church Street.[46] There is no other information about her in the local press during all the war years apart from a reference to her serving at Arnsbrae Red Cross Hospital when it was first set up in April 1915.[47]

It was not my intention to continue to demonstrate the inaccuracies in the Burgh of Alloa Roll of Honour, but there is no doubt that there were many omissions, especially of women. Some of these came to light due to the fact that the Moncrieff U F Church Roll of Honour listed the war service of so many women in their congregation who were not mentioned in the Burgh of Alloa's Roll. One key example was:

Nettie Harley: This lady (full name, Janet Glen Harley) was in QAIMNS and her full military service records can be seen online in the National Archives in Kew.[48] They show that she trained as a nurse in Edinburgh between 1 July 1912 and 30 June

1916 and rose to be Staff Nurse and Acting Sister. She then transferred to Professor Alexis Thomson's Surgical Nursing Home between August 1916 and May 1917 before applying to join QAIMNS. She was accepted by them on 19 May 1917 and was sent to Cambridge Hospital, Aldershot, where she served for the rest of the war.[49] She was demobilised on 4 April 1920 and her excellent departing reference included the note that 'Her name was brought to the notice of the Secretary of State for War for valuable services on 19/8/19'.[50] This lady was a former pupil of both the Primary Department of Alloa Academy[51] and Alloa Academy itself[52] and lived in Coningsby Place before the war, although she had an Edinburgh address while she was training. The omission of her name from the Burgh of Alloa Roll of Honour is inexcusable, particularly as two of her brothers, Major James Glen Harley and Capt. Robert Bruce Harley were both mentioned.[53]

Some of the other nurses from Clackmannanshire who served were:

Sophie Robertson, daughter of the Clackmannan minister, who went off to Petrograd in October 1915, having already served in Serbia and Bulgaria.[54]

Nellie Johnstone from Forest Mill, who was awarded the Royal Red Cross medal (2nd class) in April 1917. She was serving at the 4th Scottish General Hospital in Govan.[55]

Margaret McCallum from Clackmannan (originally from Helensburgh) served with Lady Muriel Paget's Mission. She died of typhus in Slovakia on 30 September 1919.[56] For thirteen years before the war she had been district nurse for the Parish of Clackmannan under the supervision of Lady Balfour. She volunteered for overseas duties in 1916 and the inhabitants of the parish 'presented her with a beautiful fitted bag, luminous wrist watch and a well-filled purse of money, as an expression of the esteem with which she was held...'[57] Nurse McCallum then saw service in Russia, where she was in Petrograd during the Revolution.[58] She came home and served in a hospital in Kent until the Armistice, but she then volunteered for a Red Cross relief mission which took her to Slovakia.[59] Her name is on Clackmannan's war memorial.

The Moncrieff U F Church was the only Alloa church to draw up a Roll of Honour after the war, with the names of all of their congregational members who had served.[60] Interestingly, this Roll of 210 names includes **fifteen** women, twelve of whom are listed as serving in military hospitals,[61] yet only **one** of these names is listed amongst the six nurses in the Burgh of Alloa Roll of Honour, so it appears that there have been major omissions. It could be that serving as a VAD at Arnsbrae Auxiliary Hospital was enough to qualify for a mention, in the view of those who drew up the Moncrieff U F Church Roll; or the omission of these names from the Burgh of Alloa Roll of Honour could be explained by the fact that these lady members of the church were living outside the Burgh boundary and therefore did not count, but seven of those fifteen names appear in Alloa Academy Admission Registers, so they do indeed appear to be local.[62] It seems that they were overlooked – and that the women of Alloa may have played a far more prominent part in the story of Alloa at war than some of the records have, until now, recognised.

It may not have been directly war-related, but a last aside on changing attitudes towards women in Alloa in those times was that in January 1919 Alloa West Church elected three women to its Management Committee. This was thought sufficiently ground-breaking for the Session minute book to record that 'Mrs Thomson, Miss Cock and Mrs Brown were therefore elected and are thus the first lady members of Management of the West UF Church'.[63]

ENDNOTES

1. *Alloa Journal* 28 March 1914 p. 3 col. 3
2. *Alloa Journal* 25 April 1914 p. 2 col. 4
3. *Alloa Journal* 15 Aug 1914 p. 3 col. 4
4. *Alloa Journal* 1 Oct 1914 p. 4 col. 4
5. *Alloa Journal* 7 April 1917 p. 3 col. 4
6. *Alloa Journal* 26 May 1917 p. 4 col. 1 letter from W.M. Cheshire
7. *Alloa Journal* 9 June 1917 p. 3 col. 5
8. This was the case; for a woman to vote she had to be a householder or married to a householder, and over thirty, of course
9. *Scotsman* 19 March 1918
10. *Alloa Advertiser* 2 March 1918 p. 3 col. 4
11. *Alloa Advertiser* 2 Feb 1918 p. 2 col. 5
12. *Alloa Advertiser* 9 March 1918 p. 2 col. 5
13. *Alloa Journal* 23 Nov 1918 p. 3 col. 4

14 *Alloa Advertiser* 12 May 1917 p. 2 col. 5
15 *Alloa Journal* 22 May 1915 p. 2 col. 6
16 *Alloa Circular* 18 Aug 1915 p. 3 col. 4
17 *Alloa Advertiser* 22 Sept 1917 p. 2 col. 3
18 Although the Moncrieff Church Roll of Honour records that Alice Pearson was in the Women's Auxiliary Corps
19 *Alloa Journal* 22 Sept 1917 p. 3 col. 3
20 *Alloa Advertiser* 21 Sept 1918 pp. 2 and 3
21 *Alloa Advertiser* 21 Sept 1918 p. 4 col. 2
22 *Alloa Journal* 5 Oct 1918 p. 3 col. 1
23 *Alloa Advertiser* 16 Nov 1918 p. 3 col. 5
24 Alloa Circular 13 Nov 1918 p. 2 col. 4
25 *Alloa Advertiser* 9 Nov 1918 p. 3 col. 1
26 Nurse MacDougall was clearly on war service (referred to in School Board letter book and *Alloa Journal* 5 April 1919 p. 4 col. 5) yet her name was missed out of the Burgh of Alloa Roll of Honour
27 *Alloa Journal* 16 Dec 1916 p. 3 col. 6
28 Scarletfinders website
29 Burgh of Alloa Roll of Honour
30 *London Gazette* Issue 37835 p. 17 of Supplement dated 1 January 1947
31 *Alloa Advertiser* 3 June 1916 p. 1 col. 4, *Alloa Journal* 10 June 1916 p. 2 col. 6
32 *Alloa Journal* 31 July 1915 p. 2 col. 4, *Alloa Circular* 5 Jan 1916 p. 3 col. 4
33 *Alloa Circular* 12 Jan 1916 p. 3 col. 6
34 *Alloa Journal* 19 Feb 1916 p. 3 col. 4
35 *Alloa Advertiser* 9 Feb 1916 p. 2 cols. 4–5. The national census of April 1901 listed her as a draper's assistant at that time
36 *Alloa Circular* 27 Oct 1915 p. 1 col. 6
37 Scarletfinders website
38 *British Journal of Nursing* 14 Dec 1918 p. 364
39 *Alloa Journal* 7 Dec 1918 p. 3 col. 3 (plus photo; BJN said she died in Lenzie and they are probably correct)
40 *Alloa Journal* 7 Dec 1918 p. 3 col. 3
41 From National Archives on-line medal checker
42 National Archives File WO 399/1648
43 Army Form B.103... which also helps to explain why all her money was in the Standard Bank of South Africa, Lombard St.
44 Burgh of Alloa Roll of Honour
45 National Archives File WO399/7734 contains her letter of resignation, which gives this reason
46 Burgh of Alloa Roll of Honour
47 *Alloa Circular* 21 April 1915 p. 3 col. 3
48 National Archives File WO 399/3549

49   This was the first hospital in the UK to experiment with plastic surgery, under the New Zealand surgeon Harold Gillies
50   This was reported in *Alloa Advertiser* 6 Sept 1919 p. 3 col. 1 and is the equivalent of being 'mentioned in despatches'
51   Alloa Academy Primary Dept. Admission Register No. 865
52   Alloa Academy Secondary Admission Register No. 52
53   Burgh of Alloa Roll of Honour... although Major J.G. Harley had certainly left the family home at 7 Coningsby Place by 1920 and is not even listed there on the 1911 census
54   *Alloa Circular* 27 Oct 1915 p. 2 col. 6, *Alloa Journal* 23 Oct 1915 p. 3 col. 5
55   *Alloa Journal* 21 April 1917 p. 3 col. 5
56   *Alloa Journal* 25 Oct 1919 p. 4 col. 5 gives a detailed account of her funeral in Slovakia
57   *Alloa Journal* 29 April 1916 p. 3 col. 2
58   *Alloa Advertiser* 25 Oct 1919 p. 3 col. 4
59   http://www.helensburgh-heritage.co.uk
60   Moncrieff Church held its 'Welcome Home' for the serving members of its congregation in September 1919 and the minister referred to the war service of 191 men and twenty-three women. By the time their Roll of Honour was produced these figures had been adjusted slightly. See *Alloa Journal* 27 Sept 1919 p3 col1
61   The other three women who were mentioned included one serving at a 'Church hut in France', one serving in the Women's Auxiliary Corps but whose service records do not seem to be in the National Archives, and Nettie Harley in QAIMNS
62   Living outside the Burgh boundary did not prevent William Millar from adding lots of men's names to the Roll of Honour, but another lady he missed out was Miss C.E. Cairns who was a Unit Administrator in the Queen Mary's Army Auxiliary Corps who was mentioned in dispatches and came from 1 Bedford Place. See *Alloa Journal* 5 April 1919 p. 2 col. 5. Her brother was William Cairns who died in December 1918 and was listed in the Burgh of Alloa Roll of Honour. Her sister Mary worked at Alloa Academy
63   Alloa West Church Management Committee minute book 26 Jan 1919

CHAPTER 7

DAILY LIFE IN THE WAR

The obvious place to look for evidence of the impact of war on the daily lives of the Alloa townspeople is in the local newspapers. There may have been an element of censorship, especially when the papers reported on national issues that might have affected Alloa, rather than just local topics; and in some cases there was a heavy tone of patriotism. It was probably typical of those times, but the local press also had a distinctly respectful way of writing about the activities of anyone in an elevated position in the local community; there was never much criticism in their reports of the actions of authority figures. Nonetheless, it is fortunate for any historian that Alloa had **three** local newspapers during World War I, despite being such a small town.[1] Besides the local press, the minutes of all meetings of Alloa Burgh Council also give insights into the way the town responded to the strains of war.

Rather than exploring every wartime event that ever affected the town, this chapter will consider a range of themes connected with the impact of war on the people of Alloa. However, if a group of people from those days went to the trouble of recording their experiences and activities, a history like this should allow them to have their say, whether or not it now seems important.

ANTI-GERMAN FEELING

People are aware that there is supposed to have been a strong hatred of the Germans during World War I, partly as a result of skilful government propaganda to help mobilise support for joining Britain's first mass Citizen's Army. How much did this affect the people of Alloa? Certainly, in the first two to three months of the war the local press 'toed' the national line by including references to alleged German atrocities as they invaded Belgium, generally referring to Germans as 'Huns' or 'butchers'. They do not seem to have had much actual detailed information to go on, but were content to use such generalisations as; 'In every district of Belgium and France occupied by German troops, terrorism, maintained by savage brutality and rapacity, has been used as a weapon against the civilian population; women of all ages, children and men have been victims of the new German barbarism...'[2] Without many real facts available, the local press were fairly restrained in their comments, but by May 1915 the Bryce Report on German atrocities in Belgium had been published and the *Journal* certainly agreed with all its findings on the general prevalence among German troops of abusing, raping and murdering innocent Belgian civilians.[3]

Anti-German feeling increased on 7 May 1915 when the news broke of the torpedoing of the *Lusitania* by a German U-boat. This sinking of an unarmed passenger liner with the loss of 1,197 lives led to spontaneous outbreaks of anti-German feeling in several Scottish towns against this 'outrage' and 'dastardly crime'.[4] The *Advertiser* saw it as one of 'the long list of atrocities for which Germany will be made to answer... the cold-blooded sinking of the *Lusitania* with 1,960 souls on board, constitutes the foulest crime...'[5] The *Journal* merely remarked that it had given 'a great impetus to recruiting...'

The *Circular* however, reported on 19 May on just how profoundly the people of Alloa had been affected.[6] It noted that 'Serious disturbances took place on Saturday (15 May) in several Scottish towns, notably Dumfries, Annan, Alloa and Perth'. It then described at some length the hostile demonstration in Alloa with an angry crowd in the High Street, the German pork butcher's shop being attacked and its windows broken. The owner of the shop was Alfred Becher, admittedly of German origin, but a peaceful citizen for many years who had contributed to the Red Cross and local relief funds,[7] '...so Saturday's affair was all the more striking an indication of the revulsion of feeling against all things "German" that has come about since the sinking of the *Lusitania*'. It was reported that a Territorial soldier had started the disturbance by kicking in the shop window; that attracted a crowd of up to 1,000,[8] leading to a heavy police presence guarding the shop and protecting the Becher family, with missiles then being thrown, and attempts to 'rush' the shop. It lasted for about four hours but quietened down at midnight. It is difficult to attribute all this to a drink-fuelled mob; for instance, there was a suggestion of some planning during the afternoon in that 'rumours were current in the town that an attack was going to be made on the shop...'[9] Despite the fact of the disturbance being started by the soldier, it was a local man, John Gourlay of Broad Street, who was convicted of incitement at Alloa Sheriff

Court on 7 June. He was the one who shouted 'rush them'. He was fined 20s or had the option of ten days in jail.[10]

The *Advertiser* had a very unsatisfactory editorial about the local violence, where it discussed it in the third person, starting in a very detached way, but in the end almost justifying it. Its editorial opened with the comment that 'lawlessness is never justifiable… therefore anti-German demonstrations… cannot be defended' but then went on to say 'The mere presence of a German is enough to excite among civilised people feelings of loathing and detestation…'[11]

There was certainly high feeling among the Alloa people, and the *Lusitania* made a good excuse; but it may actually have been more of a gut reaction against the Germans for the terrible mauling which the local regiment, the Argylls, had just suffered at Ypres during the previous couple of weeks. References to the 'heroic work of the Argylls' with 'heavy losses', the 'beastly use of poison gas' and the long lists of casualties were ALL in the local press at this time. That would probably have been a more potent reason for the people of Alloa to hate the Germans than the sinking of a single ship.

It was understood that Mr Becher had been taken off to an internment camp near Edinburgh[12] and certainly the Burgh Council was worried for several months about whether anti-German feeling had quietened down enough to let Mrs Becher re-open the shop. Even in September 1915 the Chief Constable recommended that it <u>not</u> be re-opened and Mrs Becher accepted the decision.[13]

ALLOA BURGH COUNCIL

The minutes of every meeting of Alloa Burgh Council and all its sub-committees are available as evidence of how the town fathers reacted to the problems of running Alloa in the four and a half years of war. In a way that is reminiscent of the school log books (ie those in charge often did not seem to want to dwell on the fact that a war was happening), the Burgh Council minutes reveal just how much it was still pre-occupied with routine Council business. It was responsible for the production and supply of gas, electricity and water; licencing, fire-fighting, slaughterhouses, the Town Hall, library, baths and education, so it may be no surprise that 'business as usual' seemed the Council's natural response to the strange times that war imposed on it. That is not to say that war-related issues did not concern it: Belgian relief, War loans, the Burgh Roll of Honour, and war bonuses to Council employees were regularly on the table for discussion by Councillors. Now and again however, war-specific issues arose.

One of the first concerned the Town Hall. As early as 14 September 1914 it became apparent that this would be requisitioned by the army as billets for the local Territorial soldiers. In a fit of generosity the Council agreed that all the soldiers billeted there should have free use of the Public Baths in Primrose Street.[14] By early October 1914 however, one may be forgiven for wondering if the Council had suddenly realised that it had a potential financial windfall, because the attractive deal they had struck with the army was that they could have the Town Hall for £2 inclusive a day, with 'the whole premises to be restored at the ending of occupancy to the same condition'. This fee was in fact reduced to 35 shillings a day on 12 October. The Army actually used the premises only intermittently during the next year, making it difficult for the Council to pursue other letting arrangements, so it lost money; it does, however, seem a bit grasping of them to see the Town Hall as some sort of wartime 'cash cow'. This was highlighted starkly by December 1915,[15] when it was reported to the Council that the Army owed £306 and had so far refused to pay. The military authorities wrote asking for a discount, due to their low use of heating in the summer of 1915. The Council gave in,[16] with the offer of a £50 discount and a new rate of 18 shillings a night for

Some of the local Territorials in front of Alloa Town Hall, ready to set off to war in 1915

future use, but by February 1916 the Council had buckled still further with an offer of £25 a month inclusive.[17] By 28 March 1916 they had still not been paid and sent the Army a stiff note. Even by mid-April the Provost reported that 'he had been unable to secure an amicable settlement of the accounts due...'[18] but in mid-May he happily announced that the £306, 'less £75 which the Council had agreed to allow off...'[19] had been paid. Having restored its working relationship with the Army, in September 1916 the Council said that officers billeted in the Town Hall could have the use of the Baths at the same rate as the men; that is, half the normal fee – rather different from the Council's initial enthusiastic generosity back in September 1914.[20]

The Council suffered another setback in its cash-raising activities when it found it difficult to let the sheep-grazing rights on the public parks for 1915. It was advertised, but only one farmer applied and he offered only £3 a season, arguing that the constant drilling by the soldiers had ruined the grazing anyway. The Council accepted his reduced offer.[21] The Council still managed to let the public park for the Spring and Autumn Fairs in 1916 and obtained £72 from Mr Herbert Green of Glasgow.[22]

It should not be thought, however, that the Council was always on the lookout for financial gain; there were plenty of occasions where it showed common sense or compassion or both in its financial dealings with its employees. It agreed for a war bonus for all Council (manual) employees in March 1915 of 2 shillings a week if wages were under 30 shillings a week, and 1 shilling a week if wages were between 30 shillings and 40 shillings.[23] There were also many meetings when it mulled over what to pay, and how to be fair to Council employees away on war duty and dependents of Council employees where that employee had been killed in action. It invariably maintained an allowance until such time as the widow concerned was able to receive the military pension to which she was entitled.

As mentioned, the Burgh Council was in charge of its own gas production works. In 1915 the government asked all councils 'to take steps to extract Toluol from the gas-making process because this was needed for munitions', but Alloa's gas managers reported that this was already being done.[24] One other initiative that the Corporation Gas Works got involved in later in the war was the collection of fruit stones and nutshells. These were in great demand to be turned into charcoal to fill gas mask filters; and the Corporation Gas showrooms in Bank Street agreed to act as a collection point.[25] The Council's control of the gas works was surely an example of it doing something right in the war, because the *Journal* was able to announce in August 1918 that 'Alloa gas remains the cheapest gas in Scotland'.[26]

THE LOCAL MAGISTRATES

Local justice and the keeping of public order were among the responsibilities of the Burgh Council. It did this chiefly through the appointment of the Chief Constable of the Burgh to run a small police force, and senior Councillors called Baillies running the Magistrates Court, which dealt with sentencing for small crime and issuing licences. Two issues occupied the Magistrates' minds at the start of the war; the local billeting of Territorial troops and the risk of public disorder or even German attack.

In response to the first issue, the Chief Constable drew up a list of likely billeting venues and the numbers they could accommodate and submitted it to the Council;[27] as an afterthought he helpfully added the amount of potential stabling.

Burgh School	126
Maclay's Barns	228
Drill Hall	136
Town Hall	135
Quarters for officers in hotels	30
Stabling	for 107 horses

Of this list, the only venue with no clear evidence of being used for billets was Maclay's Barns, despite it seeming to be the largest. The list should not be taken as final however, because in the event Greenside Hall, the YMCA Institute and the Masonic Lodge were all requisitioned for billeting purposes once the war had started.

The second issue was whether there might be a public order breakdown; and the first wartime meeting of the Magistrates 'took into consideration the question of appointing an unpaid force of Special Constables in consequence of the European war'. They asked the Chief Constable to draw up a list of names.[28] By the end of October this list had been compiled and the men were all sworn in.[29] Not surprisingly, the list did not contain many of the young men of the town; they were more likely to have rushed to join the armed forces. The fifty-four names were more a representative list of the town's middle-aged propertied class, including a good sprinkling of Councillors, (Henderson, Hepburn, Duncanson, Strang etc), David Jeffrey of the shipyard, William Buchan of the *Alloa Advertiser* and Alexander Forrester-Paton. They were given batons, armlet badges and whistles to assist them in their duties.[30] Thirteen more were appointed on 16 November, including Rev A.W. Scudamore Forbes.[31]

Their first job emerged from an early scare. In September 1914 the Magistrates received a letter from Captain A.P. Moir, Secretary of the local Territorial Association, 'Intimating that the Colonel Commanding had sent him a note of the vulnerable points on the railway that he wished guarded by the territorials, and Capt. Moir asked if it was desired that any vulnerable points in which the Burgh are interested should be so guarded'.[32] The Magistrates thought that the Gartmorn Dam filtration plants and the Burgh Gas and Electricity works should be guarded; they decided that the special constables could do the job, once they were appointed.[33] This panic did not last long, though, and it was not very often that the special constables were called out to do any sort of wartime duty. It was indeed the case that by early 1916, 'eight men who had been with the burgh police were now serving in the colours',[34] but they had largely been replaced by trained policemen. Did any special constables help to control the town's anti-German riots in May 1915, when property may have been genuinely at risk? This is not known. The Magistrates may have thought there was a risk of overstretching the energies of this group of middle-aged volunteer policemen, as in June 1917 they agreed that any special constables who were also in the Local Volunteer Battalion should resign from their police duties.[35] This new Battalion had, by 1917, in any case become much more 'the place to be'. The Chief Constable's Report for 1918 noted that '100 special constables had been sworn in but very little occasion has arisen to call upon their services'.[36]

THE GRETNA RAIL DISASTER

The *Circular* was the first local paper to give information about Alloa's anti-German riots in May 1915; likewise it was the <u>only</u> local paper to give a report[37] of the terrible Gretna Rail Disaster of 22 May 1915. This was a multiple train crash, followed by a massive fire, at the Quintinshill signal box at 6.50 in the morning, where 225 people died, mostly men from the 7th Royal Scots, and 246 people were injured.

The *Circular*'s editorial called it 'A disaster unparalleled in the history of British railways', which indeed it was and has not been equalled since, its report accurately conveying the carnage resulting from 'the terrible circumstances which laid the troop train and the local train in ruin, and which immediately thereafter hurled an express train into the midst of and over this wreckage'. It is surprising that there was so little coverage: after all, it was almost local news; the 1st/7th Royal Scots (Leith Territorial Battalion) had been in hutments on the Tryst at Larbert and left from Larbert Station on their way to Gallipoli, via Liverpool Docks, before they met with their tragic accident.

ARNSBRAE RED CROSS HOSPITAL

James Younger of the local brewing family placed Arnsbrae House at the disposal of the Red Cross in February 1915, for use as an Auxiliary Hospital;[38] effectively it became a fifty-bed convalescent home with fifteen wards for injured soldiers,[39] and received its first group of patients on 5 April 1915.

Arnsbrae Red Cross Hospital (*British Red Cross*)

Staff at Arnsbrae Hospital

James Younger had another house at Mount Melville near St Andrews, and he lived there for the rest of the war, but before he left Alloa, he fully funded Arnsbrae House's conversion to medical use. The Countess of Mar & Kellie, the President of the local Red Cross Society, wrote '...it has been beautifully equipped as a hospital in all its internal arrangements through the great generosity of Mr and Mrs Younger...'[40] It began with a staff of three trained nurses and eleven Red Cross nurses, led by an Acting Surgeon, Dr J.D. Octavius Wilson, and a Matron, Miss Emily L'Estrange. Local doctors also attended the patients. There were often printed lists of the trained and untrained staff (VADs) in the local press.

Soldiers sent for convalescence at Arnsbrae were not officers; they were generally 'other ranks'. There must have been a fairly efficient system for allocating them to their appropriate recuperation centres, because the *Journal*, for instance, reported that some of those arriving on Thursday 15 April 1915 had only been wounded (at the battles of Neuve Chapelle and St Eloi) on the previous Sunday.[41] The wounded soldiers usually arrived at Alloa Station and the press reported that they were 'often motored out to the hospital by the local gentlemen'.[42] Eight of the local families were mentioned on one occasion for lending their cars, but their chauffeurs probably did the actual work of transporting the wounded soldiers.[43] By later 1915 there was a decline in the volunteering of motor cars and a letter from Lady Mar was published in the local press to encourage a better response.[44]

Staff at Arnsbrae Hospital

There were various reports in the Alloa press from early 1915 about the arrival and treatment of the military patients,[45] since the press were keen to show how well-supported the hospital was within the local community; and most weeks they printed lists of all the gifts that the patients received. These could be anything from cigarettes, magazines and board games, eggs or jars of jam, to gifts of 3 guineas from Provost Strang, £5 from Rev Scudamore Forbes and £20 from ex-Provost Duncanson.

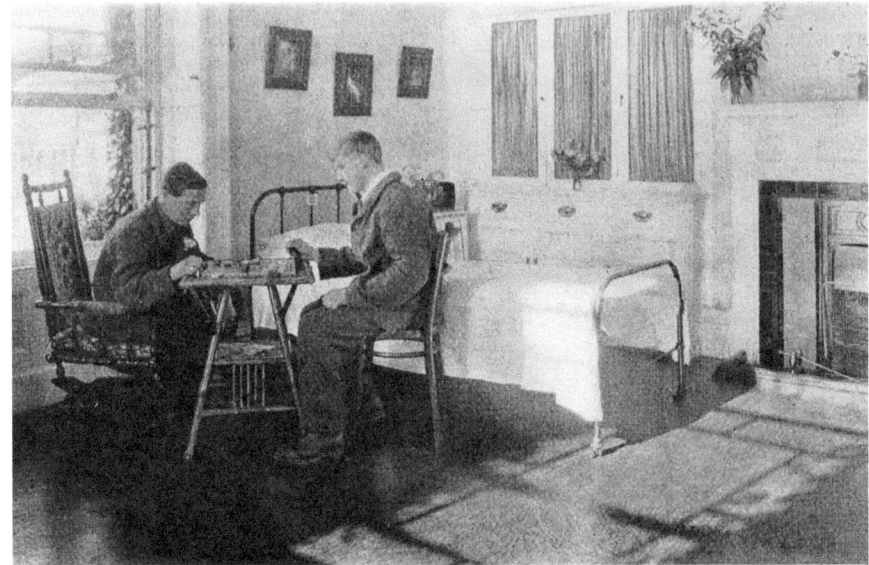

A corner of a ward, Arnsbrae Hospital

The single highlight of this wartime charitable giving was the fundraising which led to the building of a large wooden recreation hut big enough to seat 200 people, on the lawn in front of the mansion, which was officially opened by Lady Mar in July 1917.[46] In her speech she noted that the hall had been paid for by subscriptions from throughout the county, but she commented especially on how very generous the Clackmannanshire miners were; 'who had from the very first subscribed most liberally to the funds of the hospital…' There may have been contributions from the wider Clackmannanshire miners, but the employees of the Alloa Coal Company alone had a solid record for giving throughout the war. The *Advertiser* for 7 July 1917 showed that in June 1917 they made their 111th–14th weekly contributions to Arnsbrae Hospital at the rate of about £8 or £10 per week.[47] Even by July 1918 when they were making their 160th–164th contributions they had not reduced their rate of giving, it was still around £10 per week.⁴⁸ That generosity was matched by James Younger's; after lending his house to the Red Cross, at Christmas 1916 Matron L'Estrange presented each patient in the hospital with a leather pocket wallet, paid for by Mr and Mrs Younger.⁴⁹

The Red Cross was a very popular cause to support in Alloa. It had work parties throughout the county and in June 1915 reported that since the war started they had produced over 14,000 pieces of clothing to be sent on to various military destinations or hospitals.⁵⁰ In March 1916 they held a concert at the Pavilion, Shillinghill, organised by the Clara Butt-Rumford Foundation, which raised £115 for the Red Cross.⁵¹ In December 1916 Madame Clara Butt actually appeared in person in another concert at the Pavilion and received glowing reports in the press – 'Madame Butt was in magnificent voice and sang with that fine feeling, artistic expression and charming effect which have deservedly won for her the premier position...'⁵² Referring to the concert, Madame Butt said 'I was very pleased with the results and I am terribly greedy for the Red Cross'. Her efforts on this occasion raised £187. The Red Cross was also regular recipient of charity collections in the local schools, flag days in the town and, of course, an entire week devoted to raising money for it in July 1917 made over £2000.⁵³ The June 1918 Red Cross Gift Sale and Garden Fete held in the grounds of Alloa House raised even more money; over £4,000, partly helped by the glorious weather and the massive turnout of over 7,000 people.⁵⁴ Regular fund-raising concert parties were held at Arnsbrae and included performances by patients as well as visiting singers/musicians. These were usually well reported in the local press,⁵⁵ both in the detail given and in the compliments on the performances.

Arnsbrae Hospital had a royal visit in September 1916, with the arrival of HRH Princess Christian to inspect the work being done.⁵⁶ She drove over from Hopetoun House to have lunch with the Earl and Countess of Mar & Kellie, then visited the hospital, where eighty uniformed members of the Clackmannan County VAD acted as a guard of honour on the entrance way into Arnsbrae House. She spent part of the early afternoon there and 'spoke a cheering word to some of the wounded soldiers.'⁵⁷ The *Journal* reported that she stayed for about half an hour and 'was much gratified with the general appearance and complete equipment of the hospital'.⁵⁸

Red Cross records show that Arnsbrae Hospital received 1,168 patients during its time in operation, although the *Journal* has the figure at 1,396.⁵⁹ The last patients left on 15 January 1919 and the nursing staff, still led by Matron L'Estrange RRC, left on 1 February.⁶⁰ The recreation hut was given by the Red Cross to the Clackmannanshire miners as a tribute to their wartime generosity (they contributed over £2,000) and was rebuilt on a site in Fishcross next to the public school, 'with billiards and other games installed and the appointment of a caretaker'.[61] It was going to be officially opened for the second time by Lady Mar on 7 April 1919,[62] but in fact she merely chaired the proceedings and let her brother, Lord Shaftesbury, have the honour. Lord Mar was also present and, after a short speech, he handed over a German machine gun to the people of Fishcross as a war memento.[63]

AIR RAIDS

8 April 1916 was the first time the local press printed warning notices from the Alloa police authority about what might happen in air raids.[64] If an air raid appeared likely then all the street lights would be turned down to a red glow lasting three minutes, and the pressure in the town gas supply would be lowered. This panic response was obviously prompted by the Zeppelin bombing of Leith a week earlier, but it must be said that the Council had shown a concern about the impact of air raids from an even earlier date, although rather more from a financial than a human perspective. In February 1916 they had agreed to pay an insurance premium to cover all Council property from actions by hostile aircraft. This would cost £90 pa.[65] It was also agreed in April 1916 that the Burgh School, already requisitioned by the army, would in fact be used as a clearing station by the 2nd Detachment of Alloa VAD in the event of an air raid.[66] By the end of April 1916 it was also reported that '...arrangements had been made in the Old Hospital Buildings for a special ward for the treatment of any accident cases that might arise through a raid by hostile aircraft'.[67] The Council also agreed that if the fire brigade had to be called out the firemen would get an extra shilling an hour. These defensive preparations were all very well, but Councillor Hepburn wanted something a bit more offensive and asked 'What about [anti-] air-craft guns or something of that kind?'[68] He did not get any support for this idea from the Provost.

On the evening of Tuesday 2 May 1916 Alloa went through a real-life air raid drill after the town's Chief Constable had been notified that a fleet of German Zeppelins '...were making apparently for the South-East coast of Scotland'.[69] The fire brigade was put on standby, the two VAD detachments were sent to their respective clearing stations, and forty special constables came out on duty. They patrolled the streets, enforced the early closure of Alloa's three picture houses and made sure that the blackout was observed totally; 'By half past 11 o'clock the town might be said to have been in absolute darkness'.[70] They were all stood down at 2 o'clock on the Wednesday morning when it was officially notified that the raiders had left the Scottish coast. So, no hostile aircraft ever actually appeared in the skies over Alloa, but the local civil defence forces had been put through their paces and neither they nor the people of Alloa were found wanting. The *Journal* congratulated the Alloa townsfolk on their response, noting that 'The news of the possibility of a visit from the "Zepps" naturally caused a good deal of mild excitement throughout the town, but there was not the slightest indication of any tendency to panic'.[71]

On the evening of 9 August 1916 there was a second alert at just after midnight, when there was a warning of the approach of Zeppelins. The fire brigade was called out, but 'very few householders knew that anything unusual was expected and therefore there was no excitement'. The alarm was over by 2.00am.[72]

By the beginning of 1918 there were clearly some national inter-Council discussions taking place, where the Councils were trying to get the government to underwrite a national indemnity for possible war damage. Alloa Burgh Council was keen on this in order to avoid paying its own insurance and the Council minutes show that the members even expressed the hope, in the event of this national insurance policy being implemented, that there would also be a return of premiums paid previously.[73]

FOOD SUPPLIES AND RATIONING

It was almost the middle of 1917 before there seemed to be any serious concerns about food supplies in Alloa. May 1917 was the first time that the Alloa Cooperative Society put notices in the local press warning readers of likely shortages of sugar and that sugar cards would be issued which would give each buyer an allowance.[74] This allowance would be ½lb a week per family member, but in no case more than 4lbs per family. In retrospect these quantities do not seem to have been much of a limitation. However, they also put a notice on the front of the *Journal* warning that they were suspending the production of penny pastries.[75]

There were also signs that the Council was trying to get to grips with exactly how to run a food economy campaign, although in May 1917 their discussions had progressed no further than wondering how to persuade butchers and bakers to sell less.[76] By August it had set up a nine-person committee which would include five councillors and four members of the public, including one woman.[77]

Possible shortages of sugar continued to be a worry; there was an increasing concern about sugar supply throughout July and August 1917 in all Alloa papers. In the *Journal*

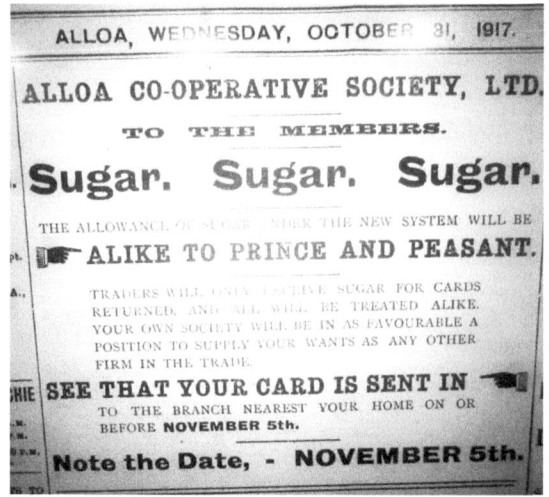

Alloa Co-op sugar notice (*Alloa Advertiser*)

on 18 August there was a whole column called 'Concerning Sugar', extolling its various delights.[78] This was not being facetious; the writer obviously believed that people were shortly to be severely deprived of one of life's major luxuries.

Then, on 1 September came the dreaded news about everyone having to fill in an official form to apply for a national sugar card.[79] Call it what you will, this was the beginning of a rationing system, although it still took a while to get it up and running. Even by the middle of October the Alloa Cooperative Society took a full column of the *Journal* to familiarise its customers with the appearance of a sugar card application form[80] and went to some lengths to convince its customers that everyone would be treated the same. The big warning notice, stating that 5 November was the final cut-off date for applicants, was supported by the reassuring message that the new system would 'be alike to prince and peasant.'[81] Sugar rationing finally started on 30 December 1917.

The *Journal* was first to use the dreaded expression 'Food queues' but managed to be positive about it.[82] By the end of December 1917 there was a set of voluntary rationing controls, agreed within the ranks of Alloa shopkeepers, overlaid by a few compulsory controls enforced by the Burgh Council, using its powers under the Defence of the Realm Act. As one of the voluntary controls, the shopkeepers became accustomed to dividing their new stock (of, say, margarine or butter) into small pre-packed quantities, then putting a notice in the windows saying when it would be on sale. This gave everyone a chance to get there and the possibility of at least buying a little bit, even if there were a lot of people. It was the queues that formed under these voluntary controls that the paper was complimenting, saying that it was only when people got nothing that resentment set in, whereas if they could all go away with a small amount, as a result of queuing, then everyone would be relatively happy.

It is tempting to think that if facing up to a slight sugar shortage and an ice cream ban[83] by December 1917 were the only nutritional deprivations that Alloa people would have to face in the first three and a half years of war, then things could not have been *so* bad. The situation deteriorated a lot during 1918, however, when other diet and household items were hit by shortages. The three areas where shortages (and therefore rationing) were anticipated were coal, butcher meat and flour grain. In all cases there were fears that food shortages would lead to high prices, causing many Alloa people to become undernourished because they could not afford to buy enough food. The answer seemed to lie, therefore, in both an 'allocation system', so that everyone got some, and a 'price control system', so that costs never rose beyond the pocket of the ordinary person. The risk that profiteering by suppliers might cause social unrest and an uprising by the masses was never mentioned explicitly, but there were enough references in the local press to the revolutionary events in Russia in 1917 to make one suspect that Alloa's local government was conscious of that possibility.

Regarding coal supplies, as from 15 October 1917 the Burgh Council took steps to fix the maximum price and put big notices explaining its statutory position, in the local press.[84] There was some hoarding though, as people tried to fill their coal cellars. There was also a fair amount of stealing of coal from the wagons standing in the sidings at Kelliebank. This was largely done by children, '...and it is strongly suspected that this is done, if not at the instigation, then with the knowledge of the parents'.[85]

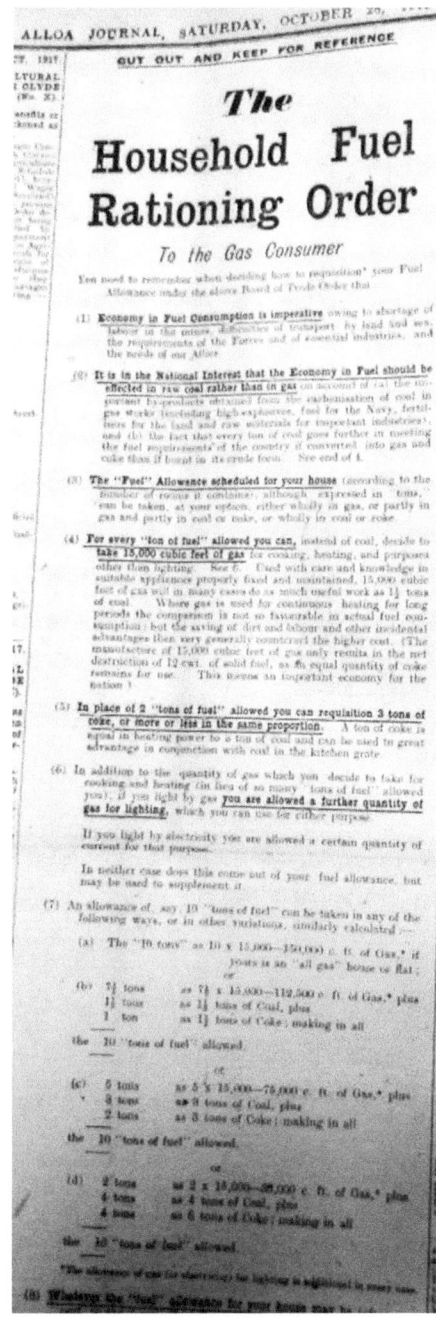

Household Fuel Rationing Order
(*Alloa Journal*)

By 26 October 1918 there was the Household Fuel Rationing Order. This was an alarmingly complex-looking schedule, covering almost a third of page 2 in the *Advertiser*, explaining how households now had to requisition their allocation of fuel and justify their usage.[86] Those businesses which used more than three tons of coal a week had to register.[87]

Regarding flour grain, the *Journal* commended the collection by children of chestnuts, for conversion into a rough sort of flour to add to flour grain.[88] The short article noted that 'a good many have been gathered locally', and estimated that if the national collection met its target of 5,000 tons, that was equal to over three million loaves of bread. In June 1917 there was a big government appeal for farmers to plant more wheat. The local farmers' committee felt that oats were more suitable to Scotland, but that they could probably convert about 400 acres from grassland to cereal production.[89] This may not have been successful enough, as on 15 February 1918 local bakers attended a lecture on how to increase the use of potato flour in baking. They resolved to 'assist the Ministry of Food in using potatoes...',[90] so there was probably still a big local wheat shortage. There was little else specifically about bread shortages in the local press.

At the end of November 1917 the Council opened a Communal Kitchen in Kelliebank. This was a heavily industrialised area of Alloa, with a lot of workers and it was chiefly for their benefit. Workers would get a two-course meal for 8d or 9d.[91] In that first week, 900 separate dinners were served.[92] In its first six months of operation it served 12,000 soups, almost 8,000 stews and 1,700 portions of potatoes.[93]

By January 1918 the Burgh Council had obviously found an answer to the problem of how to make butchers sell less, when they ordered them to close their shops on Tuesday afternoons and all day on Wednesday. The public were warned that butchers were only going to get 50 per cent of what they wanted, so buyers should purchase 50 per cent of what they normally got, and buyers should only deal with one retailer. It was considered that, with one meatless day a week, ¾lb of meat per person per week would be available

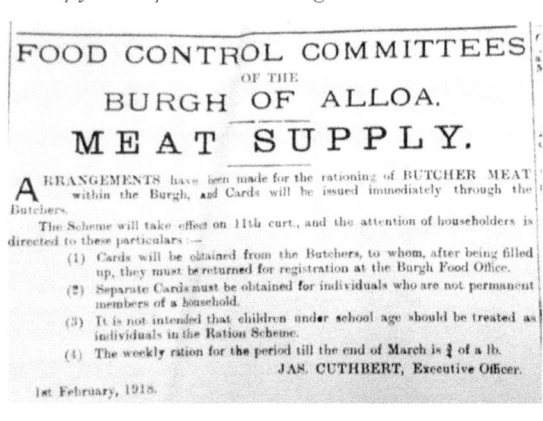

Food Control Committee meat supply poster
(*Alloa Advertiser*)

and that should be enough.⁹⁴ It all depended on butchers getting their supplies, though, and the system soon began to creak. On 26 January butchers put their own notice in the *Advertiser* saying 'Scarcity of butcher meat' and that they could not do home deliveries any more.⁹⁵ They really wanted everyone to come into shops and collect their own meat; some people might be dissuaded from eating meat every day if they had to go to the trouble of collecting it themselves.

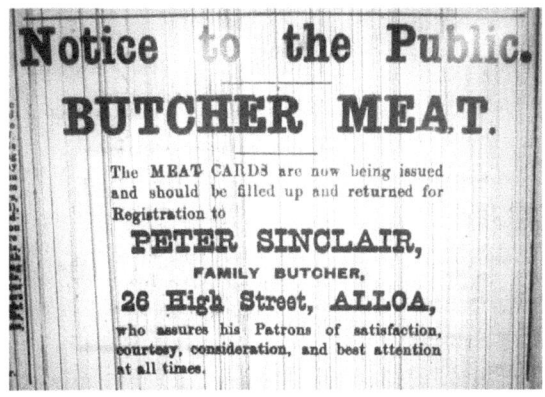

Notice to public on the issuing of meat ration cards
(*Alloa Advertiser*)

This did not really work and 'unprecedented scenes were witnessed', as buyers formed queues from 6.00 am and 'by noon some establishments were sold out and had to close their doors.'⁹⁶ In the light of the fact that 'During the week meat queues have been a marked feature of the town shopping', the Council acted and decided to introduce meat rationing from 11 February, though it still took another month for it become operational. The *Journal* reported on the apt comment, which seemed to sum up these hard times, from an Alloa lady who came up with the following verse from Psalm 59: 'Let them wander up and down for meat, and grudge if they are not satisfied.'⁹⁷

The Alloa Cooperative warned its customers that the rationing of meat would be 'worked on similar lines to that presently in vogue in the distribution of sugar' and it was hoped that there would be ¾lb per person per week.⁹⁸ Posters in the local press told the public that 'Butcher Cards were now being issued.'⁹⁹ The whole rationing scheme was getting quite serious and food cards were now to be dealt with by the Post Office; 11,000 Meat Rationing cards were to be sent out within the Burgh on 25 March 1918.¹⁰⁰ There must have been concerns that families with growing children were not getting enough; in April 1918 the age for collecting an adult's meat ration was reduced to 6.¹⁰¹ The local press reported that there was an increase in the number of poaching cases being dealt with by Alloa Sheriff Court.¹⁰² One of the accused said he 'had been scarce of meat' and it was clear that the meat shortage was beginning to have an effect. It was not only the Alloa citizens who might have been thinking of ways of getting around the meat restrictions: one Alloa butcher, William Dow from Mill St, enterprisingly but dishonestly submitted greatly inflated lists to the Food Committee of how many local people had registered their meat cards with him. He claimed for 3,647 adults and 568 children, when in reality he was only supplying the 1,665 adults and 362 children who had registered with him.[103] He was then over-supplied considerably with meat, which he seems to have sold on outside the district for his own profit. He was caught out, prosecuted, won his case on a technicality in December 1918, but lost it on appeal in January 1919.[104] The Sheriff said 'There could scarcely have been a worse attempt to defraud the public'[105] and fined him £100.

The Burgh Food Control Committee was told as early as January 1918 that there were already plans for a national rationing scheme which would be implemented when necessary. This would cover additional items such as tea, margarine and butter.[106] By the end of October 1918 that time arrived and '…12,000 individual ration books for local consumers' were in the hands of the Post Office ready for posting out on 2 November.[107] They were obviously sent out on time because the *Journal* reported the following week that 'Householders had a busy time getting their new ration books in order for registration with their grocers'.[108]

Times were tough for the people of Alloa in 1918, though they never reached a critical state. The full, government-controlled, rationing scheme was only introduced **nine days** before the end of the war; the people of Alloa had survived their wartime food shortages through some Burgh Council arm-twisting and local shopkeeper persuasion about fairness and economy. That is not to say, though, that the people of Alloa enjoyed either the quantity or the quality of their food supplies: the *Journal's* columnist noted in December 1918 that 'The other day I encountered a mysterious substance which had been sold over a local counter as cheese. It was of the consistency of putty, had the colour of wagon grease, smelt like fertiliser and …had a taste of the hereafter'.[109]

It is worth pointing out that rationing did not stop at the end of the war, but continued well into 1919. The *Circular* in September 1919 commented that 'The present rations (1 shilling and 8 pence's worth of meat, 1½oz of butter and 12oz of sugar per head per week) are likely to continue to the end of the year', and 12,000 more ration books were issued to the people of Alloa in November 1919.[110] Butcher meat was de-controlled only by the middle of December 1919.[111]

CONSCIENTIOUS OBJECTORS AND TRIBUNALS

The general picture in Alloa was of great enthusiasm for the war and there was certainly little support for conscientious objectors in the local press. The comment of the

Advertiser on 'the monstrous lengths to which conscientious objectors are prepared to go...'[112] gives an idea of its view, although on this occasion it was not actually reporting a local case.

In the early days, however, the Military Tribunal for the Burgh of Alloa did not have to deal with many conscientious objectors as such; more often it was groups of working men, or individuals who wanted clarification about their exact status in terms of enlistment. However, following the introduction of conscription in early 1916, they did have to deal with cases of conscientious objection. For instance, at the Tribunal on Friday 10 March 1916 they dealt with four cases of men who were claiming, on different conscience grounds, that they should not have to serve.[113] The Tribunal asked the obvious leading questions: 'Suppose you saw the enemy trying to shoot one of our men, would you defend him?' and 'If a man presented a pistol at your mother's head, would you not rather shoot him than let him shoot your mother?' As a result of this meeting of the Tribunal, the Gartmorn Socialist and the anti-militarist insurance agent had their claims disallowed; the Christian objector with the church testimonial was exempted with the hope that he might change his mind... while the other objector was recommended for non-combative service.

However, that was an unusual day; the Tribunal's work was usually more to do with adjudicating over giving exemption or some form of partial exemption to working men who were brought before it. For instance, the Burgh Council had declared that all of Alloa Academy's male teachers were exempt from military service due to them all being essential workers. The military authorities contested that (as did some of the councillors like Dr Harper[114]) and it therefore went to the Tribunal for a ruling.

The local churches sometimes had problems with tribunals; in February 1917 St Mungo's Church missionary at Tullibody had to appear before the local County Tribunal and was granted exemption only 'as long as he remains in his present profession'.[115] Then there was the curious case of a minister, John Strathern, who was offered the interim assistantship at St Mungo's during the overseas chaplaincy of Rev A.W. Scudamore Forbes. However, Mr Strathern wrote to say that his 'appeal as regards military service had... been rejected, since he was not [at that moment actually in the post as] a minister of the gospel...', therefore he could not take up the position because he would probably be sent off somewhere on war service. Lord Mar wrote a letter to the authorities...'[116] and this must have worked because, Mr Strathern then wrote to the Kirk Session saying that 'his calling-up papers' had been cancelled meantime.[117] It appears that tribunals could be 'convinced', although Lord Mar was in fact the chairman of the

County Tribunal so he may have had some influence over the Burgh one.

The Burgh Tribunal meeting of 30 July 1917 was probably typical of its type.[118] At this meeting, a few male workers at Paton's Mills were given conditional exemption, a bread vanman and a temporary constable had their cases dismissed while a watch repairer and a cashier in a brewery were granted conditional exemption. By November 1917 the Tribunal seems to have more often taken the approach of offering conditional exemption as long as the man concerned joined the local volunteers or VAD.[119] This became a 'ruling' from December 1917, when an article in the *Journal* reported on a Circular from the Government's Military Representative[120] saying that it was mandatory for exempted men to register with the local volunteers, otherwise they risked having their exemption certificate 'reviewed'.

Interestingly, Alloa had a branch of the Independent Labour Party, many of whose national leaders were absolutist conscientious objectors, yet in a report of their propaganda meetings in June 1917 the Alloa ILP made it clear that they were calling for 'the complete organisation of the manpower and industrial and economic resources of the nation for the defence of the Empire'.[121] This stance was socialist, not anti-conscription, and was not a message to the working men of Alloa that they should refuse to be called up.

NOT EVERY ALLOA MAN WANTED TO BE A HERO

It might be satisfying to think that the men of Alloa were all enthusiastic to go off and fight in the war, just as the evidence from those early days in August 1914 seemed to suggest; though a study of Alloa's conscientious objectors suggests there was a counterpoint to the accuracy of this view. More seriously still, however, for different reasons there were some men who could not maintain the idea or the practice of military service and deserted. The home town of such a man would normally play this down, since it reflected poorly on the 'esprit' of that community. Who knows how many men from Alloa fitted into this category of reluctant soldiers? One of them certainly behaved in such an outrageous way that he got quite a lot of coverage in the local press and achieved a certain notoriety.

John Horne, born in November 1893,[122] was from a large but reputedly good family. He lived at 8, The Shore and had six brothers,[123] two of whom served in the war (his younger brother Robert was in the Machine Gun Corps and was killed in Mesopotamia in 1917).[124] There is no suggestion that any of the other brothers had criminal intentions, but it appears that from a very early age John was in trouble. He had a criminal record by the time he was twelve, receiving three stripes of the birch rod for theft in Alloa.[125] At his trial 'Mrs Horne asked the Baillie to please himself about the stripes as, she added, it might do him good'. He was still only twelve when he committed further thefts and was sent to a reformatory. Following his release, the next eight years saw him being arrested frequently for theft in Alloa, Falkirk, Stirling, Dunfermline and Glasgow; the punishments ranged from admonishments to three months' imprisonment (twice) and two sentences of six months' imprisonment, once with hard labour.[126]

He did not join up in 1914; he continued his job as a labourer and fisherman and only joined up as a private in the 3rd Argylls once conscription was introduced in 1916. However, he did not then report for duty and was arrested in July 1916 and handed over to the military authorities.[127] He received twenty-eight days' detention. He then deserted and lived rough on Alloa Inch, an island in the River Forth, for a short while, before being captured and put on trial for the crimes he had committed whilst a deserter. This led to his conviction at Alloa Sheriff Court in September 1916, when he was given twelve months' hard labour.[128] The local press thought that his latest criminal activity was so audacious that it got its own article in the *Journal* under the heading 'A Masterful Criminal'.[129] Horne had actually committed several thefts over his time as a deserter, but the one that especially caught the attention of the sheriff was on the night of 7 August, when he broke into the Royal Garrison Artillery Hall in Dunfermline and pilfered belongings from the sleeping soldiers. The *Journal* recorded that 'He went about in such a light-footed manner... that he took practically all they had.'

His military records show that on 1 September 1917 he was to be transferred to a training battalion, but by now he had had enough of army life. On 10 August he deserted again and achieved some local celebrity over the next two months, since, as the local paper put it, he became 'Alloa's Robinson Crusoe'.[130] He came back to the area and lived rough in a well-concealed hideout on Dunmore Moss, to the south of River Forth. He survived by breaking into local primary schools to steal

ALLOA'S "ROBINSON CRUSOE."

Sent to Penal Servitude.

At a sitting of the High Court of Justiciary in Edinburgh on Monday.—A young soldier named John Horn, belonging to Alloa, who, after deserting from the Army, retired to a dug-out on a Stirlingshire moor and spent a hermit-like existence on the proceeds of various burglaries, was brought up for sentence at the High Court of Justiciary on Monday.

He had been remitted from Stirling, where he pleaded guilty to nine different charges, dating from 11th August last, when he stole a military bicycle at Redford Barracks. He subsequently broke into an office at Dunmore Moss, Airth, and into Fallin and Cowie Public Schools.

At St. Ninians and other places he stole a paraffin stove, a suit of overalls, a safety razor, a shaving brush, tea and sugar, coffee, syrup, currants, oatmeal, dripping, cocoa, whisky, watches, matches, ham, cheese, salt, some clothing, and a sum of £8.

food; he also stole money (just over £8) and whisky from the ship *Rosia*, which was lying in the river. The local police were aware that he might be back in the area, and the *Advertiser*, unable to deny itself the use of a military metaphor, reported his capture at the end of September under a heading of 'Local deserter's dug out'. The article described how 'Three constables systematically searched both banks of the river... for ten hours, and after an exciting hunt they succeeded in capturing Horne in a ditch on Carnock Moss.'[131] It was noted that he was 'in uniform when he was arrested'. This was now all too serious for Alloa Sheriff Court; he was remitted to the High Court of Justiciary in Edinburgh for sentencing and was given three years' penal servitude.[132]

In some ways the local press could be accused of romanticising this soldier's life as a deserter; referring to his 'hermit-like existence', 'living alone in a hut on an island after the fashion of Robinson Crusoe' and how his 'dug out... was cleverly concealed with heather...'[133] It might be said that these were the very characteristics that could have made him a good soldier in the trenches, but it is clear that, by temperament, here was an Alloa man entirely unsuited to the discipline of military life. So that was it: his army career was over; he was formally discharged from the Army on 1 December 1917 and served his sentence.

Even though it could be argued that John Horne did in fact have some limited military service,[134] his name does not appear in the Burgh of Alloa Roll of Honour. It seems that whilst he did achieve a measure of celebrity in 1917, it was for the wrong reasons, and no one wanted his name in the Roll as a permanent reminder of his disgrace.[135]

ALLOA BRASS BAND

Alloa had a well-established brass band, more properly entitled Alloa Instrumental Band, which performed each summer season in the bandstand in the West End Public Park, on Wednesday or Thursday nights and some weekends. It put on perhaps sixteen to twenty performances a season. It had been popular enough before the war for the *Journal* to run a column called 'Round the Bandstand' each week in summer,[136] to give notice of the programme and comment on the quality of the playing and the attendance. Alloa's Instrumental Band struggled to maintain its schedule during the war years. The minutes of its Management Committee noted in May 1915 that 'Since the outbreak of war the Conductor has laboured under serious difficulties. Quite half the members of the band are now serving in one or other branch of His Majesty's Forces, and Mr Muddiman has had to fill their places with young boys.'[137] He had received assistance, however, from three Territorial soldiers in 3rd/7th Argylls who had been members of other bands, but were billeted in the Town Hall. The situation could not have been too bad, however, because the February 1916 minutes recorded that there had been some good attendances at the bandstand in 1915, and Alloa's band had been helped out on some occasions by the pipe band of the 3rd/7th Argylls.[138] By February 1916 there were already ten members of the band serving in the armed forces, and this prompted a letter to the *Journal* asking if there were any retired bandsmen 'who may be good enough to offer their services'.[139] By May 1916 the band conductor was on the verge of despair. The Committee minutes noted that 'Mr Muddiman states that since last season he has been working under constantly adverse conditions... Compulsory Military Service however has interfered with and nullified all his plans, and he now fears that he must abandon all hope of being able to make the usual weekly appearances in the Park.'[140] He was clearly over-reacting, because the mid-season committee meeting in August reported that 'Concerts had been continued during the current season, and on the whole had been very satisfactory'.[141] However, the *Journal* more accurately reported that attendances were down and that a lot of those attending were women 'because the needs of the nation have drained a large proportion of our population to other scenes...'[142] It did go on to say that 'the programmes submitted are really good.' Indeed, in some ways one could argue that things prospered during the war years and by June 1918 Mr Muddiman thought that the band was in a better position than it had been in the past two years, with a few new players. In June 1918 he, like a lot of older men who thought the military authorities had passed them by, was caught out by the changes in the enlistment rules and faced his own call-up. He reported to the Band's Management Committee that 'in view of the likelihood of his being called up on an early date for Military Service; [he] had lodged a personal Application for Exemption with the local Tribunal. It was agreed that the Provost would represent the Committee at the tribunal in [his] support...'[143]

The band was unable to perform its Wednesday repertoire one night in mid-July 1918 due to 'the effects of the influenza epidemic on the ranks of the members'.[144] Apart from that one occasion, the press reported pretty well every week that the band was playing in the park and nothing more was reported about Mr Muddiman appearing before a tribunal. Maybe his worst fears were unfounded.

CINEMA ENTERTAINMENT

Alloa had three cinemas – La Scala, from January 1916, The Pavilion, and Green's Picturedrome. They advertised themselves in the local press via lists of their showings, and the press sometimes filled up their spare column inches with short reviews of the films themselves. The VB Picture Palace also existed in 1915 but seems to have disappeared.

Two particular films which were shown are of interest. From July to November 1916 two official war cameramen, Geoff Malins and John McDowell, went out to France and shot black and white, silent movie film of the fighting in the Somme Offensive.[145] Their footage was turned into two films: *The Battle of the Somme* (premiered in August 1916) and The *Battle of the Ancre and the Advance of the Tanks...* (known as 'the tanks film'), shown in 1917.

These films were both colossal successes throughout the country and had a profound effect on the British viewing public, who had never before seen such a graphic and realistic impression of what their menfolk were enduring. Twenty million tickets were sold in the first six weeks for *The Battle of the Somme*, and takings were even higher in the first three months for 'the tanks film'. Both films came to Alloa: the first to La Scala, the second to the Pavilion, La Scala and Green's Picturedrome. The people of Alloa could see *The Battle of the Somme* by the end of September 1916.[146] What was the reaction?

The *Advertiser* reported that 'However vivid have been the descriptions of this titanic struggle... these pictures tell the story as no words can do'. It noted that 'This remarkable film has caused a great sensation wherever it has been shown...' and went on 'it is one of the most marvellous films that has ever been shown'. It commented critically that 'it is a disappointing fact to find the Scottish regiments so scantily represented', but it complimented the film on 'its grim realism and moving incident'.[147] The *Advertiser* ended with: 'The whole film is brimful of appealing incident, most of it tragic, some of it touched with humour, but all serving to convey the terrible reality of modern battle.' The Earl and Countess of Mar & Kellie were present at one showing and at another the wounded soldiers from Arnsbrae Hospital were allowed in free. The *Journal* reported in the film's second week that 'every exhibition of this famous film has been viewed by a crowded house'.[148] It was only on for two weeks and was replaced by a Charlie Chaplin film.

'The tanks film' was shown in all three Alloa picture houses in late February 1917

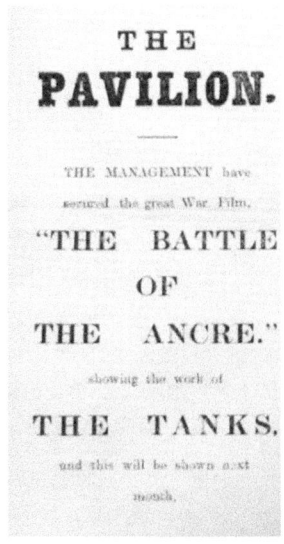

(Alloa Advertiser) (Alloa Journal)

and the Pavilion gave good notice that it had got the film. Green's Picturedrome topped La Scala's advertising by actually having a tank picture as part of its poster. The *Journal* had a piece praising the film and the cinematographer, especially admiring Malins' recklessness and the risk to his life in the way he had filmed it. It was a longish piece but it was entirely borrowed from the *Daily Sketch* and did not have anything in it about how Alloa people had reacted, though it did comment that 'it was viewed nightly by large audiences' when it was showing at La Scala.[149] The *Journal* held the view that 'While the films of the Somme held the attention as new in photography, the Battle of the Ancre pictures are better taken, and convey more of the real life of the front'.[150]

MASONIC LODGES

In 1957, a bicentenary history of the Freemasons Lodge No. 69 in Alloa was written by two members of the local lodge.[151] Pages 70-78 and page 93 of the book, plus additional references in the local press, help to build up quite a good picture of the impact of war on this local group.

When the Lodge resumed for the winter session of 1914 many office bearers and members were already in uniform. It began contributing to war charities early on; 4 guineas to the Soldier's and Sailor's Families Association on 4 Sept 1914 and 3 guineas each to the Red Cross and Prince of Wales' Fund. The Masonic Hall was commandeered for billeting by the military authorities in early October and the Lodge moved to the Parish Church Hall, which at that time was situated in the top flat of the building at the east corner of Candleriggs and Mill Street. The initial excitement of the war was reflected in the activities of the Lodge, as only four new members were initiated in 1915. There were twenty-one meetings in 1915 and a lot of them included reports from serving members. The Lodge agreed to start a Roll of Honour and recognised that serving members should be excused from paying their Test fees and be held in good standing as long as they were in the Colours. The Lodge's charitable contributions continued with donations of £3 for equipment for Bellahouston Hospital, £2 for equipment for Arnsbrae Hospital, 2 guineas to the Argylls' shilling fund, £5 for comforts to the troops and £6 for gifts to serving members.

The Army stopped using the Masonic Hall as a billet and instead it was let as an Officers' Mess. The officers, however, did quite a lot of damage to the furniture and carpet, so the Army was charged almost £13 for repairs. The Lodge was still able to use its Hall for evening meetings during most of 1916 and 1917, until it became a billet again. In September 1916 there was a letter from the Grand Lodge asking all lodges to check their membership for alien members.

In December 1916 it was decided to send seasonable gifts to all serving members; those at home would get 5s each while those abroad would be granted tobacco valued at 3 shillings. This cost the Lodge just over £20 in total. This was not really a problem, since the Lodge was quite wealthy and there were discussions in 1916 as to what to do with its money. In the end members agreed to invest £300 in a war loan.

In 1918 there was a rush to join the Lodge which lasted for two years; those years were a record for the numbers of meetings held and the number of candidates installed. The fact that those not in the forces had good jobs and were enjoying high wages may have explained some of this increase, but there were many candidates on wartime service as well. The two shipyards in Alloa were very busy and a lot of members came from their workforce; unfortunately they were not always local, therefore did not attend many meetings and left town when the yards closed. In 1918 the Lodge gave £20 for Alloa's Red Cross Week, and in June 1918 they welcomed Brother, the Rev A.W. Scudamore Forbes, Chaplain, home on furlough, who talked about his experiences in Egypt and Palestine. In September 1918 the military again commandeered their hall and the Lodge held its meetings in Kilncraigs Hall.

To celebrate the Armistice on 11 November 1918, the Lodge held a harmony in the upstairs hall on 15 November. 156 people sat down to a supper and speeches, 'and thankfulness predominated and the occasion was a memorable one'. There was a further celebration when its serving members were demobilised, and another harmony took place in the large hall at Kilncraigs on 12 November 1919. The military and naval brethren, numbering forty-four, marched into the Lodge room, headed by Colonel E.E. Dyer, Provincial Grand Master, to the strains of *Rule Britannia*, while 120 brethren stood to attention. The toast 'To Fallen Comrades' was observed in silence, after which the lament *Flowers o' the Forest* was played on the organ by Brother Ledger. The harmony cost the Lodge £37, but it was not grudged.

On 30 September 1921 a Roll of Serving Brethren in the Great War 1914-1918, in the form of an ornate, framed scroll, was prepared at a cost of just over £25. This used to hang in the members' room. At the regular meeting on 30 April 1925, a bronze memorial tablet to the memory of the eleven brethren killed in the Great War was unveiled by Brother A.L. Roxburgh (Past Master). This tablet was affixed to the north wall of the entrance hall, but in 1998 both memorials were transferred for safekeeping into the collection of Clackmannanshire Council Museum and Heritage Service, when the Masonic Hall was sold.[152] There was a report in the *Advertiser*[153] of A.L. Roxburgh's speech at the unveiling ceremony, which was more than critical of the government for neglecting the welfare of its returned soldiers.

ALLOA LIBRARIES

One of the responsibilities of the Burgh Council was the supervision of the local library and during the war years the Council contributed about £260 each year to support the library (staff salaries and purchase of books, newspapers and periodicals). The library auctioned off the magazines every so often and this raised about £13-£17 pa. One of the Council's sub-committees was the Library Book Committee, and it ran the library system. It was made up of ten councillors and ten householders, though the latter were actually chosen from the wealthier strata of local society. Among the ten men were three town ministers, two local school headmasters and the rest were other former Councillors. Provost Strang chaired this group, which also had its own sub-committee to look after the running of Alloa's Subscription Library. Both groups kept minutes of their wartime meetings which were quite regular, every two months or so for most of the war.

The minutes reveal that they purchased books, often £20-25- worth per month, throughout the war. There were few references to the impact of the war. In March 1916 it was noted within the Library book Committee that 'Certain members... with a view to economy at this time, held that only a limited number of books should be purchased'.[154] Then, concerned as they were about the Zeppelin attacks in 1916, they noted that 'the sum of £5 sterling had been paid as insurance against enemy aircraft'.[155] They regularly went through the book stock and removed old ones, but in February 1917 they withdrew 700 books from the library of which '200 were sent to the army through the medium of the Post Office.'[156]

Another point of interest in the Library Book Committee minutes was the light they shed on wage inflation during the war. Everyone knows that wars cause inflation because there are fewer goods for people to buy, therefore prices rise and people ask for pay rises to compensate. One wonders if these inflationary worries would have made much of an impact on the lives of the Alloa people: in the case of the library employees the answer seems to be 'No'. In December 1914 a new librarian, Miss Troup, was appointed at £52 pa.[157] Her new assistant, Jeanie Allan, received 10 shillings a week.[158] The librarian's salary was raised in 1916, raised again to £75 pa in December 1917 (plus a war bonus), then raised yet again in October 1918. Meanwhile, the assistant's salary had risen to 30 shillings a week. In other words, in four years the *assistant's* wages had **trebled** and by 1918 she was actually being paid 50 per cent more than the librarian herself had been earning only four years earlier,[159] which was not too bad.

As with the minutes of many of the Council's sub-committees, the first meeting of the Library Book Committee after the signing of the Armistice made no reference to the ending of the war.[160] What was more surprising was that, given the publicity in the local press, there was no reference to the actions of Dr Ferguson, the Committee's Convenor, in bringing about the creation of the John Buchan VC Memorial.[161]

CRIME IN ALLOA DURING WORLD WAR I

The question as to whether there would be a rise or fall in crime during the war is an interesting one; after all, it is suggested that most criminals were male and most of the men were away fighting, so did the local crime rate fall? Chief Constable John Johnston led the Burgh of Alloa Police force during the war – a force made up of one Inspector, two sergeants and nine constables – and every January he issued a report where he reviewed the local crime statistics for the previous year. These reports can be studied in the Council minutes; often they were given coverage in the local press.[162]

Synopsis of the Chief Constable's Reports for Burgh of Alloa 1914–1919						
	No of crimes	No of individuals committing crimes	No of juvenile offenders	No of juveniles convicted	No of males charged	No of females charged
Over 1913	561	610			508	102
Over 1914	581	643	30	26	541	102
Over 1915	491	549	79	66	390	159
Over 1916	310	342	45	23	242	100
Over 1917	320	342	18	10	256	86
Over 1918	242	306	67		249	57

These statistics speak for themselves; there was indeed a big decrease in crime in Alloa during the war years; by 1918 the number of crimes and the number of criminals just about halved, compared to the pre-war figures, although the larger ratio of crimes to criminals in 1918 suggests that they were working in gangs. Crime in Alloa seemed to remain chiefly a male pursuit, although that could be partly explained by the Chief Constable's comment in his Report on 1917's crime rates; that '51 per cent of the prisoners charged were under the influence of drink when they committed the offence.'[163] A lot of collective 'drunk and disorderly's (i.e. ten criminals but only one crime) would help to explain the 1918 figures.

The Chief Constable certainly saw 1916 as a breakthrough year and the *Journal* noted his comment that 'the figures show a remarkable decrease in crime, and that there have been no serious offences'.[164] However, at the same time as he was writing that, Chief Constable Scott's police report for the wider area of the county of Clackmannanshire noted that the number of crimes there rose from 105 to 145[165] and the Chief Constable for the Burgh of Stirling noted a 20 per cent increase in the number of crimes from 815 in 1915 to 1016 in 1916.[166] Maybe Alloa's criminals went into the neighbouring areas to do their crimes.

It is more difficult to reach a conclusion on the issue of the rate of juvenile offending. The assumption is that this would have risen due to the lack of parental supervision while the men were away at war. 1916 did see a rise in what the Council called 'Juvenile depravity', and there was much soul- searching as to its causes.[167] There was also a big rise in 1918, but how can the large decrease in 1917 be explained? Certainly, the apparent lack of control of young lads was a big concern during the war. Grange School log book for 1916 recorded the unusual and rather sad story of police investigations into a thieving ring called 'The Ace of Hearts', which was centred on four or five young lads who lacked the guiding hand of their absent fathers serving in the army.[168] The police caught the culprits, who admitted to pilfering in twenty-five local shops, and two of them were flogged; they were publicly birched in Alloa as an example to the rest.[169] One of the most serious of the young offenders was Alexander Goldie, a pupil from the Burgh School; he was given three years in Paisley Reformatory.[170] Perhaps these severe punishments actually worked as a deterrent to young offenders through 1917 and that was what kept the juvenile crime rate down that year

WAR SAVINGS CAMPAIGNS AND THE TANK 'JULIAN'

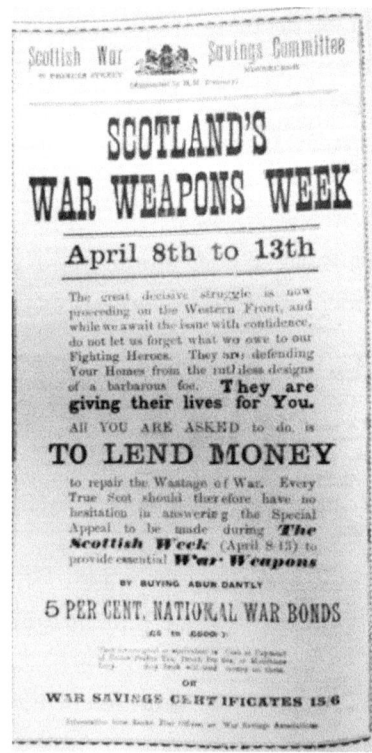

During the war, everyone (schools, churches, clubs, councils and individuals) was encouraged to put their savings into War loans to help pay for the war. There were often 'War Weapons' weeks and the competition among towns to raise money was quite intense. In April 1918 for instance, Alloa raised over £190,000, and when the County's total was added in, it was over £300,000. That was considered 'notable among the returns of the country,'[171] and according to the reckoning of the time would have paid for two destroyers.[172]

At one time Alloa was well in the running to be the best money-raising town in Scotland for its size.[173] In July 1918 Alloa's *per capita* rate was £41, second only to Edinburgh, but Alloa fell away in its total and by the end of 1918 was in 7th place with a total of £308,696,[174] though its *per capita* rate had risen to £47 by the end of August 1918.[175]

Curiously, there was still great propaganda

A rather tattered poster adorns the pillar, but otherwise a proud bunch of Alloa's fundraisers stands in front of the Burgh Chambers in Bank Street, for War Weapons Week in April 1918 (*Clackmannanshire Archives and Local History Service*)

pressure to keep up the lending, even into 1919, when there was a Victory Savings Week from 13-19 January, offering 5 per cent National War Bonds, which were clearly regarded as a good investment.[176] The Burgh of Alloa managed to raise the incredible total of just over £101,000 in that one week.[177]

One of the War Savings propaganda stunts that the government introduced during the war, were 'tank banks'. A whole set of tanks (six in all) travelled round the country showing off their paces – going over obstacle courses, often set up in the town's main street and the watching spectators were so impressed they would then put money into the tank. The idea was that the town that made the highest *per capita* contribution would be allowed to keep one of the tanks as a memorial. The tank 'Julian' was the one which visited Alloa, although it only arrived by train on the afternoon of Friday 7 February 1919, when the main campaign for raising war savings might be expected to have finished.[178] However, it did come for 'the purpose of assisting the sale of war bonds and certificates'[179] and through its performance on Saturday raised almost £2,000 as extra war loans from the Alloa townspeople in that one afternoon.

Peace Victory Bonds (*Alloa Circular*)

From the train station, 'Julian' did a fairly lengthy tour of the town, ending up at Smithfield Loan. An obstacle course of trenches, barbed wire and hedges had been erected for the tank's benefit on a piece of waste ground there, rather than being located in the town centre. 'Julian' obligingly put on its show and 'crashed through' and 'went over these obstacles with the utmost ease',[180] to the approval of the many watching spectators. Some of the local Councillors then stood on the tank and addressed the crowds, making 'a spirited appeal on behalf of the War Savings Committee.'[181] The *Journal* thought that 'Julian' undoubtedly created a great sensation during its visit to Alloa, as the size of the crowd at Smithfield Loan amply testified.'[182] A week later its columnist reported 'A belated story which is too good to lose...with reference to 'Julian's visit to Alloa. While the war engine was making its way through the streets of the town, preceded by two burly members of the Police Force, a facetious beholder was heard enquiring which of the three was the tank.'[183] Despite the great interest in this event, not unexpectedly, there was no photograph in the local press, although the internet has a fair number of photographs of 'Julian' visiting other towns, some of it actually movie footage.[184]

Curiously, Alloa <u>did</u> in fact receive an actual tank. In July 1919 'An intimation was read from the Scottish War Savings Committee, that, within the next few weeks, the War Office hoped to be able to supply a Tank for presentation to the town, in recognition of its great record in War Bond sales'.[185] This news was not universally welcomed; 'Some of the Councillors questioned the utility of the gift and were disposed not to accept it, but it was ultimately agreed to accept the proffered war monster...'[186] and in August 1919 a tank was 'handed over to the care and custody of the town council.'[187] This one was only called '6/25' and 'seemed to be coated with the mud of Flanders and had several bullet holes on one side'. 'The huge monster... attracted much attention',[188] as it was driven by Captain Everitt MC and two mechanics from the goods station to its display position to the west of the Town Hall.[189] The War Office clearly wanted this tank to be shown due respect; after all, it was, in some ways, a war memorial, so it wrote to the Council in September and suggested that a brass name plate with a suitable inscription should be attached to the tank.[190] By December 1919 there were already those in the Council who were saying 'Send it back'[191] and by May 1920 the Town Hall Committee (a sub-committee of the Burgh Council) was tired of it and wanted it removed to the West End Public Park.[192] Eventually, by November 1921, 'The Works Committee of the Town Council agreed that the tank and guns presently lying at the town hall should be removed to the Public Park and placed in position over the fountain'.[193] The question is; how long did they remain in the West End Public Park for and what happened to them afterwards?

ENDNOTES

1. These were the *Alloa Advertiser* owned by Buchan Bros, Candle St; *Alloa Journal* owned by M. Gardiner, Candleriggs, and *Alloa Circular* owned by J B Rae, Primrose St. All three newspapers were four-sided broadsheets. The *Circular* was the least likely to include photographs
2. *Alloa Journal* 7 Nov 1914 p. 2 col. 4
3. *Alloa Journal* 15 May 1915 p. 2 col. 3
4. *Alloa Journal* 8 May 1915 p. 2 col. 7
5. *Alloa Advertiser* 15 May 1915 p. 2 col. 4
6. *Alloa Circular* 19 May 1915 p. 2 col. 7
7. Despite the 1915 hostility, the Bechers continued to live in Alloa; indeed their grandson George was Alloa Academy's Dux medallist in 1955
8. *Glasgow Herald* 17 May 1917 reported that the shop was '...attacked by a mob of between 2,000 and 3,000 men and boys...' which seems to be a bit of an exaggeration
9. *Alloa Circular* 19 May 1915 p. 2 col. 7
10. *Alloa Journal* 12 June 1915 p. 3 col. 7. The Burgh of Alloa Roll of Honour lists a John Gourlay from 40 Broad Street as serving in the 3rd Seaforths. I wonder if it was the same man
11. *Alloa Advertiser* 22 May 1915 p. 2 col. 4
12. *Alloa Journal* 22 May 1915 p. 3 col. 7
13. Alloa Burgh Council minute book 13 Sept 1915
14. Alloa Burgh Council minute book 14 Sept 1914
15. Alloa Burgh Council minute book 8 Dec 1915

16 Alloa Burgh Council minute book Jan 1916
17 Alloa Burgh Council minute book 14 Feb 1916
18 *Alloa Journal* 15 April 1916 p. 3 col. 3
19 *Alloa Journal* 13 May 1916 p. 3 col. 3
20 Alloa Burgh Council minute book 5 Sept 1916, *Alloa Journal* 16 Sept 1916 p. 3 col. 2
21 Alloa Burgh Council minute book March 1915
22 *Alloa Journal* 15 April 1916 p. 3 col. 4
23 Alloa Burgh Council minute book 23 March 1915
24 Alloa Burgh Council minute book 12 April 1915
25 *Alloa Advertiser* 21 Sept 1918 p. 3 col. 2
26 *Alloa Journal* 3 Aug 1918 p. 3 col. 5
27 Meeting of Magistrates minute book 24 Aug 1914
28 Meeting of Magistrates minute book 24 Aug 1914
29 *Alloa Journal* 24 Oct 1914 p. 2 col. 6 also had a full list of those sworn in at 'An Unique Ceremony'
30 Meeting of Magistrates minute book 21 Oct 1914
31 Meeting of Magistrates minute book 13 Nov 1914
32 Meeting of Magistrates minute book 8 Sept 1914
33 Meeting of Magistrates minute book 14 Sept 1914
34 Meeting of Magistrates minute book 25 Jan 1916
35 Meeting of Magistrates minute book 11 June 1917
36 *Alloa Journal* 1 Feb 1919 p. 3 col. 4
37 *Alloa Circular* 22 May 1915 p. 2 col. 4
38 *Alloa Journal* 15 Feb 1915 p. 3 col. 6, *Alloa Circular* 17 February 1915 p. 3 col. 4
39 *An Illustrated Record of Red Cross Work in the East of Scotland* by J.C. McKechnie (1918) *Alloa Journal* 3 April 1915 p. 3 col. 1. The wards were big enough for between two to six patients. Four more rooms were set aside for nurses' accommodation. All the photographs in this section come from this book.
40 *Alloa Journal* 27 March 1915 p. 3 col. 2
41 *Alloa Journal* 17 Feb 1915 p. 2 col. 8
42 *Alloa Circular* 21 April 1915 p. 3 col. 5
43 *Alloa Journal* 17 April 1915 p. 3 col. 3
44 *Alloa Journal* 16 Oct 1915 p. 2 col. 6
45 *Alloa Circular* 21 April 1915 p. 3 col. 5
46 *Alloa Advertiser* 14 July 1917 p. 2 col. 4. Lady Mar noted that the hospital had dealt with 930 patients by that date
47 *Alloa Advertiser* 7 July 1917 p. 4 col. 1
48 *Alloa Journal* 29 June 1918 p. 3 col. 2
49 *Alloa Advertiser* 30 Dec 1916 p. 4 col. 2, *Alloa Journal* 30 Dec 1916 p. 3 col. 4
50 *Alloa Journal* 12 June 1915 p. 3 col. 5, 160 pieces of clothing went to Arnsbrae, over 300 to Lady Jellicoe for the Grand Fleet, almost 7,000 to different battalions of the Argylls and over 1,000 to Belgian refugees.

51 *Alloa Journal* 1 April 1916 p. 3 col. 2. It was reported that London artistes gave their services. The total collected was a record, so far, for a single town during the Scottish tour. Kelso only took £81 and Hawick only £82. See *Alloa Journal* 1 April 1916 p. 3 col. 1
52 *Alloa Advertiser* 9 Dec 1916 p. 3 col. 1
53 *Alloa Advertiser* 14 July 1917 p. 3 col. 2, *Alloa Journal* 14 July 1917 p. 3 of Special Supplement says it was over £2,300
54 *Alloa Journal* 29 June 1918 p. 3 col. 2. The Fete was opened by Lady Beatty, wife of Admiral Sir David Beatty of Jutland fame
55 *Alloa Journal* 26 June 1915 p. 3 col. 5. Different groups took responsibility for organising these concerts; for instance, the one on 22 June 1915 was organised by the people of Tillicoultry, the one on 15 July 1915 by Mr J.C. Boag of Alloa. See a long report of a concert with patients and a local pierrot troupe in *Alloa Advertiser* 30 Dec 1916 p. 3 col. 2
56 *Alloa Journal* 9 Sept 1916 p. 3 col. 1. Princess Christian was the third daughter of Queen Victoria and was keenly interested in medical matters, having set up the Army Nursing Reserve (which served in the Boer War) before it was absorbed into Queen Alexandra's Imperial Military Nursing Service. In World War I it seems that Princess Christian had a roving job as inspector of Red Cross facilities
57 *Alloa Advertiser* 9 Sept 1916 p. 3 col. 2
58 *Alloa Journal* 9 Sept 1916 p. 3 col. 1
59 *Alloa Journal* 8 Feb 1919 p. 3 col. 4. The figure had risen to 1983 patients in the long and detailed report of the Fishcross opening in *Alloa Advertiser* 12 April 1919 p. 3 col. 3
60 *Alloa Advertiser* 17 May 1919 p. 4 col. 4 noted that Miss L'Estrange received a clock and a cheque in recognition of her service at Arnsbrae Hospital for nearly four years
61 *Alloa Journal* 1 March 1919 p. 3 col. 2
62 *Alloa Journal* 5 April 1919 p. 2 col. 5
63 *Alloa Advertiser* 12 April 1919 p. 3 col. 3. The Government had sent Lord Mar four German machine guns to distribute and this was the first one
64 *Alloa Journal* 8 April 1916 p. 2 col. 1, *Alloa Advertiser* 8 April 1916 p. 2 col. 2
65 Alloa Burgh Council minute book 29 Feb 1916
66 Alloa Burgh Council minute book 24 April 1916
67 *Alloa Journal* 22 April 1916 p. 3 col. 3
68 *Alloa Journal* 15 April 1916 p. 3 col. 3
69 I think in fact this was a fleet of eight Zeppelins that came over the NE coast of England and bombed York at around 10.30 pm. They may have then proceeded in a northerly direction, giving the impression that they were going to bomb Scotland. One of them landed in Norway!
70 *Alloa Advertiser* 6 May 1916 p. 2 col. 5
71 *Alloa Journal* 6 May 1916 p. 4 col. 4
72 *Alloa Advertiser* 12 Aug 1916 p. 2 col. 4
73 Alloa Burgh Council minute book 29 Jan 1918
74 *Alloa Journal* 12 May 1917 p. 2 col. 3
75 *Alloa Journal* 19 May 1917 p. 1 col. 4

76 *Alloa Journal* 19 May 1917 p. 3 col. 5
77 Alloa Burgh Council minute book 6 Aug 1917
78 *Alloa Journal* 18 Aug 1917 p. 4 col. 3
79 *Alloa Journal* 1 Sept 1917 p. 1 col. 3
80 *Alloa Journal* 17 Oct 1917 p. 1 col. 3
81 *Alloa Journal* 3 Nov 1917 p. 2 col. 1
82 *Alloa Journal* 22 Dec 1917 p. 3 col. 3
83 *Alloa Journal* 5 Jan 1918 p. 3 col. 1 for account of the Ice Cream (Restriction) Order
84 *Alloa Journal* 27 Oct 1917 p. 2 col. 1
85 *Alloa Journal* 9 March 1918 p. 3 col. 3
86 *Alloa Advertiser* 26 Oct 1918 p. 2 col. 4
87 *Alloa Journal* 9 November 1918 p. 4 col. 4
88 *Alloa Journal* 15 Dec 1917 p. 3 col. 2, *Alloa Advertiser* 16 Feb 1918 p. 3 col. 1
89 *Alloa Advertiser* 2 June 1917 p. 4 col. 1
90 *Alloa Advertiser* 16 Feb 1918 p. 3 col. 1
91 *Alloa Journal* 24 Nov 1917 p. 2 col. 4
92 *Alloa Advertiser* 1 Dec 1917 p. 2 col. 5
93 *Alloa Journal* 18 May 1918 p. 3 col. 2
94 *Alloa Journal* 12 Jan 1918 p. 2 col. 1, col. 7
95 *Alloa Advertiser* 26 Jan 1918 p. 2 col. 1, 2 Feb 1918 p. 2 col. 1
96 *Alloa Advertiser* 2 Feb 1918 p. 3 col. 5
97 *Alloa Journal* 18 May 1918 p. 3 col. 2
98 *Alloa Advertiser* 2 Feb 1918 p. 2 col. 3
99 *Alloa Advertiser* 23 March 1918 p. 2 col. 3
100 *Alloa Advertiser* 9 March 1918 p. 2 col. 3
101 *Alloa Advertiser* 20 April 1918 p. 2 col. 3
102 *Alloa Journal* 16 March 1918 p. 3 col. 4
103 *Alloa Journal* 12 Oct 1918 p. 3 col. 1 for first reports of the offence
104 *Alloa Journal* 1 Feb 1919 p. 2 col. 5
105 *Alloa Journal* 15 Feb 1919 p. 3 col. 4
106 *Alloa Advertiser* 26 Jan 1918 p. 3 col. 4
107 *Alloa Advertiser* 2 Nov 1918 p. 3 col. 1
108 *Alloa Journal* 9 Nov 1918 p. 3 col. 1
109 *Alloa Journal* 8 Dec 1918 p. 3 col. 1
110 *Alloa Journal* 13 Dec 1919 noted that butcher meat was de-controlled from 15 Dec 1919 but sugar and butter were still rationed
111 *Alloa Advertiser* 13 Dec 1919 p. 2 col. 6
112 *Alloa Advertiser* 4 March 1916 p. 3 col. 2
113 *Alloa Journal* 11 March 1916 p. 3 cols. 2-3
114 Alloa Burgh School Board minute book 10 Feb 1916

115 St Mungo's Kirk Session minute book 14 Feb 1917
116 St Mungo's Kirk Session minute book 13 June 1917
117 St Mungo's Kirk Session minute book 13 July 1917
118 *Alloa Advertiser* 4 Aug 1917 p. 3 col5.
119 *Alloa Journal* 10 Nov 1917 p. 3 col. 1
120 *Alloa Journal* 29 Dec 1917 p. 3 col. 5
121 *Alloa Journal* 2 June 1917 p. 3 col. 1
122 This date is from his birth certificate. His record of military service shows his joining-up date as 16 April 1916. At that time he was twenty-two years and five months, which pretty well agrees with this. Curiously, the April 1901 census says he was 'age six last birthday', which would have put his date of birth as 1894
123 His younger brother Robert's Army Form W.5080, giving a statement of all blood relatives, lists his six brothers and three sisters
124 The Burgh of Alloa Roll of Honour gives further details of his brothers' military service and records the address as 8, The Shore. The 1901 census records his address as 4, The Shore, but he could have moved. In 1901 his surname was spelt as Horn
125 *Alloa Advertiser* May 1906 called it 'A Daring theft by a boy' from Alloa boathouse. He stole a gold watch, two half sovereigns and 6d
126 The documents showing his criminal record from 1906-1915 can be inspected in the Fife Constabulary 2nd Photo Criminal Register
127 *Devon Valley Tribune* July 1916
128 By now he appears to have transferred to the Royal Garrison Artillery. According to *Alloa Advertiser* 23 Sept 1916 p. 3 col. 2 he appeared for trial as a private soldier in the uniform of that regiment.
129 *Alloa Journal* 23 Sept 1916 p. 2 col. 4
130 *Alloa Journal* 20 Oct 1917 p. 3 col. 5
131 *Alloa Advertiser* 29 Sept 1917 p. 3 col. 4
132 *Alloa Journal* 20 Oct 1917 p. 3 col. 5
133 *Alloa Journal* 29 Sept 1917 p. 3 col. 1 and 20 Oct 1917 p. 3 col. 5. The *Stirling Observer* (quoted in the *Alloa Advertiser* 20 Oct 1917 p. 4 col. 3) was most guilty of this romanticisation. It reported that '...there is always some good in the worst of us...' and went on to say that '...during the six weeks that he was hiding in a "dug out", he tamed a wild rabbit. He taught it to come and feed out of his hand, and anybody who could gain the confidence of a timid animal to that extent cannot be entirely bad'
134 His military record states that he was technically in the army for 1 year 220 days
135 In the interests of accuracy it must be reported that despite his appalling early record, John Horne did not remain an incorrigible criminal throughout his life. He may never have been a model citizen but he held down a job on a Calder's Brewery boat, married in the late 1920s and had two children. He died in 1965. My thanks to J.D.H. and John McClelland (the grandson of John Horne) for drawing my attention to this story, which I think provides an interesting counterpoint to the cosy general view of all-round enthusiasm for the war

136 *Alloa Journal* 31 July 1915 p. 3 col. 1 shows that this feature column was still intermittently printed
137 Alloa Instrumental Band Management Committee minute book 10 June 1915
138 Alloa Instrumental Band Management Committee minute book 2 Feb 1916
139 *Alloa Journal* 15 April 1916 p. 3 col. 4
140 Alloa Instrumental Band Management Committee minute book 2 May 1916
141 Alloa Instrumental Band Management Committee minute book 14 Aug 1917
142 *Alloa Journal* 8 July 1916 p. 3 col. 1
143 Alloa Instrumental Band Management Committee minute book 24 June 1918
144 *Alloa Journal* 13 July 1918 p. 3 col. 1
145 *Alloa Journal* 30 Sept 1916 p. 3 col. 1 noted that the two cameramen were paid £1 a day for their work
146 *Alloa Advertiser* 30 Sept 1916 p. 2 col. 5
147 *Alloa Advertiser* 7 Oct 1916 p. 2 col. 4
148 *Alloa Journal* 7 Oct 1916 p. 4 col. 3
149 *Alloa Journal* 3 March 1917 p. 3 col. 4
150 *Alloa Journal* 3 March 1917 p. 3 col. 1
151 *A History of the Lodge of Alloa No 69 1757–1957* Brother James Saunders and Brother Robert Wright (1957)
152 For photograph, see Chapter 11
153 *Alloa Advertiser* 2 May 1925
154 Alloa Burgh Council Library Book Committee minute book 2 March 1916
155 Alloa Burgh Council Library Book Committee minute book 27 Sept 1916
156 Alloa Burgh Council Library Book Committee minute book 9 Feb 1917
157 Alloa Burgh Council Library Book Committee minute book 9 Dec 1914
158 Alloa Burgh Council Library Book Committee minute book 16 Dec 1914
159 Alloa Burgh Council Library Book Committee minute book 12 Dec 1917, 8 Oct 1918
160 Alloa Burgh Council Library Book Committee minute book 16 Dec 1918
161 See Chapter 14 for details of the town's memorial to J.C. Buchan VC.
162 *Alloa Journal* 16 Jan 1915 p. 3 col. 2, 29 Jan 1916 p. 3 col. 7, 13 Jan 1917 p. 3 col. 4, 2 Feb 1918 p. 3 col. 1, 1 Feb 1919 p. 3 col. 1
163 *Alloa Journal* 2 Feb 1918 p. 4 col. 1 [in 1916 his report noted that it was 67 per cent!]
164 *Alloa Journal* 6 Jan 1917 p. 3 col. 1
165 *Alloa Journal* 6 Jan 1917 p. 4 col. 5
166 *Stirling Observer* 6 Jan 1917 p. 2 col. 5
167 *Alloa Advertiser* 22 July 1916 p. 4 col. 2. It chiefly blamed the cinema and absent fathers
168 This was also extensively reported in the *Alloa Advertiser* 1 July 1916 p. 4 col. 4.
169 Grange School Headmaster's Log Book 31 May 1916
170 Alloa Burgh School Headmaster's Log Book 31 May 1916
171 *Alloa Journal* 20 April 1918 p. 3 col. 1
172 *Alloa Journal* 20 April 1918 Editorial p. 2 col. 4

173 *Alloa Journal* 6 July 1918 p. 3 col. 4
174 *Alloa Advertiser* 7 Dec 1918 p. 3 col. 2
175 *Alloa Advertiser* 31 Aug 1918 p. 2 col. 4
176 *Alloa Advertiser* 4 Jan 1919 p. 2 col. 3
177 *Alloa Advertiser* 25 Jan 1919 p. 3 cols. 1+3
178 *Alloa Journal* 10 Aug 1918 p. 3 col. 5 reported that 'Julian' had already visited the neighbouring town of Stirling during the war
179 *Alloa Advertiser* 15 Feb 1919 p. 3 col. 1
180 *Alloa Journal* 15 Feb 1919 p. 4 col. 2
181 *Alloa Advertiser* 15 Feb 1919 p. 3 col. 1
182 *Alloa Journal* 15 Feb 1919 p. 3 col. 1
183 *Alloa Journal* 22 Feb 1919 p. 3 col. 2
184 The WPA Film Library on the internet has movie footage. There is also a nice picture of 'Julian' visiting Elgin in October 1918, found on p. 204 of Derek Bird's *The Spirit of the Troops is Excellent* (2008)
185 Alloa Burgh Council minute book 29 July 1919
186 *Alloa Journal* 2 Aug 1919 p. 3 col. 2
187 *Alloa Advertiser* 23 Aug 1919 p. 3 col. 1
188 Alloa Journal 23 Aug 1919 p. 2 col. 5
189 7th Battalion Argylls Regimental History p. 83 and Burgh of Alloa Roll of Honour. Captain W.A. Everitt was a local man from 29 Ludgate. He was in the 7th Argylls before transferring to the Tank Corps. His photograph and details of the award of his MC are in *Alloa Journal* 26 Jan 1918 p. 3 col. 3. He also appears in the photo of the officers of the 7th Argylls on p. 243.
190 Alloa Burgh Council minute book 30 Sept 1919
191 *Alloa Journal* 13 Dec 1919 p. 2 col. 6. 264 of these presentation tanks were given to communities around the UK as a reward for their war savings efforts. By 1945 all but one had been scrapped. The only present survivor is in Ashford, Kent
192 Alloa Burgh Council minute book 25 May 1920
193 Alloa Burgh Council minute book 28 Nov 1921. By 'over the fountain' they presumably meant that it was placed on the bit of higher ground **overlooking** the drinking fountain by the public entrance at the Claremont end of the Public Park

CHAPTER 8

CHURCHES AND THE WAR

The main sources of evidence for the reaction of local churches to the impact of the war are the Kirk Session or Deacons' Court records of the main Presbyterian churches in the town. St Mungo's, West Church (now Ludgate Church), St Andrew's Church, Chalmers Church and Moncrieff Church all kept records of their (usually) monthly meetings. St John's Episcopal Church kept minutes of the meetings of its Vestry Committee and Finance Committee, and there are also records from the Greenside Mission, Park Lane Mission, Alloa Baptist Church and the YMCA/YWCA. From these and the local press it is possible to get a fair impression of the responses of local religious groups to the strains of war. The only great omission is the St Mungo's RC Church: the priest, Rev John McDaniel, kept no wartime records which have been passed onto the Catholic Archives in Edinburgh and the local press seems to have had very little interest in reporting the activities of the Catholic population of Alloa, even omitting them from their church service listings.

WARTIME ACTIVITIES OF THE CHURCHES WITHIN ALLOA

The first response to the outbreak of war by nearly all the local churches was to hold intercessory services. The sermon given at the first of these services at St Mungo's was reported as 'eloquent and inspiring'.[1] These services were still being held well into late 1915 and became a shared duty amongst the different churches, although there was some discussion amongst the ministers about how long to continue with them.[2]

Within six weeks of the declaration of war, the local churches had decided to postpone the idea of joint mission services.[3] The West Church Kirk Session noted that this cancellation was '…in consequence of the War breaking out [in] Europe, Germany and Austria against Britain, France, Russia, Belgium and Servia (sic)…'[4]

Alloa's churches did make arrangements with the local military authorities to welcome them to church services[5] and offered soldiers special occasions for celebrating Holy Communion.[6] St Mungo's also introduced special Communions for the wounded soldiers at Arnsbrae Hospital,[7] and Rev D. Moir from St John's Church followed suit on two or three occasions in late 1916 when he was home from his chaplaincy duties in France.[8]

Elders were encouraged to get a reasonable list of the names of congregational members who were ' ... assisting the country in the present grave crisis'[9] and an early draft list for the West Church appeared in the Kirk Session minute book on 25 September 1914,[10] a list that was occasionally updated thereafter. It was not long, of course, before the churches were sending out letters of condolence to wives or parents of members who had been killed[11] and then holding memorial services. The West Church sent a special letter of condolence/congratulations in May 1918 to congregation member Mr David Buchan, when his son, John Crawford Buchan, was awarded the VC but was also missing in action.[12] On Sunday 3 September 1916, St Andrew's Church was the first to hold an 'In Memoriam' Service for those of its congregation who had been killed in action. The *Advertiser* noted of this service that; 'The scourge of the War which has swept over the country during the past two years has left an indelible mark upon our community...' and observed that eighteen congregational members of St Andrew's Church had been killed so far.[13] The Chalmers Church held a similar memorial service on Sunday 12 November 1916, the West Church held one on the last Sunday of July 1917,[14] and St Mungo's held one in early November 1917 'to commemorate those who had fallen in action and give comfort and consolation to sorrowing relatives and friends'.[15] The Chalmers Church also noted its feelings at a meeting of its Deacons' Court; 'The very great loss sustained by many of the members of the congregation, and of them, deep sorrow at the sacrifice of young and gallant lives at the battle front, in the great war, now raging... The Court desired to give heartfelt expression of their deep feeling of sympathy for those who sorrowed, and the irreparable loss sustained by this congregation.'[16]

By 1915 most of the churches had started their own rolls of honour.[17] St Mungo's proudly noted that its roll 'included 8 commissioned officers and 187 non-commissioned officers and privates.'[18] perhaps betraying a strange sort of one-upmanship. Greenside Mission's roll, dated July 1915, included no officers at all, in fact no-one ranked higher than a corporal. The Chalmers Church had produced their roll by April 1917, with 117 names on it, of whom seventeen had died.[19] After the war, most of Alloa's churches produced war memorials to honour the fallen in their own congregations; full details of these are given in Chapter 11.

From the start of the war, members of congregations (normally Ladies Committees) were quick to make what contribution they could; '...it was heartily agreed to provide material for the making of comforts for soldiers and sailors taking part in the war...'[20] Local churches took part, often by offering the church hall, in charity events to raise funds for the war. There was a recital in St Mungo's on 9 December 1914[21] and the congregation was much involved in raising money for the Belgian Relief Fund in 1915.[22] However, when the West Church was asked to consider giving its hall over for billeting troops in December 1916 the response was as follows: 'it was unanimously agreed to offer the cellar and infants room for storage purposes gratuitously if required',[23] which was not quite the same thing.

The West Church Guild produced a wartime *Manuscript Magazine* on 9 February 1915, with an evening's entertainment, with singers, to accompany its publication. This magazine was an occasional scrapbook-cum-journal (last previous issue was in 1912) and the editor, R.G. Duff, [24] noted that 'little did we dream that our beloved country would be passing though the gravest crisis that had faced her for a century, and that the sombre clouds of a war, the greatest in the world's history, and beside which other, what we used to call "Great" wars sink into insignificance, should be hovering like a dark and dismal shadow over the hearts and lives of our people'.[25] The editorial continued with three more pages of this lyrical and noble prose on the theme of sacrifice and loss. The *Manuscript Magazine* in the archive is handwritten, presumably a copy of the original printed version. It contained articles on indirectly war-related themes like the French Marseillaise, Burns' poems and 'Notes from the Trenches' by a serving member of the congregation. Interestingly, it also included an article cut out of a non-local newspaper entitled 'Amongst the Bernese Alps' by J.C.B. This is clearly John Crawford Buchan VC, who was stranded in Switzerland in 1914–15.

All local churches seemed concerned about the new Lighting Act which the government introduced in 1916. It was widely discussed about whether to cancel or change the times of evening services due to this blackout.[26] St Mungo's seemed best prepared, when it reported in February 1916 that 'As to lighting, Mr Robertson received instructions to reduce the lighting so to obviate any objection under the new regulations'.[27]

However, there was still the question as to whether it was practicable to run evening services. At St Mungo's, 'The Session considered what action should be taken in view of the effect of the lighting restrictions upon the evening service... The experiment held in spring with an afternoon service was felt to have proved that it was desirable, if at all possible, to hold the evening service...'[28]

Whatever action they took must have helped preserve their evening service because by October, 'The Session approved of the manner in which the lights of the church had been obscured, with the view to the continuance of Sunday Evening Services.'[29] Curiously, the West Church did not show the same degree of urgency until much later; with 'The question of changing the hours of Evening Services at close of summer time' only being discussed in July 1917.[30] The West Church must also have come up with the same idea of obscuring lights and windows as St Mungo's, after having had '...discussion with the Chief Constable about whether it would be sufficient to have the lights of the church properly shaded in some manner without having to fit up dark blinds...'[31]

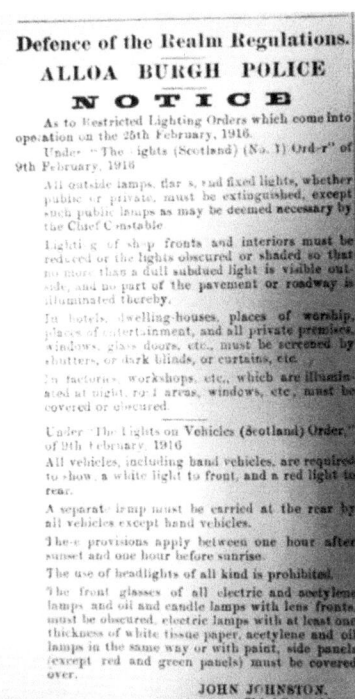

Lighting regulations notice for churches (*Alloa Advertiser*)

In the light of the risk of bombing, most local churches were not prepared to just put their trust in God and the blackout; they wanted better cover than that. The Baptist Church noted in regard to Zeppelin Raids that 'In view of the destruction caused by such raids made by the Germans in many parts of the country just now... it was agreed that we insure the Church Buildings against such raids for the duration of the war.'[32] The Chalmers Church also 'agreed to increase the (insurance on) the Church and Manse properties against damage done by enemy Air-Craft'.[33] The West Church was the first to feel confident that it could do without insuring its property against enemy aircraft, and it dropped the policy in January 1917.[34]

Most of the Alloa churches got involved to varying degrees in the same sort of wartime activities – fund-raising, war savings, comforts for soldiers etc. The Baptist Church, however, held true to some of its more special beliefs which were not necessarily shared by the other churches; the chief of these was temperance. On two occasions it communicated the strength of its feeling on this issue to the government.

In a widely publicised speech in January 1915, Lloyd George had told the Shipbuilding Employers Federation that Britain was 'fighting Germans, Austrians and Drink, and as far as I can see the greatest of these foes is Drink'. He wanted the labour force to move towards the habit of temperance and he was supported by the King, who made a pledge that no alcohol would be consumed in the Royal household until the war was over. The Alloa Baptist Church clearly took heart from this and in April 1915 a Resolution was made 'That this congregation is strongly convinced that the serious evils caused by the liquor traffic, especially at this time of grave national crisis demand drastic action, [it] welcomes the declaration of the Chancellor of the Exchequer that nothing but root and branch methods will be of any avail in dealing with this evil, and earnestly calls upon His Majesty's Government in the highest interest of the Country, to entirely prohibit the sale of intoxicating liquor during the period of the war.' Copies of this Resolution were sent to the Prime Minister, the Chancellor of the Exchequer and the local MP Eugene Wason.[35]

Three months later the Baptist pastor reported that the Resolution had *not* been adopted in the House of Commons, but certain 'steps had been taken to restrict the sale of the same, for which we were deeply thankful'.[36] With all its breweries you might almost say that Alloa was a town built on alcohol, but that did not stop the Baptist Church from writing to the government again in early 1918, during the food controls, expressing their disbelief at the inconsistency the government was showing, in a time of great shortage, in letting the best grain in the country be allocated to liquor production[37] rather than bread.

There is no evidence in the local press of any of the churches getting involved in the national Days of Prayer which seemed so popular in England. The interim minister of St John's Church, Dr MacIntosh, noted on 5 August 1917 that it was 'Third Anniversary of War' and on 4 August 1918 that it was a 'Special Service on anniversary of Declaration of War',[38] but there is no record as to what he said in his sermon on that theme.[39] A big, joint commemorative service for the fourth anniversary of the outbreak of the war was held in St Mungo's on Sunday 4 August 1918 with the minister of the Moncrieff Church sharing the preaching.[40]

Uniquely among the local churches, the Baptist congregation cemented its pacifist credentials more deeply by observing 22 December 1918 'as a day to further the advisability of having a League of Nations so as to make it impossible for us as a nation to experience the terrible [*word omitted*] of such a war now finished'. They also had a petition signed by members of the congregation in favour of the League.

DID CONGREGATIONAL GIVING OR CHURCH ATTENDANCE CHANGE DURING THE WAR YEARS?

There are no references in the local press to the scale of congregational giving during the war. One might have expected that average church attendance would have dropped due to the men being away, but there is no hint that local churches lost much by way of congregational income or suffered a decrease in congregational size. The records that the churches kept themselves are not always very helpful; they are often incomplete or it is difficult to work out from their accounts what was the real level of income.

One full set of accounts came from the West Church:

	Income
1911	£842
1912	£879
1913	£937
1914	£861
1915	£856
1916	£860
1917	£926
1918	£896

These figures certainly don't give an impression of any dramatic reduction in church income, nor do they reveal the fact that the West Church had an increasing 'balance in hand' <u>for every year</u> of the war, ending up with a surplus carried forward of £419.[41] In 1916 they were able to invest £100 in Exchequer bonds at a 5 per cent interest rate. The West Church seems to have been careful with its money: in March 1915 there was the issue of a large repair needed to the boundary wall of the manse grounds in Claremont, which they 'agreed to let lie over until the war is over owing to the high cost of labour and materials.'[42] The next time this was discussed was in 1920, when they wanted to put the manse in good order for the incoming new minister... but even then they agreed to delay repairs again for a year.[43]

Another set of accounts from the Chalmers Church shows that they also maintained their finances quite well during the war years,[44] although they did not reveal how much their expenditure exceeded their income.

Income to the Central Fund

1913	£275	
1914	£267	1914 ended with a credit balance of £9
1915	£261	1915 ended with a debit balance of £4
1916	£262	1916 had deficit of £35
1917	£258	
1918	£283	
1919	£310	
1921	£334	

It seems that St John's Church struggled financially during the war. It had a debit balance of £102 in 1917 and at the Vestry Committee meeting Lord Mar pointed out that '...there was a falling off in the Offertories'[45] and 'it was arranged that Dr MacIntosh should make an appeal to the congregation to be more liberal in their offerings'. By November 1918 the debit balance had risen to £163 and it was noted that 'offertories have declined from £246 in 1913-14 to £228 in 1917-18'.[46]

There is plenty of evidence that St Mungo's was also, though **just in 1918** feeling the financial pinch. By June 1918, the Kirk Session 'Agreed to postpone discussion of what steps should be taken to remove the deficit of last year's congregational collections and improve the finances of the church'.[47] By September 1918 they had to face up to the brutal truth when 'the treasurer told the session that the deficit at the end of last year was £60, despite the fact that there was no choir and at the end of the year would be worse unless steps were taken to provide against such a deficit. Salaries and wages had been increased by £30, coal was more expensive and the wine used at Communion was double its price in pre-war times.'[48] As a short term measure, £22 was transferred from the Poor Fund into the general funds of the church, but things got worse; by November the treasurer said the deficit for 1918 was £186. To help defray that debt there would be a special collection on Christmas Sunday to raise £100. This collection actually raised £101.

CHURCH MEMBERSHIP DURING THE WAR YEARS

West Church membership remained fairly stable, as these figures indicate:
   Over 1914 decrease of 13 members
   Over 1915 decrease of 2

Over 1916 increase of 11
Over 1917 increase of 4
Over 1918 increase of 11

The Baptist Church has some evidence which showed a similarly steady membership:

	Members	
January 1914	227	(1914 total was regarded as including largest membership increase for 7 years
January 1915	228	
January 1916		(Secretary reported 'numbers on the roll were being well maintained…')
January 1917		(No figures given for 1917 and 1918, and no comment in Church records)
January 1918		
January 1919	227	

However, in November 1919 the Baptist Church held their 81st anniversary service and expressed a slightly more pessimistic note about their wartime membership. The minister commented that 'During the absence of the pastor in France… the membership, through death, removals and other causes, had seriously decreased'[49] but he did not give the membership numbers.

Evidence from St Mungo's Kirk Session minutes allow two ways of checking if church attendance declined in the war: we can get an accurate picture of the size of the Church Roll and also see the attendance at the two Communions held each year.

St Mungo's Church Roll and number of communicant members:

	Members	Took communion at least once
31 December 1913	2451	1967
31 December 1914	2530	1899
31 December 1915	2552	1816
31 December 1916	2591	1833
31 December 1917	2594	1698
31 December 1918	2610	1671
31 December 1919	2663	1937

From these figures you would be hard pressed to argue that church membership decreased dramatically. Apart from in 1917, there was a wartime rate of about 72 per cent for the number of members who took communion at least once.

St Mungo's Communion attendance:

Communion	Attendance	Comment in Session minute book
June 1914	1411	
Dec 1914	1371	
June 1915	1410	
Dec 1915	1092	'the weather was unusually severe.'
June 1916	1361	
Dec 1916	1312	'... gratifying considering that almost all the young men...were in the army.'
June 1917	1241	
Dec 1917	1230	
June 1918	1254	
Dec 1918	1123	'not un-satisfactory considering the large numbers of persons absent on service in the army and the prevalence of disease in the parish.'
June 1919	1250	

These figures for those who actually took communion certainly suggest that attendance at the two big events of each year held up fairly well, although the first post-war Communion had almost 20 per cent less attendance than the last pre-war Communion. Overall, it might appear that the religiosity of the people of Alloa did not decrease significantly during the war, despite the length and suffering of the conflict and the scale of family loss among churchgoers. It is widely believed that a disillusionment with religion set in during World War I, but figures for church attendance and congregational giving in Alloa do not really support that claim, nor do the figures for baptisms; this particular ritual maintained its popularity as a part of family faith. The figures are available for the number of baptisms at St John's Church,[50] St Andrew's Church[51] and St Mungo's during the war years. Do they reveal any signs of the rejection of the church? At the very moment that St Andrew's had a dip, St John's had a rise, although numbers in St Mungo's do seem to have declined significantly.

	St John's	St Andrew's	St Mungo's	
1913	32	39	104	baptisms
1914	31	33	105	
1915	26	38	129	
1916	37	19	no figure given	
1917	27	28	78	
1918	25	17	79	
1919	41	19	83	
1920	39	27		

The West Church had the Park Lane and Kelliebank Mission as part of its area of responsibility (Park Lane was a narrow alley linking Forth Street with Castle Street the entire area is now part of O-I Manufacturing (UK) Ltd.). This Mission was under the charge of a paid Missionary, Rev Thomas Wilson, up until January 1916, when he resigned, 'having arranged with the YMCA to do work among the troops in France'.[52] He had been given a missionary assistant, Rev Adamson Findlay, in December 1915 and he then took over as the full time missionary, but he also resigned in February 1917.[53] The West Church offered an extra £10 a year to persuade him to stay but he counter-offered with a demand for an additional £10 on top of that, which the West Church accepted.[54] That situation did not last long however, since Rev Findlay was called to a parish in Aberdeenshire in April 1917, so he resigned again. The Mission struggled to find a good replacement but eventually, in May 1917, appointed Mr John Scorgie, an Alloa Academy FP but now a divinity student in Glasgow. He held the job until October 1919, when he was called to a post in Cardonald.

Within five weeks of the outbreak of war, the leaders of the West Church and the Park Lane Mission held 'a long discussion with regard to the Church's duty in connection with relief work owing to the war'.[55] In the event, they apparently continued with a Christian 'business as usual' policy, because their minute books had reported very little on any war-related activities, but a great deal on their regular activities. Throughout the war they ran Sunday schools, a PSA[56], a young lads' guild, girls clubs, bible classes,[57] sewing classes, distributed Christian literature and held sales of work etc. All the evidence in the minute books suggests that they continued their work, attendance and funds quite happily throughout the war. They ran a choir which had fifty-four members by 1916.[58] They were not short of money either, because they received £500 in Mr David Thomson's will in 1917.[59]

The Moncrieff Church was connected to the Greenside Mission and the reports in their minute book show continuing good work during the war years with their own Guildry, Band of Hope and Sabbath schools. In the early years of the war the Greenside Mission seem to have had less money than the Park Lane Mission and they asked the treasurer of their parent church for funds, especially to pay for the lay missionary. They had a deficit of 17 shillings for 1914, as shown in their annual financial statement on 21 January 1915.[60] However, by late 1916, the minutes reported that '...funds to date showed that they were in an exceedingly flourishing condition. In the nine months passed of this year the church's own collection had already exceeded the total collected for the whole of the year 1915'[61] and there would be a probability of 'a large excess of income over expenditure... for the current year.'[62] Because Greenside Hall was used for billeting troops, the Mission was forced to meet in one of the dining halls at Kilncraigs Mill [63] for much of the war.

The Greenside Mission held a Roll of Honour service in July 1915.[64] Following this they issued a set of printed notes from this service to be sent out to all those from the congregation who were on active service. These notes recorded twenty-nine names of former members of the Mission who were serving in the war. On that list, only one was recorded as having been 'killed in action'. By October 1915 one more from that list had been killed and three wounded.[65] The Mission held an 'In Memorium' service for its members who had lost their lives in the war, on the last Sunday of 1916.[66] One other war-related impact on the Mission was that it cancelled its annual Hogmanay social event in 1917 because of a shortage of foodstuffs and 'on account of the attitude of the Food Controller towards such social meetings'.[67] Somewhat belatedly, in 1920, they recognised that since 'All our members who had been on active service have now been demobilised; it was thought appropriate that the committee should meet in a social capacity to welcome them home...'[68] This social event was held on 20 March 1920, nine months after the Burgh of Alloa had held its own 'welcome home' function.

CHRISTIAN ORGANISATIONS

During the war years Alloa had both a YMCA and a YWCA. Evidence for the YMCA's activities can be found in a minute book in the National Archives,[69] while the best evidence for the YWCA is from their 1916 and 1917 Reports; no minute book is extant. For both organisations there was some coverage in the weekly columns of the local press. The organisations' progress during the war was inter-linked, since on two different occasions they shared the same premises.

YMCA

Within less than three weeks of the start of the war, the *Journal* noted that 'no fewer than ten members of the intermediate class [*of the* YMCA] are serving with the local Company on active service...This should prove that the YMCA does not make a man a milksop, but rather, makes him a manly man...'[70] It is no wonder, then, that in September 1914 the YMCA noted that meetings might be short of members due to enlistment.[71]

In the Annual Report in May 1915 the Secretary noted that 'A great European War is proceeding, the effects of which have completely disorganised our usual agencies'.[72] He also noted that '...at least 75 per cent of our membership fit for service have answered the call.' They made up for this shortfall by imaginatively opening up their rooms for use by the Territorials (for letter writing, refreshment and recreation), so much so that 'every evening the rooms are crowded out with men who are most appreciative.'[73] The YMCA might not have been so generous had they known that the Territorials would requisition their entire premises for billets less than two years later. These evening meetings were so popular that they had to be transferred to the Moncrieff Church hall in order to get enough room.[74] Although keen to promote 'gospel temperance', the YMCA also ran a group of hand-bell ringers and the 1st Clackmannanshire Boy Scout troop. The local territorials had their musketry camp at Jellyholm, just outside Alloa, and for eighteen weeks each summer the Alloa YMCA operated a tent at that camp.[75]

In the first years of the war the YMCA met at their Institute in Shillinghill at 10.00 am every Sunday. Their little members' cards with their syllabuses still exist, revealing the regularity of their meetings and the religious topics to be discussed. The minute book however, with one main exception, shows little more than that the main business of their committee was to draw up lists of subjects for their syllabus and 'securing essayists...'[76] One speaker they were pleased to get in September 1915 was the famous authoress and suffragist Annie S. Swan, who gave a talk on 'War and YMCA work'.[77] The *Journal* gave a long report of her 'simple yet powerful address'.[78]

The Alloa YMCA did not have a great attendance of members. Their minute book included a list of 1916-17's membership of thirty-one men, with some honest comments scrawled next to the names; six were unsatisfactory or irregular, two were gone from Alloa and two were in the navy. The most interesting and certainly war-related piece in the whole minute book is the Secretary's Report for 1916,[79] giving as it does both actual detail of the impact of the war on this small organisation and a flavour of its approach to it. He wrote:

> 'It was evident to members of the meeting, that when we commenced our present session, last Sept, we did so under very uncertain circumstances. One or two of the Committee were under marching orders for Military Service, and early in the session, our late Secretary John Russell, was called to the Colours. Then the Military again assailed our association, we were unceremoniously expelled from our meeting room in the YMCA in Shillinghill. The probability is that we may be exiled from the latter for the duration of the war; however, this is by the way.' They were able to move to the Townhead Institute and the Secretary reported that '...in view of the material comfort gained by our compulsory removal from Shillinghill, we bear no grudge towards the Military.'

The Secretary noted that 'At present our membership is thirty-two – the average attendance being fourteen', but proudly continued 'With the exception of the Parish Church Guild...we are the only YMCA presently in Session. Such conditions are entirely due to the war.' It is clear that the small numbers for regular attendance could also be attributed to the war, because the Secretary then went on to discuss 'Members on Active Service: We have great pleasure in bringing before you tonight the names of our soldier members serving under the Colours for their Country and Humanity:– [There follows **sixteen** names] and he continued his Report by commenting that 'You were good enough to subscribe to a fund which aimed to provide Xmas gifts for each of those members, and personally, I feel very grateful to you for having enabled me to forward, to each of these members a Xmas remembrance in your name. May the goodness of our God grant to all of these men an early return to Peace, Happiness and Home.' It is a shame that nothing else was written in the minute book after September 1917, as the Secretary, Lewis Park, had a refreshing turn of phrase.

During the war, the YMCA built huts wherever it felt there was a need to provide for the welfare of largish numbers of passing servicemen. There were YMCA huts in many big cities and ports in the UK, and also at most British army bases. In October 1917, Alloa YMCA held a Flag Day to raise money for these huts, and put a fairly prominent piece in the *Advertiser* under the heading 'The YMCA Hut,' accompanied

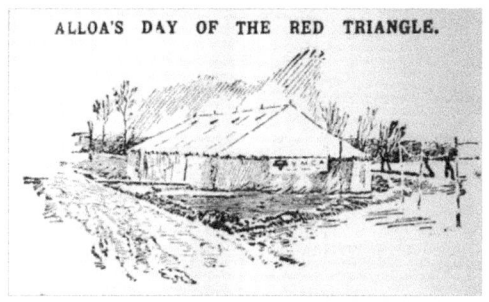

YMCA Tent (*Alloa Advertiser*)

by a picture of a big tent in the middle of nowhere showing the YMCA banner.[80] The article explained all the good work they were doing in France (200 YMCA centres serving the troops), and made a plea for money.

The *Journal* had a more interesting picture of a YMCA hut in the middle of a muddy camp and an article explaining that there were twenty-four YMCA dugouts actually in the trenches and that one of those dugouts had given out 26,000 cups of cocoa in a week.[81] There was strong support in the local press for the YMCA; the *Advertiser* praised it for its success in 'the formidable task of universal caterers for the social, moral and religious well-being of everyone on active service...'[82] and the *Journal* featured a charming picture of Lady Mar outside the YMCA flower stall in Alloa High St.[83] The Flag Day raised £180.[84]

YMCA Hut (*Alloa Journal*)

Lady Mar selling flowers (*Alloa Journal*)

The nearest wartime YMCA hut to Alloa was probably the one in Tillicoultry opposite the Devonvale Mill.[85] Another one was opened in January 1917 at Cornton Military Camp in Bridge of Allan, where 'a very considerable number of soldiers are stationed'.[86] The hut had a large hall plus a reading room, and cost £1,200. Though not really part of this story, it is worth mentioning because the proceedings for the ceremonial opening of the hut were chaired by Alexander Forrester-Paton and the hut was declared open by Lady Mar.[87] Four very nice pictures were taken of her and the troops at this ceremony, which are held in the YMCA archives at the University of Birmingham.[88]

It seems that Alloa finally got its own YMCA hut, but not until well after the war was over. In May 1919 there were plans to set up a hut on a site at Mars Hill in the centre of Alloa. The large '… and very well finished structure' had previously been used by American servicemen in Inverness but was now being re-sited in Alloa.[89]

Alloa YMCA was left £500 in Alexander P. Forrester-Paton's will following his death in 1915,[90] but they may not have received much of that during the war. Their tax returns in May 1918 indicate that they tried to get a tax rebate for the previous four years (they were given £7 18s 11d), where part of their income was £6 17s 6d from the Territorials' use of their building in Shillinghill; there is no reference to income from the interest on any bequest in the bank.

YWCA

There is very little in the local press about the early wartime meetings or activities of the YWCA. The first reported meeting in March 1915 was more concerned with their response to the death of Miss Catherine Forrester-Paton than anything else.[91]

The YWCA's original little syllabus booklets for 1916 and 1917 are still in existence;[92] a much more sophisticated effort than the YMCA's little card. The syllabus booklet included information on the Committee of nine ladies, a Secretary's Report, a Treasurer's Report and details of the progress of specific Christian projects around the world that the branch was supporting. In the first years of the war they met in their rooms in Mill St, planning to move to a new building in 1916, which 'owing to difficulties arising through the terrible European War, was not completed'. However, they then got the use of a room in the YMCA Institute. In terms of war-related work, they eventually copied what most of the ladies' groups in Alloa were doing, and by January 1916 were 'knitting socks and other useful garments for our soldiers and sailors' and were duly registered as a war work party in April 1916.[93] By the time of their 1917 Report they noted that 'The war work party begun in January 1916… had made 79 woollen garments to be sent to the war work depot.' In the YWCA 'Little girls under 14 also made bags for the wounded soldiers *[in Arnsbrae Hospital]* to keep their personal possessions in'.

Their new premises in the Townhead Institute were ready for the YWCA by the end of 1916, and they repaid the favour to the YMCA by letting them have a room there, following the YMCA's ejection from their Shillinghill premises by the Territorials.

One thing that shows the members' wider appreciation of the impact of the World

War was their understanding of events in Armenia. The Armenian genocide is still a very sensitive subject today, but Alloa YWCA had a personal interest in 1916-17 because of their support for orphans there. In 1916, the Secretary's Report noted 'We would ask that members especially remember the Armenians in prayer. They are passing through a fiery trial and in 1917 they were still reporting "It is a source of sorrow to us that no news has been received... of our Armenian orphans". May we ask you to unite with us in praying for the Armenian people in this time of suffering and persecution.'[94]

As far as membership and income went, it was reported by the end of 1916 that 'There was a considerable loss of membership... it now stands at seventy-four which includes twelve honorary' (it was seventy-eight in 1917) but it was still larger than the men's side of the organisation. There was some thriftiness about the Alloa YWCA; its income in 1916 was £38 (£37 in 1917) and expenditure was about £10 less. They had been lucky enough to receive £300 as a bequest from Miss Forrester-Paton and that was transferred to being a War loan, providing an income itself of about £24 a year by the end of the war.[95]

WARTIME ACTIVITIES OF THE MINISTERS OF ALLOA'S CHURCHES

The assistant minister at St Mungo's, Rev J.G. Edwards, was ahead of everyone else to make his contribution to the war.[96] He volunteered to be an army chaplain in Portsmouth and left for duties on 19 September 1914.[97]

Within a year of the start of the war, Rev David Moir, minister of St John's Episcopal Church, volunteered as chaplain for the forces and went to France.[98] His last service at St John's was on 4 July 1915.[99] He enlisted in the 7th Service Battalion of the Royal Scots Fusiliers for his first tour as a chaplain, before being transferred to 45th Ambulance Corps (15th Division) in September 1915.[100] He was back as the minister in St John's from July 1916 for the rest of the year,[101] but then went off to France for his second stint as a chaplain in January 1917. He must have moved on somewhat, because by April 1917 he was sending home reports of his time with the 7th Gordon Highlanders.[102] He clearly took to the work and was promoted to a Chaplaincy of the 2nd Class in June 1917, with the rank of Major.[103] He was then based at No. 10 General Hospital in Rouen. He stayed out in France, making further reports back to his congregation and one was printed in the *Advertiser* in July 1918. He had now been given the task of organising church services for the lumbermen in a group of ten forestry camps at Lyons Forest, somewhere still close to the front because he commented that he was 'within sound of battle'.[104] He was back preaching at St John's on 7 January 1919.[105]

The minister of St Mungo's, Rev A.W. Scudamore Forbes, became officiating clergyman to the Presbyterian troops in Alloa as from 1 January 1915.[106] In March 1917 he 'informed the Session that he had that week received a nomination to a Chaplaincy in the Army. Having indicated that he had strong desire to do something for the army…it was unanimously agreed… the Kirk Session cordially approves of the step Mr Forbes proposes to take.'[107] He therefore became a chaplain to the overseas forces in Egypt from about Easter 1917.[108] The Women's Guild gave him a 'send-off' and presented him with a wrist watch on Good Friday.[109] By February 1918 he had fallen ill while he was abroad and the Kirk Session 'referred to the serious illness of Mr Forbes who was presently lying in the Citadel Hospital, Cairo … according to the most recent information, Mr Forbes was making fair progress towards recovery'.[110] By April 1918 Mrs Forbes had received a cable from Egypt, saying that Mr Forbes might be expected home in a few weeks and,[111] sure enough, by early May he was home from his chaplaincy in Palestine and by 19 May was chairing Kirk Session meetings.[112]

The Baptist minister, Rev Alexander Clark, made his own military contribution. He told his Deacons' Court in September 1917 that he had 'made arrangements to go to France for four months to work with YMCA from January 1918'.[113] He did his four months' service and came home. His church held a 'Welcome Home' reception for him where, in his speech, he stated that fifty-five members of the Alloa Baptist congregation were serving in the armed forces. The congregation obviously held a collection for him, because the *Journal* quaintly informed us that he was 'handed a packet of Treasury Notes as a kindly remembrance…'[114] In July 1918 he again requested leave of absence to go and 'work for the YMCA again in France for a year among the boys at [the] Front'.[115] He left for France in the second week of November 1918 and only returned at the end of July 1919.[116] During his second stint in France he was in charge of YMCA huts in Cambrai, then near Doullens. Finally, he was Area Secretary at Dunkirk where he supervised huts as far away as Ostend and the Zeebrugge Mole.[117]

We have already noted that Rev Thomas Wilson, the missionary with Park Lane Mission, went off to France to work with the YMCA in January 1916. Mr Alex Aitken, the lay missionary at Greenside Mission, joined the local Voluntary Aid Detachment in early 1918, leading him to alter the times of the Wednesday night prayer meeting.[118]

Rev John Cumming, minister of St Andrew's Church was offered an army chaplaincy in July 1918. It was thought that he would be away for two years;[119] however, he was back by June 1919.[120]

IMPACT OF WAR ON OTHER CHURCH STAFF

The West Church lost the services of its organist/choir master, Mr George Allan FRCO, in February 1916 when he attested and was placed on army reserve[121] then sent out to Egypt.[122] He was in the Cameron Highlanders and came back to serve in France, where he was killed in October 1918.[123] The organist at St Mungo's requested a pay rise in October 1916, saying he 'had been "hard hit" by the war'.[124] The Kirk Session agreed to an increase of £5 a year.

William Maltman, the church officer for the West Church, was called up in June 1918. It was agreed to not fill the vacancy but that his wife would fulfil his duties, with some assistance.[125] He, however, refused to allow his position to be held for him until 'he returned to civil life', so it was advertised and filled by Mr Don, a member of the congregation.[126]

ENDNOTES

1. *Alloa Journal* 15 Aug 1914 p. 2 cols. 5-6
2. Alloa West Kirk Session minute book 21 Sept 1915
3. St Mungo's Kirk Session minute book 16 Sept 1914
4. Alloa West Kirk Session minute book 17 Sept 1914
5. St Mungo's Kirk Session minute book 14 Nov 1914
6. St Mungo's Kirk Session minute book 14 April 1915
7. St Mungo's Kirk Session minute book 12 Jan 1916
8. St John's Church Register of Services
9. Alloa West Kirk Session minute book 17 Sept 1914
10. Alloa West Kirk Session minute book 25 Sept 1914
11. St Mungo's Kirk Session minute book 6 Dec 1914
12. Alloa West Kirk Session minute book 29 May 1918

13 *Alloa Advertiser* 9 Sept 1916 p. 3 col. 3. By 1918 this figure had risen to 48
14 Alloa West Kirk Session minute book 15 July 1917, *Alloa Journal* 4 Aug 1917 p. 2 col. 4
15 St Mungo's Kirk Session minute book 27 Oct 1915
16 Chalmers Church Deacons' Court minutes 11 Sept 1917
17 *Alloa Journal* 20 Feb 1915 p. 3 col. 6, 27 Feb 1915 p. 4 col. 1
18 St Mungo's Kirk Session minute book 10 Feb 1915
19 *Alloa Journal* 7 April 1917 p. 3 col. 1. By 1918 this figure had risen to 32
20 Alloa West Kirk Session minute book 17 Sept 1914
21 St Mungo's Kirk Session minute book 9 Dec 1914
22 St Mungo's Kirk Session minute book 2 Nov 1915, 24 Nov 1915
23 Alloa West Kirk Session minute book 13 Dec 1916
24 The teacher at Grange School then Sunnyside
25 Alloa West Kirk Manuscript Magazine 9 Feb 1915
26 St Mungo's Kirk Session minute book 25 July 1916
27 St Mungo's Kirk Session minute book 21 Feb 1916
28 St Mungo's Kirk Session minute book 13 Sept 1916
29 St Mungo's Kirk Session minute book 11 Oct 1916
30 Alloa West Kirk Session minute book 15 July 1917
31 Alloa West Kirk Session minute book 9 Sept 1917
32 Alloa Baptist Church Deacons' Court minute book 16 Feb 1916
33 Chalmers Church Deacons' Court minute book 14 March 1916
34 Alloa West Kirk Session minute book 17 Jan 1917
35 Alloa Baptist Church Deacons' Court minute book 15 April 1915
36 Alloa Baptist Church Deacons' Court minute book 13 July 1915
37 Alloa Baptist Church Deacons' Court minute book 24 Jan 1918
38 Both references are in St John's Church Register of Services
39 That would have been a sad day; he had just had news of the death of his second son in France, from wounds sustained in action. His son was a Cambridge athletic 'blue' who was a former 100 yards champion in England and Scotland and had run in the 1912 Olympics. *Alloa Journal* 3 August 1918 p. 3 col. 1. Dr MacIntosh's two other sons were both prisoners of war in Germany, one of them having been interned in 1914 during a holiday in Germany which unfortunately coincided with the outbreak of war. *Alloa Journal* 30 March 1918 p. 2 col. 5
40 *Alloa Advertiser* 10 Aug 1918 p. 4 col. 1
41 Alloa West Kirk Session minute book 8 Jan 1912, 7 Jan 1913, 6 Jan 1914, 11 Jan 1915, 17 Jan 1917, 16 Jan 1918
42 Alloa West Church Management Committee minute book 15 March 1915
43 Alloa West Church Management Committee minute book 1 March 1920
44 Chalmers Church Deacons' Court minute book
45 St John's Church Vestry minute book 20 Sept 1917
46 St John's Church Vestry minute book 19 Nov 1918

47 St Mungo's Kirk Session minute book 12 June 1918
48 St Mungo's Kirk Session minute book 11 Sept 1918
49 *Alloa Journal* 8 Nov 1919 p. 3 col. 5
50 St John's Church Baptismal Register
51 St Andrew's Church Baptismal Register
52 Park Lane and Kelliebank Mission minute book 10 Jan 1916
53 Park Lane and Kelliebank Mission minute book 11 Feb 1917
54 Park Lane and Kelliebank Mission minute book 11 Feb 1917 and 18 Feb 1917
55 West Church Missionary Society minute book 8 Sept 1914
56 PSA stood for Pleasant Sunday Afternoon and was a temperance organisation to provide men with an alternative to their weekend drinking. There were 45 members of the Kelliebank PSA in 1913, 26 in 1914, but it had dropped to 15 in 1915 when they stopped keeping attendance records
57 West Church Missionary Society minute book 20 May 1917 showed that they did give Miss Bainbridge, the leader of the Bible Class, a £10 war bonus back-dated to 1 May 1917
58 *Alloa Journal* 22 April 1916 p. 2 col. 5
59 West Church Management Committee minute book 15 April 1917. David Thomson was a director of John Paton, Son & Co. Ltd
60 Greenside Mission Committee minute book 21 Jan 1915
61 Greenside Mission Committee minute book 3 Oct 1916
62 Greenside Mission Committee minute book 7 Nov 1914
63 Greenside Mission Committee minute book 3 Oct 1914
64 Greenside Mission Committee minute book 15 July 1915
65 Greenside Mission Committee minute book 15 Oct 1915
66 Greenside Mission Committee minute book 5 Dec 1916
67 Greenside Mission Committee minute book 27 Nov 1917
68 Greenside Mission Committee minute book 2 March 1920
69 National Archives GD476/8/13, IRS 21/1140 and IRS 21/1086
70 *Alloa Journal* 22 Aug 1914 p. 3 col. 4
71 *Alloa Journal* 5 Sept 1914 p. 2 col. 6
72 *Alloa Circular* 12 May 1915 p. 3 col. 3
73 *Alloa Journal* 10 Oct 1914 p. 2 col. 4
74 *Alloa Journal* 31 Oct 1914 p. 2 col. 5
75 *Alloa Advertiser* 8 July 1916 p. 2 col. 4
76 Alloa YMCA minute book 20 Dec 1915
77 *Alloa Journal* 18 Sept 1915 p. 2 col. 5
78 *Alloa Journal* 2 Oct 1915 p. 3 cols. 1-2, also *Alloa Circular* 6 Oct 1915 p. 3 cols. 5-6
79 Alloa YMCA minute book 19 Dec 1916
80 *Alloa Advertiser* 29 Sept 1917 p. 3 col. 3
81 *Alloa Journal* 22 Sept 1917 p. 4 col. 1
82 *Alloa Advertiser* 6 Oct 1917 p. 3 co. 1

83 *Alloa Journal* 13 Oct 1917 p. 3 col. 2
84 *Alloa Advertiser* 13 Oct 1917 p. 2 col. 4. As a slight comparison, one of the few references to the work of the Roman Catholic Church in Alloa is a note in *Alloa Journal* 21 Dec 1918 p. 2 col. 4 referring to Catholic Hut Flag Day, which raised just over £56
85 *Alloa Advertiser* 4 Oct 1919 p. 3 col. 4 refers to it being used in the war then handed over to the Red Triangle Club in 1919
86 *Stirling Observer* 27 Jan 1917 p. 8 cols. 1+2
87 *Stirling Observer* 27 Jan 1917 p. 8 cols. 1+2
88 The photos can be seen in the on-line catalogue of the Special Collections Department. They are YMCA/K/1/22 106-109
89 *Alloa Advertiser* 24 May 1919 p. 3 col. 3, *Alloa Journal* 9 Aug 1919 p. 3 col. 1
90 Names get confusing when sons are called after their fathers, but this Alexander P. who left the will was the father of the Alexander who presided over the opening of the YMCA hut
91 *Alloa Journal* 27 March 1915 p. 2 col. 6. She was their President and patroness and had provided the money to pay for their new premises
92 In the Scottish National Archives
93 Alloa YWCA 1916 Report
94 Alloa YWCA 1916 Report and 1917 Report
95 National Archives IRS 21/1140
96 St Mungo's Kirk Session minute book 7 Oct 1914 refers to the Congregational Meeting which mentions why he left
97 *Scotsman* 19 Sept 1914 p. 5, *Alloa Journal* 26 Sept 1914 p. 2 col. 6
98 *Alloa Circular* 4 Aug 1915 p. 3 col. 3, *Alloa Journal* 31 July 1915 p. 3 col. 3
99 St John's Church Register of Services
100 *Alloa Journal* 4 Sept 1915 p. 2 col. 5
101 St John's Church Register of Services
102 *Alloa Advertiser* 24 March 1917 p. 3 col. 3
103 *Alloa Advertiser* 23 June 1917 p. 3 col. 2
104 *Alloa Advertiser* 27 July 1918 p. 4 col. 4
105 St John's Church Register of Services
106 St Mungo's Kirk Session minute book 20 Jan 1915
107 St Mungo's Kirk Session minute book 15 March 1917
108 *Alloa Journal* 31 March 1917 p. 3 col. 5
109 *Alloa Journal* 14 April 1917 p. 2 col. 5
110 St Mungo's Kirk Session minute book 14 Feb 1918
111 St Mungo's Kirk Session minute book 10 April 1918
112 St Mungo's Kirk Session minute book 8 May 1918
113 Alloa Baptist Church Deacons' Court minute book 20 Sept 1917
114 *Alloa Journal* 15 June 1918 p. 2 col. 2

115 Alloa Baptist Church, Church Meetings minute book 17 July 1918. The way that it was expressed in the *Alloa Journal* [20 July 1918 p. 2 col. 4] suggests that the YMCA made an urgent request that he should be released for a year's term in France, not that he had asked for it himself
116 Alloa Baptist Church, Church Meetings minute book 29 June 1919
117 *Alloa Advertiser* 2 Aug 1919 p. 2 col. 5
118 Greenside Mission Committee minute book 11 Jan 1918
119 St Andrew's Kirk Session minute book 3 July 1918
120 St Andrew's Kirk Session minute book 5 March 1919
121 Alloa West Kirk Session minute book 13 Feb 1916
122 St Mungo's Kirk Session minute book 11 Oct 1916
123 Alloa West Kirk Session minute book 1 Dec 1918. CWGC and Burgh of Alloa Roll of Honour say he was serving in the Argylls
124 St Mungo's Kirk Session minute book 11 Oct 1916
125 Alloa West Kirk Session minute book 16 June 1918
126 Alloa West Kirk Session minute book 7 July 1918

CHAPTER 9

LOCAL POLITICS

DURING THE WAR

At the beginning of the war the national leaders of Britain's major political parties agreed to maintain a political truce and their example was followed by the local party organisations. This was noted in the Alloa press as early as 15 August 1914[1] and on 5 September the *Advertiser* commented that 'One of the most gratifying features in connection with the crisis... is the total and complete subordination of party politics to the higher interests of the nation.'[2] There was to be no canvassing, political sniping or jockeying for position or power. The local political parties all agreed to help with recruitment, relief work and other patriotic enterprises,[3] and there was very little political activity in Alloa throughout the war years. Alloa would see no politically contested municipal elections until November 1919. Naturally there were elections for the municipal positions of Provost, Town Clerk, Burgh Fiscal etc. during the war, but there seems to have been no electioneering of any sort along party lines.

There were regular reports in the local press of meetings of the Alloa Liberal Club and the Alloa Unionist Association, but there was little going on; they were social clubs with whist drives, dances, Burns Suppers and fundraising events for the war effort.[4] The local businessman, Sir George Younger, was MP for Ayr Burghs from 1906–22, being elevated to the position of Chairman of the Unionist Party in 1916. That seems to have pleased everyone, not just the Unionists.[5] In late 1917 he was responsible for proposing the amendment to the 1918 Representation of the People Act, which disenfranchised conscientious objectors.[6]

The local Liberals had reconstituted their Association in March 1918 in order to reflect the new voting arrangements, both in terms of women getting the vote and also the changed constituency boundaries.

In May 1918 the local Unionists similarly dissolved their old Association and reconstituted themselves to incorporate women and recognise that since 'Kinross had been torn from them',[7] they now had to work with their fellow Conservatives on the south side of the River Forth.

The local press seem to have regarded as almost the highlight of the month the 'visit' of the Prime Minister David Lloyd George, when he 'passed through Alloa in a motor car'[8] on his way to Dunfermline on 25 May 1918; this probably shows the lack of political activity in wartime Alloa. His car was stopped outside Younger's Brewery offices in Bank Street by the Chief Constable, who 'informed the Premier that Sir George Younger desired to have a few words with him'. Sir George Younger came out and shook hands with the Prime Minister and had his few words, then a few other local dignitaries like Capt. A.P. Moir and Provost Pearson came out of the Burgh Buildings which were directly opposite, and took the chance to be introduced, before Lloyd George got back into the car 'amid hearty cheers from the large crowd' and sped away. There were no political speeches, but at least he was there.[9]

AFTER THE WAR WAS OVER

The first election after the war was based on the new constituency boundaries drawn up in August 1917,[10] where the Redistribution of Seats Act had detached Clackmannanshire from Kinross and joined it to East Stirlingshire.[11] The *Advertiser* recognised the significance of this, and of many women getting the vote due to the 4th Reform Act of 1918, when its editorial commented that 'The change in the geographical limits of the constituency and the great increase in the number of voters would baffle attempts to forecast results...'[12] Eugene Wason of the Liberal party had been MP for the previous nineteen years, but he decided not to stand in this first post-war General Election due to advancing years (he was seventy-two) and ill-health.

There were three candidates for the local constituency in the December 1918 election:

Major William A. Chapple	Liberal
Major Ralph Glyn	Unionist Coalition
Mr Henry J. May	Cooperative Societies and ILP

Alloa Academy was the local polling station and the school closed early on Friday 13

December, since time was needed to get rooms ready and to set up the polling booths for the Saturday voting.¹³ This was the first parliamentary election in which British women voted, although the local press hardly concerned themselves with that at all. Some of the candidates did, however, hold meetings especially for women. At one of Major Chapple's, the *Advertiser* reported that 'the gallant Major congratulated the women on their enfranchisement... and he trusted that all women would make it a matter of duty and conscience to attend the poll...'.¹⁴ At other election meetings attended by men, the local press often went to some length discussing what the men wanted and what the candidate's policies were towards these demands. It obviously considered that at women's meetings the gallantry and compliments of the candidate were all that mattered.

Somewhat bemused, the *Advertiser* commented during the election that all three candidates were 'pronounced supporters of the Coalition Government' and that 'electors may well wonder why there should have been a contest at all'.¹⁵ Clackmannanshire had long been a Liberal stronghold, but as the *Advertiser* said, the Liberal candidate, Major Chapple 'was the only candidate who started with a political millstone round his neck¹⁶ because a Socialist candidate was also standing. This would split 'the progressive vote', and this was what had persuaded the Unionists to put forward their own candidate in a seat they would normally have had no chance of winning. However, on this occasion for the Unionists, 'there was at least a sporting chance of success and they were prepared to take it'.¹⁷

Major Chapple (*Alloa Journal*)

The 1918 General Election was sometimes known as the Coupon Election, because the Coalition Government authorised certain candidates to stand for them by issuing a coupon or certificate; this person then became 'ticketed' as the accredited candidate.

Major Chapple¹⁸ regarded himself as the sitting candidate – he was already the MP for Stirlingshire; that area now making up about half of the new constituency – and was already a member of the coalition. He did not see the need to apply to his own party for the coupon. But Major Glyn applied for and got the coupon, though quite late, and in a sense therefore became the preferred candidate. This led to some fuss about whether Major Glyn should stand, since although he had the coupon he was standing against the man who already considered himself the sitting candidate for the new Clackmannanshire and East Stirlingshire constituency. The *Advertiser* was more outraged about this than the *Journal*, wondering how on earth Major Glyn had managed to get his coupon, and criticised the Unionist Party by commenting '...one must protest against British politics being degraded to the level of Tammany Hall methods of electioneering'.[19] The Liberals regarded it as a cunning plot by the Unionists (Conservatives) to get their ticketed candidates into constituencies where there might be a split vote... and regarded them as using 'Hun-like methods of circumventing an honourable opponent...'[20] Major Chapple himself made a serious verbal attack on Sir George Younger himself; accusing him of being the brains behind this plan. He said that 'The Tories were the evil geniuses of this country, and today they were dominated by Sir George Younger'.[21]

Major Ralph Glyn (*Alloa Advertiser*)

The Liberal-supporting *Advertiser* also took the Unionists to task for sending their candidate to talk, 'to the utter surprise of those present who were not "in the know"',[22] at a meeting of the Federation of Discharged Sailors and Soldiers. This organisation was supposed to be non-political; and had not, apparently, extended a similar speaking invitation to the Liberal candidate. It was made worse by the additional claim made by Major Glyn at the meeting that he 'had signed up to the Federation's programme and that Major Chapple had declined to do so'. This led to outraged letters to the *Advertiser*; that firstly Major Chapple had never been offered the declaration to sign, and secondly, that there was no-one, more than him, who 'had a more active sympathy with those who had been broken by the war.'[23]

It may be that the Liberals were fuelling this sense of outrage because they were genuinely concerned about having to fight a three-cornered contest where the third candidate, the Socialist Mr May, had a lot of policies which overlapped with theirs. Major Chapple did indeed lose a lot of votes to Mr May,[24] although the *Journal* did not think much of the *Advertiser*'s argument about splitting the progressive vote, saying that Major Chapple was losing support anyway.[25] Major Chapple's manifesto showed that he favoured the League of Nations, Free Trade, Housing reform, a minimum wage and Home Rule for Scotland.[26] Curiously, given that Lloyd George's famous 'Homes fit for heroes...' speech was in Wolverhampton on 23 November, there was no specific reference to this in any of the local election speeches in Alloa, despite the crying need for better housing in the burgh, to which the local Medical Officer, Dr Cassie, had previously drawn attention.

The election was then made even more interesting by the fact that, at various ladies' meetings for the Unionists in the neighbouring burgh of Alva, it was put about that Major Chapple was an atheist. Miss Johnstone from Alva had to publicly apologise in the local press for this 'Malicious Slander'.[27] The *Advertiser* observed that 'No-one can predict the extent of harm that a slanderous rumour may inflict', but then noted that the Cooperative candidate, Mr May, had also put the knife in to Major Chapple by casting doubt on how often he had voted in the last session of Parliament whilst he had been an MP (only in about five out of sixty divisions apparently).[28]

After this unexpectedly energetic election campaign that lasted just over three weeks,[29] the result was that Major Glyn was elected,[30] with the 'sitting candidate' coming last.

	Votes
Major Glyn	6,771
Mr May	5,753
Major Chapple	5,040

The turnout was only 54 per cent, compared with 84 per cent in the last pre-war election. There should have been an electorate of 32,003 and only 17,640 votes were cast.[31] The result was also a lesson in financially effective electioneering; the one who spent the most won; election expenses for Major Glyn were £954, for Mr May £779 and for Major Chapple £591.[32]

The winning candidate had no local connections; he was probably a 'career' MP who had tried to get elected before the war in the two 1910 elections, by offering his candidacy in such disparate constituencies as Elgin and Nairn, Glasgow Colleges and Edinburgh South.[33] Having a sound war record mattered in the election of December 1918 (for two of the three candidates, at least) but there is almost an indication that the Alloa people were 'voting for toffs'. The man they chose as their elected representative was the son of the Bishop of Peterborough and his mother a daughter of the 8th Duke of Argyll. He was a product of Harrow and Sandhurst and he lived in Bramber in Sussex.[34] Nowadays that would be called 'parachuting in' a candidate and most of the electorate would scorn him, but it seems to have been 'the done thing' in those days.

Ralph Glyn lost the local seat in the 1922 election, coming third. He went to Abingdon, Oxfordshire and won that seat in the 1924 election, holding it for thirty years. He married the widow of Brigadier General Walter Long, who had been killed in action in January 1917.[35]

ENDNOTES

1 *Alloa Journal* 15 Aug 1914 p. 2 col. 2
2 *Alloa Advertiser* 5 Sept 1914 p. 3 col. 2
3 *Alloa Journal* 2 Jan 1915 p. 3 col. 2
4 It may not have any significance, but Alloa Unionist Club's account books exist and show that the Club became steadily less wealthy during the war years. Its financial assets were £766 at the end of 1914, £700 at the end of 1915, £643 at the end of 1916, £561 at the end of 1917 and £535 at the end of 1918
5 *Alloa Journal* 6 Jan 1917 p. 3 col. 3. The *Journal* was the Tory-supporting local paper, whilst the *Advertiser* supported the Liberals
6 *Alloa Journal* 24 Nov 1917 p. 3 cols. 3-4
7 *Alloa Advertiser* 18 May 1918 p. 4 col. 5
8 *Alloa Journal* 4 Jan 1919 p. 3 col. 5
9 *Alloa Journal* 1 June 1918 p. 3 col. 3, *Alloa Advertiser* 1 June 1918 p. 2 col. 4
10 *Alloa Advertiser* 4 Aug 1917 p. 3 col. 2
11 *Alloa Advertiser* 28 Dec 1918 p. 3 col. 4
12 *Alloa Advertiser* 16 Nov 1918 p. 3 col. 5
13 Alloa Academy Rector's Log Book 13 Dec 1918
14 *Alloa Advertiser* 14 Dec 1918 p. 3 col. 4
15 *Alloa Advertiser* 23 Nov 1918 p. 3 col. 2

16 *Alloa Advertiser* 4 Jan 1919 p. 3 col. 2
17 *Alloa Advertiser* 23 Nov 1918 p. 3 col. 2
18 Major Chapple was an interesting man. He was a New Zealander who in 1908 had briefly been an MP in the New Zealand House of Representatives. He was a qualified doctor and served in the RAMC during the war. He won the Stirlingshire seat in 1910. After losing the 1918 election he stood again in 1922 and won the Dumfriesshire seat which he held until 1924. It was later rather held against him that he was a keen supporter of eugenics
19 *Alloa Advertiser* 30 Nov 1918 p. 3 col. 2. I am impressed that the Advertiser could include an American metaphor for political corruption! However, Tammany Hall had been such a metaphor since the 1850s or earlier, and it must have been fairly widely known as such
20 *Alloa Advertiser* 7 Dec 1918 p. 3 col. 3
21 *Alloa Journal* 7 Dec 1918 p. 3 col. 1
22 *Alloa Advertiser* 7 Dec 1918 p. 3 col. 3. This was under a column heading of 'Not Playing the Game'
23 *Alloa Advertiser* 7 Dec 1918 p. 3 col. 2
24 *Alloa Advertiser* 4 Jan 1919 p. 3 col. 2
25 *Alloa Journal* 4 Jan 1919 p. 2 col. 5
26 *Alloa Advertiser* 23 Nov 1918 p. 3 col. 2
27 *Alloa Advertiser* 14 Dec 1918 p. 2 col. 2
28 *Alloa Advertiser* 14 Dec 1918 p. 3 col. 1. Major Chapple's explanation was that he was a serving doctor in the RAMC and could not always attend to his parliamentary duties and that was thoroughly understandable
29 *Alloa Journal* 4 Jan 1919 p. 4 col. 1
30 *Alloa Advertiser* 4 Jan 1919 p. 3 col. 3. The count did not take place until two weeks after the election date to allow for all the postal votes from demobilizing soldiers. There was a deliberate policy of mixing all the ballot papers together at the count so that 'nobody can say how the Servicemen have voted'. It does indeed look like Major Glyn only got in because the progressive vote was split
31 *Alloa Advertiser* 4 Jan 1919 p. 3 col. 3
32 *Alloa Advertiser* 8 Feb 1919 p. 2 col. 5, *Alloa Journal* 8 Feb 1919 p. 2 col. 1
33 *Alloa Journal* 4 Jan 1919 p. 3 col. 3
34 *Alloa Advertiser* 14 June 1919 p. 3 col. 3
35 See The Long, Long Trail website

CHAPTER 10

THE END OF THE WAR

Just as the outbreak of the war on Tuesday 4 August 1914 caught most Alloa citizens by surprise (as we saw in Chapter 1, no one really predicted its coming) so too did the end of the war, on Monday 11 November 1918, seem to come rather out of the blue. One day it was 'war as usual' for the people of Alloa, then the next day it was suddenly over. They can be forgiven, however, for overlooking an incredible article in the *Circular* **in 1915,** which gave them good warning that the war would end on 11 November. The author of that prediction, however, was not prepared to commit himself to exactly what year that might be![1]

It must be acknowledged, however, that there were a few clear signs in October and November 1918 that the Allies knew they were on the verge of victory. In a column in the *Advertiser* on 12 October 1918, the writer (going under the pen name 'The Censor') scathingly discussed the 'Peace notes' which the Austrian Emperor and Prince Max of Baden had been sending towards the American President Woodrow Wilson and went on to say that this showed 'Germany has come to see that there is not the shadow of a hope of achieving ultimate victory...'[2] The article continued with the claim that 'the enemy is being driven from post to pillar on all the battlefronts', and 'it may be that Germany will be compelled to formally accept unconditional surrender before the winter sets in...' This all shows a fairly upbeat sense that the last lap before victory was in progress, but no precise date was given for when it might all end.

A week later this same columnist, who seemed fairly well informed (had censorship become less strict by then?) still wrote enthusiastically that 'In all the theatres of war our armies have achieved extraordinary success, and, obversely, the enemy has sustained irretrievable disasters'.[3] He must have thought that the end was imminent, because he commented that; '... everybody's mind is occupied with the question of peace'.

However, a glance at **all** of the local press for Saturday 9 November revealed **not the**

slightest hint that the end of the war was just two days away. Regarding its political news, the *Advertiser* especially, seemed preoccupied with the forthcoming general election.⁴ However, perhaps Lady Mar had 'inside information' because in a small article she gave a strong hint that '...peace, she hoped – a Glorious Peace – was much nearer than it was a week ago.'⁵

The *Circular* again, also first to report the outbreak of war in 1914, was lucky in appearing mid-week and was therefore the first local newspaper to report on the Armistice. The rest of the Alloa press were published on Saturday 16 November and by then must have seemed like old news to anyone reading it then to see how it had affected the local people!!

THE RECEPTION OF THE NEWS IN THE TOWN

The *Circular* had an editorial called 'The End of the War' and gave details of the terms of the Armistice, including the evacuation of all occupied countries, reparations for damage done, revocation of the Treaty of Brest-Litovsk and that it was to last for thirty-six days with possibility of extension.⁶ It then reported the local reaction; 'The end of the greatest war in history was celebrated with enthusiasm throughout the County... It was a time of great rejoicing and will live long in the memories of those who took part...'⁷ The paper went on to say that 'News was received about 11 o'clock on Monday morning... The glad tidings rapidly circulated all over the town... and there were ample evidences of joy and satisfaction in the faces of the townspeople.'

According to the *Advertiser*, news of the Armistice arrived in Alloa at about 10.00am on 11 November,⁸ although the *Journal* concurred with the *Circular*'s view that it was 11.00am.⁹ Both agreed though, that shortly after 11 o'clock the bells in the Parish and Episcopal Churches rang out and 'In several of the local works the employees were so over-joyed at the permanent cessation of hostilities that they "downed tools" and made for the main thoroughfares of the town.' Recognising that they would not get their workers back, most of the managers of the local offices and factories put up notices declaring a half-day holiday from 1.00pm. 'As the day advanced, the streets were densely thronged with people in holiday garb and in holiday spirit, and an air of great satisfaction and thankfulness reigned supreme.'¹⁰ All round the town there was 'cordial handshaking', flags were hoisted on all public buildings, and there was 'a profuse display of bunting, flags and bannerettes' in many of the local shops. Some of the children formed themselves into bands and paraded the streets with whistles, tin cans etc., and there were some miniature fireworks.

The Provost called a special meeting of the Council in the afternoon and explained 'that he had called the meeting at very short notice because the declaration of the Armistice had that morning been agreed, and that they should meet and express their thankfulness and gratitude that they had got to the end of the greatest war in the history of the world'. In the meeting it was agreed that telegrams of congratulation should be sent to The King, Admiral Beatty, Field Marshall Douglas Haig and the Prime Minister[11] 'expressing their profound joy, satisfaction and thankfulness on the conclusion of the armistice...'[12]

It was also agreed that the next day (12th) should be a public holiday and that there should be a church service of thanksgiving and, at night, a bonfire in the Public Park.[13] To assist the Councillors in making the loyal and patriotic toasts, champagne was provided, paid for out of the generous pocket of Councillor Duncanson.

The public holiday on Tuesday 12th was well received, the *Circular* soberly pointing out that although: 'A fine spirit of jubilation was manifest among the holiday-makers... it was not forgotten that the path the nation had trodden to the glories is deeply strewn with the sacrifice of its sons.'[14] During the day, the Gordon Highlanders Pipe Band paraded in the town and the Public Park, there were plenty of people out in the streets and 'comparatively few people were seen under the influence of drink'.[15] The *Advertiser* reckoned there were between 5,000–6,000 people present in the park for the evening entertainment, but the *Journal* put it at 8,000 and thought it was the biggest assembly of people that the park had ever seen.[16] From 7.30pm onwards there were quite a few speeches. The first was from the Provost who managed to get in a few digs about

THE ARMISTICE.

LOCAL CELEBRATIONS AND REJOICINGS.

The signing of the armistice between the Allies and Germany was celebrated in Alloa and district in a matter befitting the occasion. The news of the great event arrived in the town shortly after eleven o'clock, and was received with fervent yet restrained and orderly jubilation by the people, who had been waiting for the official pronouncement all morning. Signs of public rejoicing were immediately forthcoming. As if by magic innumerable flags appeared on public buildings and private houses. The public works in the district ceased work as soon as possible, some till Wednesday morning, others for the most part of the week. The bells of the Alloa Parish Church and St. Johns Episcopal Church rang out merrily. As the day advanced, the streets were densely thronged with people in holiday garb and in holiday spirit, and an air of great satisfaction and thankfulness reigned supreme. After dusk the temporary relaxation of the lighting restrictions sanctioned by the Board of Trade became apparent. High power lamps were substituted for the war time fixtures on the electric standards in the principal streets, and many of the shopkeepers took advantagt of the liberty given them to improve the lighting of their windows and premises. The crowds in the streets increased in numbers, and the joy of the multitude found vent in occasional cheering and the explosion of squibs and small fireworks. The Pipe Band of the 53rd Y.S. Battalion of Gordon Highlanders from Tillicoultry, paraded the streets, and their enlivening strains were greeted with the utmost enthusiasm. The general rejoicings were continued till a late hour in the evening.

Armistice report (*Alloa Journal*)

the Kaiser, but generally praised the Alloa people for their fortitude and sympathised with those who had suffered loss. The other speakers, mostly Councillors, echoed his sentiments, although Sheriff Dean Leslie said that 'Germany must be made to pay'. As with most of the other events celebrated in Alloa's history during the war, it passed by without anyone apparently feeling that it was worth taking a photograph!

By 9 December, the Council minutes noted that they had received courteous replies in response to all four telegrams of congratulation that they had sent.[17] Also on 9 December the Council recorded that it had received a note from Scottish Military Command saying that five captured German guns had been allocated to Alloa as trophies for a temporary exhibition.[18] These guns were displayed in Meadow Place [which was in the Bank Street, Coalgate area of town, by the old Meadow Brewery] and were finally removed by the Army to Stirling Ordnance Depot at the end of March 1919.[19] It didn't end there though since Alloa was clearly sent more guns in May 1919 when the Council minutes noted that the War Trophies Committee of the War Office had offered 'for safe care and custody, three German Field guns and carriages'.[20] It was these guns that were 'dumped' in the Public Park along with the tank in 1921.

SCHOOLS

The Spanish flu epidemic, as noted earlier, had closed all the schools in the burgh, although some opened on that Monday morning. Only St John's School recorded in its log book that there had been an armistice, although we do not know the children's reaction to it, apart from them singing a few patriotic songs.

The next meeting of the Alloa School Board was on the Thursday following the Armistice and the Chairman had some moving comments to make:

'The Chairman stated that as this was the first meeting of the Board since the signing of the Armistice, they could not do less than express their thankfulness to Almighty God for having given them peace and victory. It had not always looked as if this would be the outcome of the War, but he was thankful to say that they had overcome their enemies, and he thought they could extend their felicitations to the King and Queen on the happy issue of the conflict, also to those who led the forces and the nation during the past four and a half years. In the midst of their rejoicing, they could not forget the many sad hearts in their midst to whom their sincere sympathy was extended...'[21]

CHURCHES

The West Church Kirk Session had a scheduled meeting on the evening of 11 November 1918 and 'Reference was made to the cessation of hostilities in the European War... and gratitude to Almighty God for the signal victory, granted to our nation and its allies, after four years and three months of unexampled warfare, and for the splendid devotion and sacrifice of the men summoned to defend the country... they mourn the loss of so many gallant young lives...'[22]

A Special Service of Thanksgiving was held in St Mungo's Church on Tuesday night, led by Rev A.W. Scudamore Forbes. He commented that 'no words could describe the feeling of gratitude that was present in the human heart at such a time...'[23] The Earl of Mar & Kellie read one of the lessons. The Moncrieff Church, West Church and St John's Episcopal Church all had thanksgiving services in the following days.

It was not until the evening of Wednesday 13 November that St Mungo's Kirk Session held its first post-war meeting, when 'the Moderator made reference to the great crisis through which we have passed and the signing of the armistice which brought to a close a war unparalleled in the history of the world. We should also express our gratitude and admiration that the young men of our own community... had heroically endured and contributed to ever-memorable achievements. The Session resolved to express its sympathy with the relatives of the heroic dead.'[24]

It is worth making the point that the war did not actually end on 11 November 1918; that was the Armistice, in effect a ceasefire. The end came only when German representatives signed the terms of the Treaty of Versailles on 28 June 1919. That event was, naturally, reported in the Alloa press.

ENDNOTES

1. *Alloa Circular* 1 Sept 1915 p. 3 col. 2
2. *Alloa Advertiser* 12 Oct 1918 p. 3 col. 3
3. *Alloa Advertiser* 19 Oct 1918 p. 3 col. 3
4. *Alloa Advertiser* 9 Nov 1918 p. 3 col. 3
5. *Alloa Advertiser* 9 Nov 1918 p. 3 col. 1
6. *Alloa Circular* 13 Nov 1918 p. 2 col. 3. The Treaty of Brest-Litovsk, signed in March 1918, ended the war between Germany and Russia
7. *Alloa Circular* 13 Nov 1918 p. 3 col. 2
8. *Alloa Advertiser* 16 Nov 1918 p. 3 col. 3
9. *Alloa Journal* 16 Nov 1918 p. 3 col. 3
10. *Alloa Journal* 16 Nov 1918 p. 3 col. 3
11. *Alloa Advertiser* 16 Nov 1918 p. 3 col. 3
12. *Alloa Circular* 13 Nov 1918 p. 3 col. 2
13. Alloa Burgh Council minute book Monday 11 November 1918
14. *Alloa Circular* 13 Nov 1918 p. 3 col. 3
15. *Alloa Advertiser* 16 Nov 1918 p. 3 col. 3
16. *Alloa Journal* 16 Nov 1918 p. 3 col. 5
17. Alloa Burgh Council minute book 9 Dec 1918
18. Alloa Burgh Council minute book 9 Dec 1918
19. *Alloa Advertiser* 29 March 1919 p. 3 col. 1
20. Alloa Burgh Council minute book 12 May 1919
21. Alloa Burgh School Board minute book 14 Nov 1918
22. Alloa West Kirk Session minute book 11 Nov 1918
23. *Alloa Circular* 13 Nov 1918 p. 3 col. 2
24. St Mungo's Kirk Session minute book 13 Nov 1918

CHAPTER 11

COMMEMORATION

Most people expect to see a war memorial as a commemoration of the sacrifice made by the people of a town in World War I, but many would be surprised at the extent of the commemorative events which took place in Alloa, both in tribute to the fallen and to returning servicemen.[1] They are examined in this chapter mostly in order of implementation, rather than importance.

ALLOA'S OFFICIAL WELCOME HOME DINNER

By January 1919 the Council was already proposing some sort of civic welcome for returning servicemen, and a committee was set up to organise it. It had got £700 in subscriptions by April 1919 and was thinking of holding a civic reception and giving out a wallet with a 10 shilling note inside.[2] Incredibly, there was a suggestion within the Council from some of its temperance enthusiasts that the reception should be a non-alcoholic event! This was eventually voted down 10-2 after arguments such as 'All classes of men went out to fight for them and they knew they received alcoholic stimulants when required [*a reference to the rum ration before a big attack*] and it did them much good...'[3] This argument within the Council received quite a lot of coverage in the local press, who called it 'The beer versus lemonade discussion'[4] and criticised the temperance lobby for 'pushing their temperance wares when the opportunity does not lend itself to such advertisement'. There was a fair amount of teasing in the local press in late April 1919,[5] with several rudely suggestive verses being printed, alluding to what might be the consequences for the soldiers if the reception was a temperance event. The best of them was:

> *Sergeant D who was boss of the snipers*
> *Heard great noises each day around Ypres*

But the noise that he made
After four lemonade
Beat the Argyll and Sutherland pipers

The date for the function was fixed for Saturday 21 June 1919. By this date, almost £1,100 had been received as donations so there were no anxieties about the expense. About 1,150 officers and men accepted the Council's invitation, although an extra 150 turned up. They assembled at Sunnyside School at 12.15pm, marched through the streets of Alloa to the Drill Hall for a meal, then on to the Public Park for entertainment. Evening concerts were put on in the Town Hall and the Drill Hall. There was a major supplement in the *Advertiser* the following Saturday called *Local Heroes Welcome-Home* which had complete details (but no photographs) of the great event.[6]

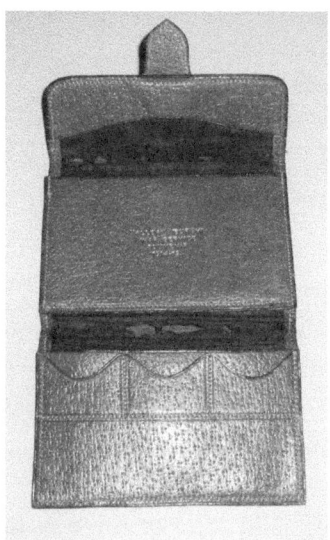

Soldier's souvenir wallet

The Council decided to give each man a 'souvenir pocket book' and Provost Pearson was responsible for organising this. However, Mr William Millar, who was in charge of the Roll of Honour and sending out the invitations, noted that more men had turned up than expected and therefore they did not have enough of these wallets to go round (382 short)[7], so it was agreed to delay giving them out until they could be sure that every returned serviceman would get one. What actually happened was that every serviceman who had won a gallantry medal got a little book of all the medal winners inserted inside his pig-skin pocket book, while every serviceman who had not won a gallantry medal got a slim pigskin wallet with the words 'Alloa Burgh War Service Souvenir 1914-1919' stamped in gold inside it. Councillor Duncanson had been worried about putting the little medals book into the wallet, but his concerns were not shared at the Council meeting.[8] In the end, 2,000 wallets were handed out.[9]

There were free cigarettes after the meal and many speeches complimenting every branch of the armed forces, plus replies. The speeches were enlivened by the telling of several jokes by Capt. A.P. Moir; the best of them, taken from *Punch*, was 'A brawny highland soldier was asked by his girlfriend, "Jock, why haven't you told your mother you got the VC?" "Ach, woman, it wasnae my turn to write".'

Only three weeks after the civic welcome, Baillie Moir reported to the Council that 'a very good series of photographs had been taken by Messrs Green of the procession and other events on the Celebration Day. The pictures had been shown in their Cinema House and it had occurred to him that it would be an interesting memento of the occasion if the film could be secured.'[10] Mr Green then offered it to the Council free of charge, and it is a disappointment verging on a tragedy that the fate of such a rare and important visual document of Alloa's war-related life is unknown.[11]

Both the *Journal* and *Advertiser*, in reporting the Homecoming Celebrations in the following Saturday's issues on 28 June 1919, remarked that the Treaty of Versailles was about to be signed, bringing a formal end to the war.

Only the *Circular* reported on the final German action a few days earlier that had pushed the Allies into an attitude towards the Germans of 'sign or else', when the German navy scuttled its own fleet in Scapa Flow after surrendering it as part of the Armistice agreement.

The *Advertiser* reported that 'The coming of peace was celebrated in a spontaneous and unofficial way... at a late hour in the evening the principal thoroughfares were converted into a zone of danger-spiced excitement by reason of the large amount of fireworks and squibs being set off.'[12] There were further Peace celebrations on Saturday 19 July, when the shops were closed for a half day and there were entertainments and bands playing in the Public Park. The Council may have regretted giving the go-ahead for the fireworks that evening, since 'an unfortunate accident occurred... the fireworks were to be let off from a lorry, but after several sky rockets had gone off, the whole stock of fireworks went up in a blaze.'[13] The Council's Finance sub-committee later reported that their insurers had paid out on claims worth a total of £12 11 shillings for '...damage done to clothing by fireworks at the Peace celebrations'.[14]

> **GERMAN FLEET SUNK.**
>
> Practically the whole of the German fleet interned at Scapa Flow were scuttled and sunk on Saturday by the German crews remaining on board these vessels. Of the huge battleships and battlecruisers forming the German High Seas Fleet, in whose developement the ex-Kaiser took so great an interest, the battleship Baden alone remains afloat. Five light cruisers have been sunk and three beached. Local tugs succeeded in beaching 18 destroyers. Four destroyers are still afloat, but all others have been sunk.

> THE COMING OF PEACE was celebrated in Alloa last Saturday night in a spontaneous and unofficial way. The Cadet Bugle Band paraded the streets, and at a late hour in the evening the principal thoroughfares were converted into a zone of danger-spiced excitement by reason of the large amount of fireworks and squibs being set off. Some rockets that ought to have produced a coruscating spectacle in mid air, came to their climax in the gutter or on the roofs of houses. In addition to these unskilful pyrotechnics, the dancing craze found its place in the impromptu rejoicings; and Meadow Place and the open space in front of the Post Office were monopolised by young people who footed it neatly to the strains of the mouth-organ or melodeon. Dancing was also a great feature of the evening's celebrations up Tillicoultry way.

The *Circular*'s reporting of the coming of peace was much more low key than that of the *Advertiser*. Its laconic view of the signing of the Peace Treaty itself in Versailles was that 'When called, the German delegates rose, walked to the table and signed without a word' and it reported Alloa's reaction under a headline of 'The Signing of Peace, No excitement shown'. Its view was that 'When news that the peace had been signed reached Alloa, there was nothing of the nature of a demonstration...'[15] Some local organisations, however, took the opportunity to celebrate: 100 members of the Alloa Boating and Swimming Club had a 'Peace Picnic' at Rumbling Bridge on 28 June,[16] the members of Alloa Tennis Club had a 'Victory Tournament' on 5 July,[17] and over 100 employees of Calder's Shore Brewery had a 'peace' trip to Lochearnhead on 12 July.[18]

ARMISTICE DAY 1919

The idea of a national two minutes' silence to mark the Armistice on 11 November had already taken hold in the popular consciousness by its first anniversary. This was fully honoured in Alloa. The Council put a note in the *Advertiser* three days earlier to warn local people what to expect.[19]

ARMISTICE DAY TWO SILENT MINUTES

The attention of the citizens is respectfully directed to the Royal Message desiring that at the hour the Armistice came into force, that is to say, on the morning of Tuesday first, 11th curt. (11.11.19), there may be for two minutes 'a complete suspension of all our varied activities' in reverent remembrance of our glorious dead.

It has been arranged that the bells will be rung at three minutes to Eleven o'clock. Immediately thereafter the citizens are requested to interrupt their business and pleasure, whatever it may be, and unite in the simple service of silent remembrance.

James Cuthbert
Town Clerk

The following week's *Advertiser* had a brief report on 'the hush that fell over the town, all traffic being suspended. In factories and workshops machines ceased running, and for two minutes the thoughts of all were turned to our glorious dead, the immortal heroes by whose self-sacrifice the civilized world was saved from destruction'.[20] The *Journal* echoed this, commenting that 'The Two Minute Silence was carried out in Alloa and district with becoming reverence...'[21]

BURGH OF ALLOA ROLL OF HONOUR

Informal rolls of honour were being drawn up by the local press, sports clubs, schools and churches from the first months of the war. Most of these lists were then arranged more systematically, corrected in 1919 and became the basis for the formal memorials that emerged in the 1920s. Alloa Burgh Council had already started a draft list of those who were serving by April 1915,[22] but wanted a full and formal Roll of Honour and the task of drawing it up was put in the hands of Mr William Millar, the Headmaster of Sunnyside School.[23] It was decided that everyone who had served should be included, so the Roll was drawn up in five sections; dead officers, dead servicemen/women, surviving officers, surviving servicemen/women, and medals/decorations. Mr Millar reported to the Burgh Council by 14 December 1918 that he had completed the roll, with approximately 3,000 names. He recommended that the permanent roll should be 'an album, the cost of which would be between £100 and £200'.[24] They put this plan in motion but it was not until May 1920 that 'Baillie Hunter submitted proof sheets of the Burgh Roll of Honour and suggested that copies should be exhibited in certain public places for a fortnight...' for the purposes of notifying corrections. It was also agreed to put adverts in the local press to warn people of this.[25]

By July 1920 the Council went for the production of a final proof copy, since 'The Roll of Honour had been practically completed' and 'The Convenor intimated that the printer would be prepared to print off a cheap copy for 10/6.'[26] By September 1920 therefore, William Millar 'laid upon the table a copy of the Roll in dummy form, with which the Council expressed its satisfaction and directed that the work should be completed. It was decided that five copies should be obtained,[27] then it was agreed to order an extra copy of the Roll to present to Mr Millar. He died suddenly in July 1921 and one wonders if he ever received his copy.

So, an album was indeed produced and it is a most dignified and comprehensive document. It contains, in fact, the name, medals, rank, regiment/military force and

Burgh of Alloa Roll of Honour

address of 2,258 military personnel from Alloa who served in World War I. According to the Roll of Honour, Alloa suffered 380 losses in the war, although the War Memorial contains 385 names.[28]

The final two sentences in the preamble to the Roll of Honour sum up how much this commemorative document mattered to the people of Alloa. It reads:

'The names of our dead are writ in every heart; and the sorrow at their loss is commingled with admiration of the great deeds of heroism performed in many a hard-won fight. This generation will never forget the sacrifices made by these valiant youths; and future generations will turn to this record with swelling breasts, proud that those who lived in the days of stress and storm served their country with zealous devotion, not counting the cost.'

Two extra pages containing information on the 125 losses in World War II were later added. One copy of this roll is presently held by Clackmannanshire Council Archives and is open to view when requested.

ALLOA'S ARNSBRAE PLEASURE GROUNDS

The planned War Memorial in Bedford Place may have been a start, but many Alloa townspeople, including the Burgh Council, felt that there would be a value in having some sort of memorial garden as well as a monument. Dean of Guild Hepburn was prominent in promoting the idea that the Council should buy Arnsbrae Woods, a seven-acre strip of land along the Stirling Road opposite the Arns and the Redwell playing fields and more commonly known as 'The Plantation', from the Earl of Mar & Kellie. Provost Mitchell went as far as arguing that 'If I had the power I would put the war memorial in this place... it is a place where they might scan at leisure, rather than in the hubbub of town, the names of those brave lads who gave their lives that we at home might live in peace and comfort.'[29] This particular part of the idea was not taken up, but the Burgh Council bought the land (it cost about £765)[30] and created a memorial park to be called, after much debate, the Arnsbrae Pleasure Grounds.[31] Many Councillors and others of the town, who had lost sons in the war, showed their support for the project by personally paying, at a cost of £1 12s 6d for each seat[32] for the fifty public seats as a tribute to them, and placing a small plaque on the back of each with a simple inscription of 'Gifted by...' and the name of the donor. These seats were often in bad repair by the late 1990s and now all of the original seats seem to have been removed.[33]

Photograph of a seat taken in 1990s

The little metal plaque can be still be seen, attached to the middle of the back of the seat, the moulding showing the name of the donor.

Detail of a different seat

The formal opening took place on Wednesday 19 July 1922 at 7.30pm. There was a crowd of about 3,000, the Alloa Instrumental Band under Mr Muddiman performed several musical items and speeches were made. At that time 'The Pleasures' was just a bit of bare, open, somewhat scrubby looking hillside, yet in their speeches Councillors talked fulsomely of the 'beautiful situation and zig-zag paths' and said it was a 'Red Letter day for the town'. Time and the natural growth of the vegetation proved the Councillors right in their vision and in the use of town funds to create this memorial park. Honesty however compels one to say that the Ministry of Works (the national body) was largely responsible for laying out the paths[34] and Mr Alexander Forrester-Paton paid for 'the whole cost of the shrubs'.[35] The Council had estimated that installing just the beech hedge along the Stirling Road would cost in the region of £500, so it was very grateful that someone else had paid for it.[36] The Council was anxious to have some ceremonial iron gates at the entrances to the park but they would not have been ready due to a moulders' strike at the local foundry. Since the apprentices were not on strike they were given the job of completing the gate posts on time. Those same gate posts are still there today, with the name 'Pearson and Ramage Ltd, Alloa' embossed on the side, all made by the (involuntary) young strike-breakers.[37]

The Council planned to put in an ex-army hut for refreshments[38] but they capped this in 1929 when they constructed a brick-built pavilion with a covered seated area with adjacent male and female toilets.[39] This was paid for entirely with a £3,000 legacy[40] from Councillor Duncanson, who had also paid for the champagne at the specially called Council meeting on Armistice Day. This building was demolished in 1989.

Photograph of the Pleasure Grounds in the early 1930s, soon after the pavilion was built. Even by then the trees and shrubs planted in 1922 had still not grown much, so the walks and views were still clear. (*Clackmannanshire Archives and Local History Service*)

ALLOA WAR MEMORIAL IN BEDFORD PLACE

The Burgh Council had a fairly clear idea of where it wanted to site the memorial and considered purchasing land in the Bank St, Coalgate, Stripehead area, and demolishing the properties there to create an open space for it.[41] In the early days of 1919 it is clear that it believed that it would have to buy the land from the major property owner there, Sir George Younger. The Council minutes noted that it would 'treat with him for the purchase of his property on the best possible terms'.[42] However things looked much brighter by the end of the year, when the Provost 'intimated that Sir George Younger had indicated his willingness to convey to the Town Council, free of any charge there for, the property belonging to him at the corner of Bank Street and Wellington Place...'[43]

The site of the memorial was therefore '...the gift of Viscount Younger to the town'.[44] One property which was in the way was <u>not</u> demolished; instead, Wellington

House was dismantled and moved to Alexandra Drive.[45] The Council did not stint on any aspect of the memorial, employing only the best: Sir Robert Lorimer designed it, Charles Pilkington-Jackson sculpted it, and in the end it cost £5,000.

In 1920 Sir Robert attended meetings with the Works Committee of the Burgh Council to discuss his general proposals[46], while Pilkington-Jackson came along on other occasions to present his ideas, though even by 1923 he was still 'only developing the figure for the memorial'.[47] In July that year he met with the Council's War Memorial Committee and put forward some draft ideas; the main one seemed to be '…four kilted soldiers advancing to battle, with a figure superimposed representing Scotland'.[48] He must have changed his mind quite a bit over the following year, because what Alloa finally got (for its money) was a large, crowned, bronze female figure (representing the Thought of Alloa) mounted on a granite pedestal with the figures of three soldiers crouched in defensive positions at her feet. The whole memorial was 6 metres (20 feet) high.[49] During the war there were surprisingly few references in the local press to the Burgh of Alloa's motto, which was 'In the Forefront'. By 1924 though, their description of the arrangement of the three soldiers could not resist the allusion to one of the soldiers being 'in the forefront', protecting the figure and the other two soldiers.

The memorial was finally ready for its unveiling ceremony towards the end of 1924 and on 28 September, 'with reverent and touching ceremonial, Alloa paid tribute to her dead sons…'[50]

The ceremony officially started at 3.00pm but the streets were full well before then. There were perhaps 5–6,000 spectators. Provost Henderson made the opening speech, starting with 'We are met here today to pay a heartfelt tribute to the immortal honour of the men of Alloa who fell in the Great War…' before referring to Alloa's cost; 2,258 had joined up, 384 died.[51] He then invited Lord Mar to say a few words, who in turn invited Field Marshall Sir Douglas Haig to unveil the memorial.[52] Before doing so, Haig made a suitable speech himself, praising the local military contribution, especially those in the 9th, 15th, 51st and 52nd Divisions. Whilst talking about the importance of memorials, he did not shirk from mentioning an unintended consequence of the war and the post-war economic slump; 'there is in our midst a vast and terrible memorial to the Great War in the shape of many thousands of out-of-work ex-Servicemen.'[53]

The 7th Battalion of the Argylls provided the Guard of Honour. A piper played the lament *The Flowers o' the Forest*, then Sergeant-Drummer T.M. McGuire and seven buglers from the battalion sounded *The Last Post* and *The Reveille*. Many wreaths were laid, the one on behalf of the town of Alloa by David Buchan and James Maitland, two of the four men from Alloa who had lost three sons.[54]

There was an official brochure for the unveiling of the war memorial (Order of Service, hymns, speeches, Last Post, wreath laying etc.) and it contained a list of the fallen. The photograph of the memorial included in the brochure had been taken before the eight bronze panels listing the fallen had been placed on the wall behind the memorial. Those panels were in position by 28 September, as can be seen from the photograph of the unveiling ceremony.

Alloa War Memorial unveiling. (*Clackmannanshire Archives and Local History Service*)

A week later, on 4 October 1924, the *Journal* used that list of the fallen from the brochure as the basis for a Special Supplement called ALLOA ROLL OF HONOUR. It was a single sheet of paper folded to give four sides and on it was a list of names, ranks, regiments and decorations of Alloa's fallen. It was a miniature version, without addresses, of the full Burgh of Alloa Roll of Honour, which had eighty-four pages.

On the 4 October, a note of dissent about the proceedings was published by someone representing VADs, who had written to one of the local papers expressing disappointment that there was no place for them at the ceremony.[55]

CHURCH WAR MEMORIALS

Most of the churches held memorial services in early 1919 for the members of their congregations who were killed[56] and 'Welcome Home' parties for those who had survived the war. Then, in due course, most of the churches in the town unveiled memorials to the fallen, presented by their own congregations. The references below show where further information can be found in the local press:

Chalmers Church	*Advertiser* 18 June 1921	*Journal* 18 June 1921
Moncrieff Church	*Advertiser* 11 September 1920	
St Mungo's Church	*Advertiser* 23 April 1921	*Journal* 23 April 1921
St Andrew's Church	*Advertiser* 21 May 1921	*Journal* 21 May 1921
St John's Church	*Advertiser* 31 December 1921	*Journal* 31 December 1921
West Church	*Advertiser* 15 October 1921	*Journal* 15 October 1921

Due to the closure and amalgamation of some of Alloa's churches over the past 100 years, three of these war memorials – West Church, St Andrew's Church and Chalmers Church – have ended up in the same place; they can be seen in Alloa Ludgate Church, originally called the West Church, at the junction of Grange Road with Ludgate. The memorials at St Mungo's, St John's and Moncrieff Churches are still where they were placed in 1920-21. Two of the memorials – St John's and St Mungo's – were designed by Sir Robert Lorimer and two churches had two memorials. In the case of Moncrieff Church there is a memorial and a framed Roll of Honour, while for St Andrew's there is a memorial tablet, but the 'principal memorial is a window erected in the centre of the chancel'.[57] This remains *in situ* and the building now functions as The Gate, a community charity.

Only St Mungo's Church listed its fallen precisely by rank, beginning with officers; most just had a terse list of names and regiments, usually organised alphabetically. St Mungo's also included Bessie Coltman on its memorial. As might be expected, there are almost as many names on the St Mungo's memorial as the rest of Alloa's churches added together.

West Church   St Andrew's Church

St Andrew's Church memorial window, with its subtle reference to the war through the dates 1914 and 1919 at the bottom of each window,[58] below the text saying 'Peace to everyman who worketh good'

Chalmers Church

St John's Church

St Mungo's Church

Moncrieff Church War Memorial and the Roll of Honour of those who served. (*J.D. Henderson*)

One small mystery is the presence of a fourth war memorial tablet, bearing seventeen names, in Alloa Ludgate Church. It is believed that it came from the Greenside Mission, but its minute books up to 1921 and afterwards, when the Mission was raised in status to being a fully-fledged church make no reference to the creation of any war memorial (at least not up to 1925). In July 1915 Greenside Mission produced a roll of honour of twenty-nine serving members of its congregation, but only six names from that list appear amongst the seventeen names of the fallen on this as yet 'unattributed' war memorial. This seems insufficient to confirm it as the war memorial of the Greenside Mission – yet where else might it be from?

Greenside Mission Memorial?

There is no evidence that Alloa's Baptist or Roman Catholic churches produced a war memorial to the fallen of their congregations at the end of the war.

SCHOOL WAR MEMORIALS

Apart from its Roll of Honour, Alloa Academy did nothing else at that time to commemorate the loss of its former pupils in World War I. It was only after World War II that the Rector, D.N. Stewart felt that the sacrifice of yet another generation of the Academy's FPs deserved more than just another framed list. He was the prime mover in organising a committee that raised funds,[59] chiefly from former pupils and their families, to create a set of memorials to the dead FPs of both wars.

The stained glass **Memorial Window** was designed and executed between January 1947 and June 1948 by Mr J.C. Macleod, Head of Art. (*Photo by Anthony Cervi*)

The **Book of Remembrance,** where the cover was designed and worked by Miss W.M. Young in the Art Department and the wording inside was transcribed by Mr Macleod

The **Oak Lectern** for the Book of Remembrance to rest on which was designed and constructed by Mr R.W. Robertson in the Technical Department

The Book of Remembrance is a fine volume and on its illuminated pages was written:

> 'Here then is the golden book of Alloa Academy. You and I turn its pages, but to us the names that appear are not mere names; they call up for us men we knew, men we respected, men we loved. Some there are who grew up with them, marched shoulder to shoulder with them and fought alongside them...'

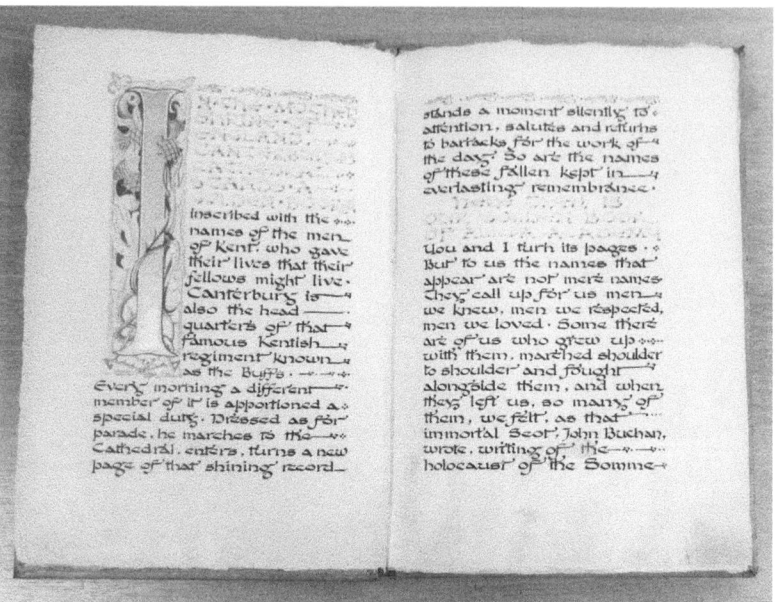

As a memorial from World War I, Alloa Academy also had the John Downie Willison Award For Leadership, which was presented to the most worthy pupil in that category until the 1960s. John Downie Willison, a former pupil,[60] was killed in France on 25 July 1918. The prize was given to the school by his father, owner of the brass foundry in Grange Road, in commemoration of his son.

ST JOHN'S PRIMARY SCHOOL

There was no reference to a Roll of Honour anywhere in the St John's School log book, but they must have kept one or had one drawn up at the end of the war, because a very decorative war memorial listing the names of sixty former pupils who had been killed was unveiled by Lady Mar in April 1921. It was on public view in the hall of the building in Grant Street, then sadly and somewhat sacrilegiously part of the end of it was hacked off to fit into the available space on the wall next to the boys' toilets when the school moved to its new premises in the former Grange School building in 1990. It is now in the Clackmannanshire Heritage Collection.

LOCAL INDUSTRY, OTHER GROUPS AND PRIVATE MEMORIALS

Alloa has three other war memorials which were created in the 1920s, in memory of the servicemen killed. These are in memory of the fallen of:

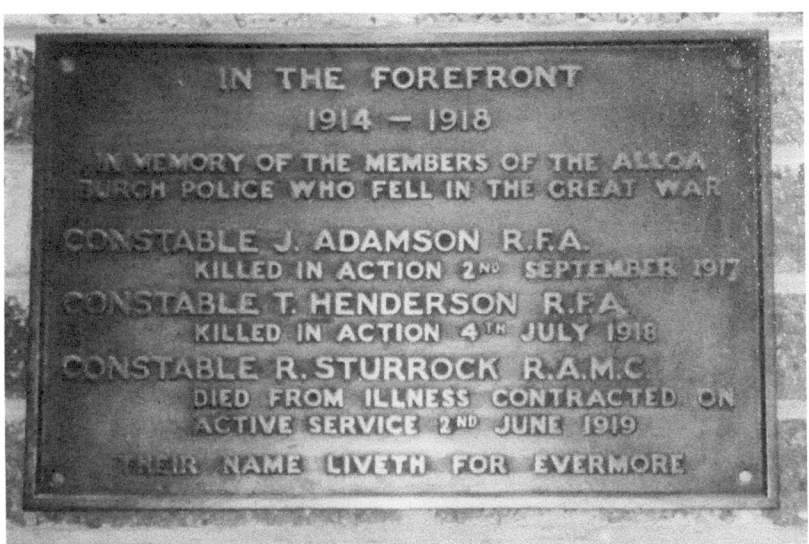

Alloa Burgh Police Force[61]

Alloa's Freemasons Lodge No. 69 (*Clackmannanshire Heritage Collection*)

Paton's Mills

There was also a private memorial to 2nd Lieut. John Millar Scott of Grange Road, Alloa. He was in the Black Watch and was killed on 18 August 1916 on the Somme.[62] In his memory, in February 1917, his friends produced a nicely presented volume of his Poems, Letters and Sermons. He was an FP of Alloa Academy, went to St Andrew's University, obtaining an MA in English literature, and was studying Divinity when war broke out. The book has an introduction by his great friend William Dunn, who somewhat quaintly opens with the expression that he 'was most intimate with Lieut. Scott', which would be open to misinterpretation now. Getting a memorial book was an unusual thing for a soldier from Alloa who had been killed in action; the best most could have hoped for was that their service medals and their bronze memorial plaque would be framed by their families and hung in a position of respect in their home.[63]

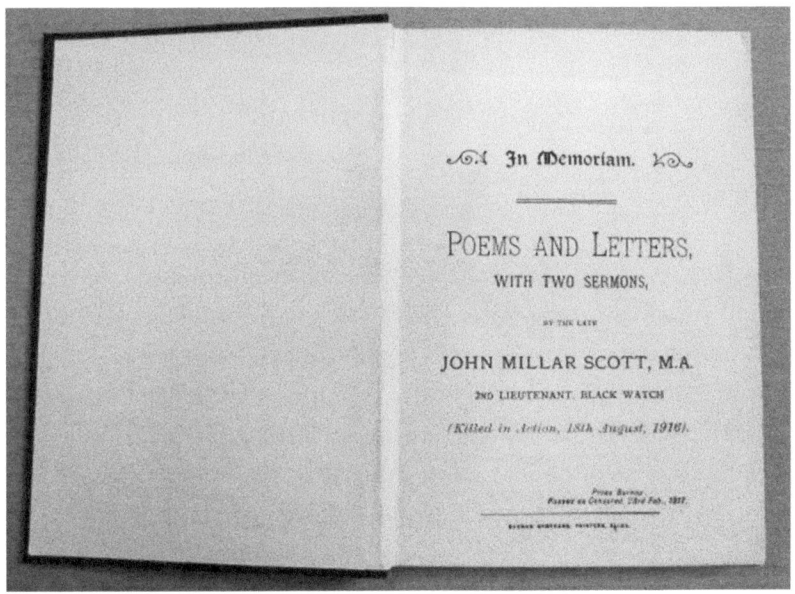

Another memorial to a single individual is the plaque on the wall of St John's Church to commemorate Lieut. Archibald Gifford Moir, who was killed in April 1915 and was buried at Bedford House Cemetery, Ypres.[64]

Archie Gifford Moir and his memorial in St John's

It would have been good to end this chapter with another local story of commemoration; of how the end of the war meant so much to one family in Alloa that (in the 1920s?) they named their daughter Armistice. I thought I knew this because the girl was born on 11 November and that she later became a pupil of Alloa Academy, I recall talking about Armistice Mitchell during the Academy's Remembrance Day service in the mid 1990s. Yet there is no record of her name in the school admission registers. Could this be an example of Alloa Academy folklore and I have just 'mis-remembered'?

ENDNOTES

1. Regarding the broader picture of commemoration in Scotland: when the Scottish National War Memorial Committee was set up in October 1918, it was chaired by the Duke of Atholl and had twenty-nine members taken from the 'great and the good' of the land, including a disproportionate number of people with a strong connection with Alloa and Clackmannanshire; Lord Balfour of Burleigh, Sir George Younger MP and Eugene Wason MP
2. *Alloa Advertiser* 19 April 1919 p. 3 col. 3
3. *Alloa Advertiser* 19 April 1919 p. 3 col. 3
4. *Alloa Journal* 19 April 1919 p. 2 col. 1, p. 3 col. 2
5. *Alloa Journal* 26 April 1919 p. 3 col. 2
6. *Alloa Advertiser* 28 June 1919 Special Supplement
7. *Alloa Advertiser* 19 June 1919 p. 3 col. 2
8. Alloa Burgh Council minute book 14 April 1919
9. *Alloa Advertiser* 18 Oct 1919 p. 4 col. 1
10. Alloa Burgh Council minute book 14 July 1919
11. Frustratingly, La Scala was the only Alloa cinema still advertising or having its programme reported in the local press in mid-1919, so we cannot verify how long this film was shown at Green's Picturedrome, or even what its title was
12. *Alloa Advertiser* 28 June 1919 p. 3 col. 1
13. *Alloa Advertiser* 26 July 1919 p. 3 col. 4
14. Alloa Burgh Council Finance Committee minute book 29 July 1919 and 2 Sept 1919
15. *Alloa Circular* 2 July 1919 p. 2 col. 4
16. *Alloa Journal* 5 July 1919 p. 2 col. 4
17. *Alloa Journal* 12 July 1919 p. 2 col. 4
18. *Alloa Journal* 19 July 1919 p. 2 col. 5
19. *Alloa Advertiser* 8 Nov 1919 p. 2 col. 3
20. *Alloa Advertiser* 15 Nov 1919 p. 3 col. 2
21. *Alloa Journal* 15 Nov 1919 p. 3 col. 1
22. *Alloa Journal* 17 April 1915 p. 2 col. 6
23. *Alloa Advertiser* 17 Feb 1917 p. 4 col. 3
24. *Alloa Advertiser* 14 Dec 1918 p. 3 col. 1
25. Alloa Burgh Council minute book 10 May 1920
26. Alloa Burgh Council minute book 12 July 1920
27. Alloa Burgh Council minute book 13 Sept 1920
28. Besides the discrepant number of names (see footnote[42]) J.D. Henderson's researches suggest that a further anomaly is that Private John Combs (No. 55 in the Roll of Honour) and Private John Combs McLaughlin (No. 205) are the same person. See CWGC website for information on him serving under the alias. His name is also recorded twice on Alloa War Memorial
29. *Alloa Advertiser* 22 July 1922

30 Alloa Burgh Council minute book 3 March 1922
31 *Alloa Advertiser* 16 Sept 1922
32 Alloa Burgh Council Arnsbrae Pleasure Ground Committee minutes 20 June 1922
33 The seats were made by Robert Mercer & Co, Alloa, to the Council's specifications. The Council paid for them to be painted and installed
34 *Alloa Advertiser* 22 July 1922
35 *Alloa Advertiser* 14 April 1923
36 Alloa Burgh Council minute book 27 Nov 1922
37 Alloa Docks Oral History Project 1987, Interview with Will, aged 83
38 *Alloa Advertiser* 17 June 1922
39 *Alloa Journal* 20 April 1929, 15 June 1929
40 *Alloa Journal* 20 April 1929
41 *Alloa Advertiser* 19 April 1919 p. 4 col. 1
42 Alloa Burgh Council minute book 29 April 1919
43 Alloa Burgh Council Special Meeting minute book 29 Dec 1919
44 *Stirling Observer* 30 Sept 1924 p. 8 col. 6
45 *Alloa Journal* 10 Dec 1949 in Special Supplement about Younger's Brewery is the first and only reference I have seen to the fact that this dismantled and rebuilt house, previously called Brewery House, was the actual birthplace of Sir George Younger in 1851
46 Alloa Burgh Council minute book 16 March 1920
47 Alloa Burgh Council minute book 9 July 1923
48 Alloa Burgh Council minute book 23 July 1923
49 I.G. Stewart *The Past Around Us* (2004)
50 *Alloa Circular* 1 Oct 1924 p. 3 cols. 2–6
51 There is no simple answer to this. Provost Henderson announced the wrong number. There are 385 names on the War Memorial, not 384. He may have got the figure from the list of the fallen in the War Memorial brochure, which itself had missed out the two members of the North Staffs Regt; Coy Sgt Major James R. Barrett and Pte James McGuire. The Roll of Honour, produced over three years earlier, missed out six names which *are* on the War Memorial (Pte William Greig of Royal Fusiliers, Pte William MacFarlane of Highland Light Infantry, Pte Matthew MacKay of Machine Gun Corps, Pte James P. Middleton of Queen's Own Cameron Highlanders, Gunner William P. Sinclair of Royal Garrison Artillery and Pte Robert Stobie of Royal Army Medical Corps). That still leaves a discrepancy between the War Memorial and the Roll of Honour of one soldier. No one knows why this happened, but an interesting question is where six extra names came from by 1924?
52 Alloa Burgh Council minute book shows that Earl Haig was approached on 4 June 1924 to unveil the memorial. He was probably asked to unveil many war memorials, but he had got a strong local connection to Alloa, so perhaps he honoured that. *Alloa Circular* 22 Dec 1915 p. 3 col. 1, following Haig's appointment as Supreme Commander, proudly noted that 'he spent his boyhood at Greenfield House'

53 *Alloa Advertiser* 4 Oct 1924 p. 3 cols. 2–5
54 Alloa Burgh Council minute book 5 Aug 1924 gave full details of all the arrangements for the unveiling
55 *Alloa Advertiser* 4 Oct 1924 p. 3 col. 5
56 *Alloa Journal* 8 Feb 1919 reported on the West Church's service for the twenty-seven officers and men of its congregation who were killed
57 *Alloa Advertiser* 21 May 1921 p. 3 col. 2
58 An 'accidental' memento to World War I also exists in the former St Andrew's Church, in the form of two vases on the ledge below another stained glass window in that church. These two 'vases' are in fact 1917 brass shell casings from a 7cm German artillery piece, which somehow found their way back to Alloa
59 The original accounts books, containing lists of all the donors and donations, are still held in the Alloa Academy Archives
60 Alloa Academy Secondary Admission Register No. 449. *Alloa Journal* 3 Aug 1918 p. 3 col. 1
61 *Alloa Journal* 22 Feb 1919 p. 3 col. 2 reported on the distinguished war record of the Alloa Burgh Police Force
62 *Alloa Advertiser* 26 Aug 1916 p. 3 col. 2
63 Lieut. J.M. Scott's memorial book can still be seen in Alloa Library; several other copies still exist
64 Archie was the elder brother of Lieut. Colonel Robert Gifford Moir, whose story appears in Chapter 14

CHAPTER 12

THE IMPACT OF WAR

People do seem to be fascinated by pondering the issue of the degree of suffering experienced in the war: was their town affected more than a neighbour? Was it worse for one family or one street than another? Who was the youngest/oldest soldier to die? Was one class at school more patriotic than another or suffered greater losses? etc. This chapter addresses, if not answers, some of these questions.

IMPACT ON THE TOWNS IN THE AREA

It really is impossible to find out which town in the county was the most badly affected. Every town was unique; there is no town with which to compare Alloa. The number of fatalities alone does not help, nor will number of fatalities as a proportion of population because it is difficult to know the age/gender profile of each town and who was liable to serve It is possible, however, to consider the fatalities from each town. Alloa, Larbert, Stirling and Denny published rolls of honour after the war and enables us to check the exact numbers.[1] In other cases the number is derived from either counting the names on the war memorials or looking in the local press in 1918-1919. In some cases the figure may be inflated by including 'and district' [Falkirk][2] or by combining the town's rate with a school's former pupils, as in Dollar. It is noteworthy that, where a local town or village was able to give a reasonably accurate number for those who served, the fatality ratio was invariably about one in six of the men who served.[3]

Town	Numbers who died
Alloa	384
Alva	135
Bo'ness	400
Clackmannan	52

Denny	154
Dunblane	98
Dollar	179
Falkirk	610
Grangemouth	276
Larbert	300
Sauchie	105
Stirling	692
Tillicoultry	69
Tullibody	25

THE IMPACT ON THE STREETS IN ALLOA

Can it be shown which part of Alloa was hardest hit by losses in World War I? Was there a worst-hit street? The Burgh of Alloa Roll of Honour reveals this, since the home addresses of all servicemen/women are included. The servicemen themselves may have lived elsewhere by the time the war was going on, but for the purposes of drawing up the Roll, their parental or family home was generally what counted.

OFFICERS

Thirty-eight officers from Alloa were killed and the worst hit streets were Claremont with seven and Bedford Place with six. The map shows the fairly concentrated middle-class areas from which most of the officers came; the bottom of Claremont and the Church Street/Grange Road area. Only six of the officers lived in more outlying parts of the burgh. As a matter of interest, the single dot in Forth Street is for Harcourt Ommundsen, who represented Britain in the 1908 and 1912 Olympics, winning a silver medal in the team rifle shooting on both occasions. He died in September 1915 at Ypres. The two dots on the Clackmannan Road are for the Teggart twins, killed in October 1917 and July 1918; the three dots in Kellie Place are for the Buchan Brothers.

NON COMMISSIONED OFFICERS (NCOS) AND OTHER RANKS

There were 342 NCOs and other ranks from Alloa who lost their lives; by far the worst hit street was Greenfield Street with 37, followed by Castle Street with 18; Erskine

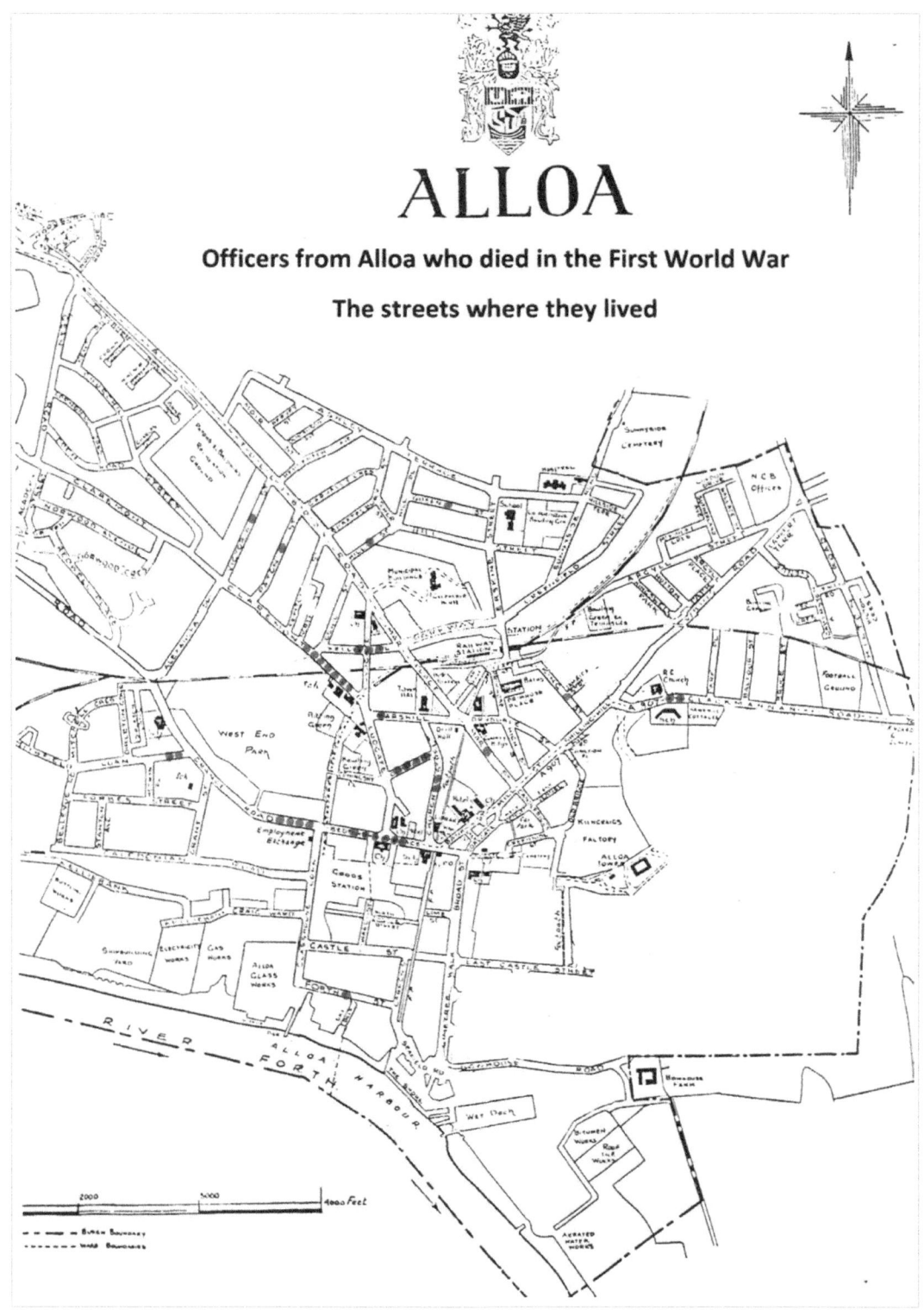

THE IMPACT OF WAR

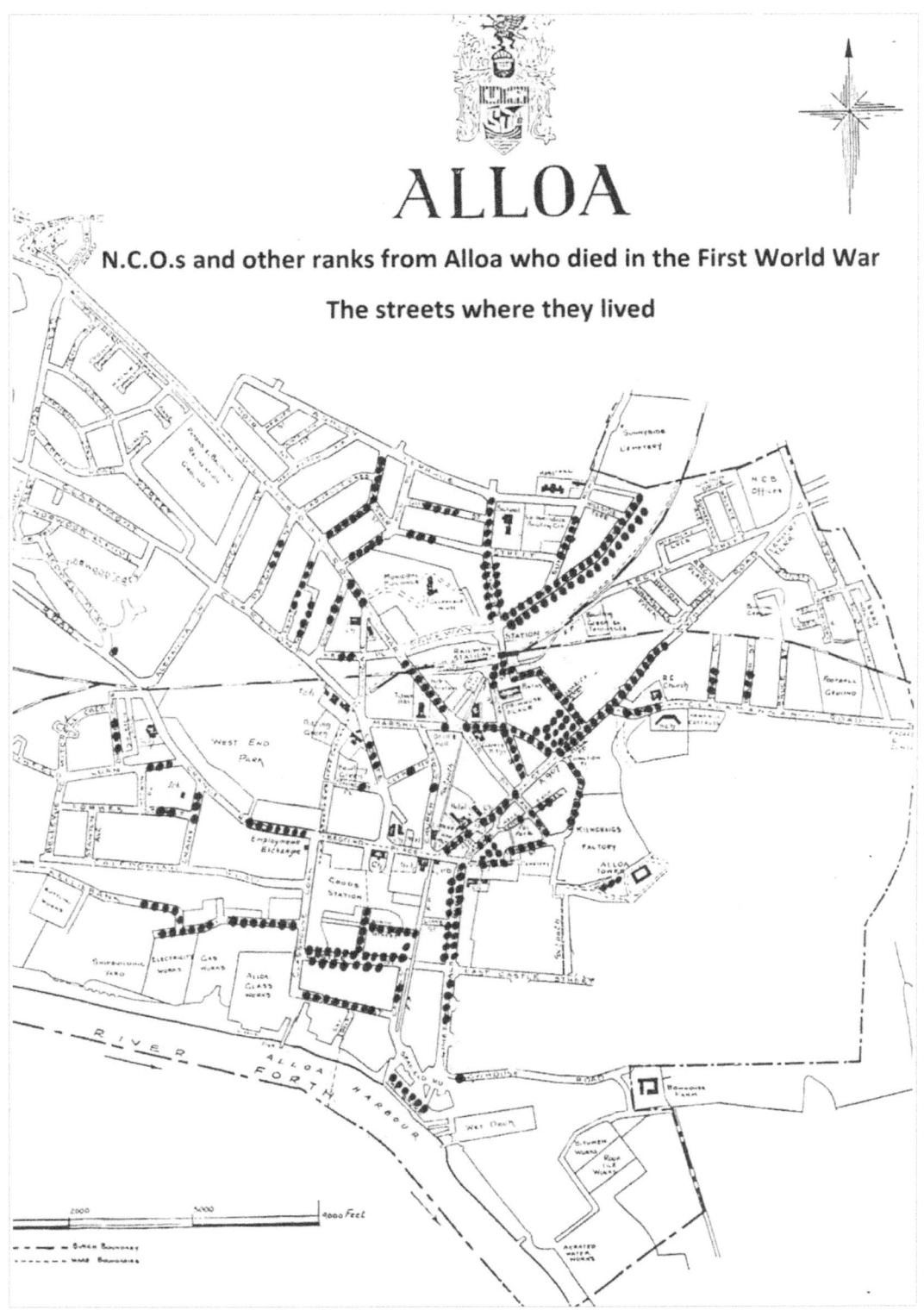

Street and Broad Street with 17; Back O' Dykes with 12; and Shaftesbury Street, King Street and Kelliebank with 11. Greenfield Street was the most heavily tenemented, with a dense population which included many young male lodgers. A comparison of the two maps shows that the two main streets in the list of 'officers that died' did not contain <u>any</u> from the 'NCOs and other ranks' category at all.

ALLOA'S WORST AFFECTED FAMILIES

The names of four Alloa families stand out as having suffered the most grievous loss in World War I. Each of these families lost three sons. Their names are Buchan, Forrest, Maitland and Waller.

The following roll shows rank, name, regiment, date of death and place of commemoration of the men from these four families:

Buchan family 5 Kellie Place

Lieut. David Buchan	1 Gordon Highlanders	09-04-17	Arras Memorial
2nd Lieut. Francis H. Buchan	11th Rifle Brigade	07-08-18	Sucrerie Cemetery, Ablain-St Nazaire
2nd Lieut. John C. Buchan	8th A & S Highlanders	22-03-18	Roisel Communal Cemetery Extension

Forrest family 44 Broad Street

Private David A. Forrest	1st Black Watch	27-10-14	Menin Gate Memorial
Private Andrew C. Forrest	1st Black Watch	10-02-15	Le Touret Memorial
Private James C. Forrest	Machine Gun Corps	09-06-17	Menin Gate Memorial

Maitland family 44 Shaftesbury Street

Drummer David H. Maitland	7th A & S Highlanders	25-04-15	Menin Gate Memorial
Private James Maitland	7th Seaforth Highlanders	17-11-15	Boulogne Eastern Cemetery
Private Malcolm M. Maitland	10th Gordon Highlanders	25-09-15	Loos Memorial

Waller family 4 Glebe Terrace

Lance Corporal Jack A. Waller	5th Q's Own Cameron Hrs.	25-09-15	Loos Memorial
2nd Lieut. Philip D. Waller	S. African Heavy Artillery	14-12-17	Red Cross Corner, Beugny
2nd Lieut. Richard P. Waller	Royal Air Force	22-05-18	Sunnyside Cemetery, Alloa

More than half of these men have no known grave, their names being recorded only on the walls of one or other of the great memorials to the missing. None of the Forrest boys have a known grave and all three Maitland boys were killed in the same year.

Recognition of the loss of the Maitlands in the *Alloa Advertiser*.
This was printed just before the death of James Maitland

The Buchan and Waller families were fairly prominent in the community and therefore there was quite a lot of coverage in the local press about the military careers and deaths of all their sons. The Maitland and Forrest families were less prominent and the deaths of the Forrest sons received little coverage in the local press: the first was on 26 December 1914 and referred to the death in October of the first Forrest boy,[4] the other was on 7 July 1917, when it was noted that the family had suffered their third loss when their youngest son was killed.[5] The Maitland sons were all killed in 1915 and the *Journal* noted by 9 October that two sons had died and a third had been seriously wounded in September, leading to a leg amputation.[6] In fact, both legs were amputated and he was always in a critical condition. He died of his wounds in November 1915.[7] The three sons were aged eighteen, twenty and twenty-eight.[8]

Within the limits of the accuracy of the Burgh of Alloa Roll of Honour, the 'luckiest' family in Alloa might have been the McMillans of 34 Hill Street. Six of the sons served in the war and they all survived.[9] A glance at the Roll further reveals that two Alloa families had five serving members of whom three survived,[10] seven families had four serving sons who all survived, ten families had four serving sons, of whom three survived, and forty-four families had three serving sons who all survived; the last figure includes four families where **all** their sons were officers.

LOSS RATES OF ALLOA SERVICEMEN: OFFICERS VERSUS OTHER RANKS

There is a common perception of World War I, probably started by the film *Oh What a Lovely War* and confirmed by the television series *Blackadder Goes Forth*, that the war was fought by officers who were safely in the rear whilst their men (the other ranks) were being callously sent 'over the top' in their thousands to face the slaughter of the battle. People believe, therefore, that the men were simply seen as 'cannon fodder' and suffered their losses at a far higher rate than their supposedly cowardly officers.

It is relatively easy to test whether this view has any basis in reality by considering the men of Alloa. The Burgh of Alloa Roll of Honour recorded all those who went to war, but divided the list into those who were killed and those who survived. The statistical analysis is not therefore very complicated, although it does not take account of those who were promoted from the ranks during the war.

Officers   201 served and 38 died. That is almost a 19 per cent loss rate. In other words, any Alloa officer who served on the battlefields had almost a **1 in 5** chance of being killed.

Men   2,057 served (including six women) and 342 died (inc. 1 woman). That indicates a 16.6 per cent loss rate, showing that any Alloa military/service personnel who were not officers had about a **1 in 6** chance of being killed.

Servicemen/women from Alloa had a better chance of surviving the war if they were **NOT** commissioned officers; and that analysis surely scotches the myth that officers were more cowardly or suffered more lightly than the men they led.

THE YOUNGEST AND OLDEST SERVING SOLDIERS FROM ALLOA

Who was the oldest man to serve?

This probably could be discovered, but it would take an extremely long time to do it. One approach would be to look at every name at a given address on the Burgh of Alloa Roll of Honour, then cross check it with the National Census of either 1901 or 1911, to get the person's age. Even then, there is the likelihood of many omissions from the colossal 2,266 pieces of individual research which would have to be done, due to the great residential mobility of those days; very often people did not stay in the same address for long periods of time. Armed forces records held in the National Archives are too incomplete to be of any use.

There is, however, a clue in Alloa's Roll of Honour which helps to identify the men who were probably the oldest soldiers. When William Millar was compiling the document in 1920 he realised that there were several instances of fathers and sons who had joined up; in these cases he wrote the word 'senior' against the father's name to distinguish them from the younger man. In the Roll of Honour there are eleven examples of this and the fathers are listed below:

Private William Candlish	7th Argylls	28 Castle St
Private Thomas Gordon	7th Argylls	36 King St
Private Andrew Haig	7th Argylls	1 Erskine St Cottages
Private William Honeyman	7th Argylls	55 Mill St
Private John McArthur	7th Argylls	28A Erskine St
Private Daniel McDonald	Royal Naval Air Force	10A Erskine St
Sergeant Andrew McEwan	7th Argylls	3 Back O' Dykes
Sergeant Alex C Napier MM	16th Canadian Infantry	30 Mar Place
Private William Prentice	11th Gordons	29 Coalgate
Private Charles Sharkey	7th Argylls	1 Low Craigward
Private William Thomson	8th Black Watch	8 High Craigward

The 1901 and 1911 national censuses indicate that only three of these men for the

1901 census, and seven for the 1911census had the same address as that recorded in the Roll of Honour. In 1914 Daniel McDonald and Andrew Haig were 39, William Thomson was 40, William Prentice was 44, William Candlish was 46, Charles Sharkey was 54 and William Honeyman was 56. It should not necessarily be assumed that these oldest serving Alloa soldiers actually saw military action in the war; the *Advertiser*, for instance, stated that William Honeyman was a reservist in Stonehaven.[11] There was nothing in the local press to show that they had any particular interest, at that time, in who might have been the oldest serving Alloa soldier.

The most likely candidate for the oldest serving Alloa soldier is Sergeant Andrew McEwan, for the following reasons;[12] he lost two of his four sons in the war (they died a fortnight apart in 1918)[13] and their names – and their memorial plaques – were added to the family gravestone in Sunnyside Cemetery. When Andrew McEwan died at the age of eighty-four on 22 December 1943, in the middle of World War II, his name was inscribed there too. Following the death of his sons in 1918, the *Advertiser* revealed that '…he was an old Quarter-Master Sergeant and although approaching sixty years of age has volunteered for home service and has been accepted.'[14] The gravestone therefore confirms the date given in the *Advertiser*. He was, therefore, born the year before Captain A.P. Moir (born 1860), who was a leading local figure in the Territorials and did home service in Alloa right through the war,[15] but whose name, for some reason, does not feature in the Burgh of Alloa Roll of Honour.

Who was the youngest man Alloa to serve?
It might be possible to identify this person, but it would require a great deal of work, partly because the CWGC records include only dead servicemen and the youngest might well have been a survivor.[16] Finding the birth date of the youngest of the six serving pupils from Alloa Academy in the 'class of 1913' (James Forsyth; born 30 June 1901) might help, but he may not have served in the actual war; instead, he could have been in the occupation forces after 1919 but still would have been included in the military roll. There may, of course have been a group of ex-Grange School pupils who were younger than the youngest Academy pupil; the absence of records from that school or, indeed, from any other private school attended by wealthier Alloa pupils makes it impossible to check this. What about someone who joined early as a boy-seaman, for instance, Midshipman Archie Douglas Moir[17] from Dunmar House, who was only seventeen when his ship HMS *Mary Rose* went down on 17 October 1917?[18] It is also possible that, given the general rush to join up in 1914-15, that there was

more than one fourteen-year old who managed to sneak in unnoticed[19] and, was either killed early, thus making him the youngest casualty, or who survived until 1918 and was still younger than James Forsyth? It is, therefore, difficult to determine definitively who was the youngest Alloa man to serve in the war. People at the time would probably soon have found out about any underage volunteer and it would have appeared in the local press, so it is unlikely that such a person existed. This leaves only Archie Douglas Moir, who seems to be the youngest to have been killed, and James Forsyth from the 'class of 1913, or any unidentified former pupils from the Grange School, as candidates for the honour of being the youngest man from Alloa to have served.

WHICH WAS THE MOST 'PATRIOTIC' OR THE WORST AFFECTED CLASS IN ALLOA ACADEMY?

The question might be asked if it is possible to find out which was the most 'patriotic' class, ie. the greatest number from one class who served, or which was the most badly affected class, ie. had the highest number of fatalities, in Alloa Academy?

It **is** possible to try attempt to answer both questions; but with **great** reservations. First, let us define our terms. 'The class of 1905' for instance, indicates the group of boys aged twelve to thirteen who had just enrolled in secondary school in September that year. Cross-referencing the names in the Alloa Academy Admission Registers against the Alloa Academy Roll of Honour indicates the contribution and loss of each class. The Secondary Admission Registers start only in 1901 – Primary Admission Registers go back to 1887 – so some pupils are bound to be omitted already.

On the following chart, the first eleven years were derived from the Primary Admission Registers. The oldest name found was in the 'class of 1890'. That pupil would have been only about thirty-eight when the war started, so it is highly probable that there are many more names from before that which just cannot be found.

Year Group or 'class of..'	Numbers NOT serving	Numbers serving
1890		1
1891		0
1892		0
1893		2

Year Group or 'class of..'	Numbers NOT serving	Numbers serving
1894		2
1895		3
1896		3
1897		4
1898		8
1899		10
1900		14
1901	1	6
1902	15	12
1903	29	24
1904	13	18
1905	21	19
1906	18	22
1907	13	36
1908	9	30
1909	18	27
1910	10	27
1911	11	34
1912	18	24
1913	29	6
1914	33	0
1915	46	0

THE MOST 'PATRIOTIC' CLASS

It must be pointed out there were many perfectly acceptable reasons why young men might **not** have served in the armed forces; there were many reserved occupations, such as mining, engineering/shipbuilding etc., which were prominent local industries. These industries absorbed a lot of the local school leavers whether they wished to fight or not.

The 1916 Military Service Act also introduced conscription, so every single male former pupil would have come under military control at the age of eighteen and would have done as they were told. This would have affected pupils from about the 'class of 1910' onwards. The list shows that no pupils joining the school in the 'class of 1914' actually served. Such a pupil would only just be eighteen in 1918, the year the war ended. Taking into account military training time, this meant that no pupil from that year group was ready to face the enemy in wartime. Equally, no one from the 'class of 1915' served because they were all still below military age when the war ended.

If war is regarded as a young man's business, concerning mainly those aged eighteen to twenty-five, then, checking backwards from the 'class of 1908', who were eighteen in 1914, a rise in the numbers joining could be expected. This is exactly the case; to a large extent, about half or more of each of those year groups joined up.

It is tempting, therefore, to conclude that the most patriotic class was the 'class of 1907'– with thirty-six serving, that is almost 75 per cent. They would all have been twenty or so when war broke out and they may well have all been volunteers. This is not certain, however, as 1916 conscription rooted out any who had avoided military service in 1914 and made them do what the government wanted - unless, of course they had fled the country!

The 'class of 1911' seems to be second in the 'patriotism' league table, but that year group would have been wholly controlled by conscription and the eleven who did not serve were presumably exempt and should not be regarded as shirkers.

There must, therefore, be great reservations about drawing up this 'patriotic' list: the evidence for the analysis is probably so limited as to make it worthless. The real value of the list is to demonstrate the consistent support that the boys of the school showed towards the idea of fighting for their country once they had become young men. Searching for the most 'patriotic' class is perhaps a futile exercise.

THE CLASS WHICH SUFFERED THE GREATEST LOSSES?

It is, once again, fairly easy to find out about this by cross-referencing the names from the Academy Roll of Honour against the Admissions Register to see which year group they were in, although there may be omissions of names from some of the early classes. Our overall conclusion will be distorted slightly, however, by that fact that there are five pupils who are listed as dead beside their names on the Academy Roll of Honour, but who cannot be found in the Admissions Registers. The obvious explanation is that they were older, had joined Alloa Academy and completed their secondary education before 1901, so there is no extant written record of their presence in the school. This means they are likely to figure near the start of any graph for losses per year group.

The analysis shows that Alloa Academy former pupils from **every** year group from 1894 to 1913, **apart** from the 'class of 1901' (a lucky year) were killed in the war. Only six of the 1901 year group served and none were lost. The oldest pupil found who was killed was from the 'class of 1886' but there may have been earlier classes with losses. The worst hit year group was the 'class of 1907' with seven deaths, followed by the 'classes of 1900 and 1911', both of which had five losses. Statistically speaking, though, the worst hit class was that of 1900, since five out of the fourteen who served were killed (i.e. almost one in three), which is a far higher death rate than the average for Alloa (almost 1 in 6 of those who served). One in seven of the total number of the boys in the 'class of 1907' were, however, killed, a record unmatched by any other year group. The 'class of 1907' holds the record, therefore, for being the most 'patriotic' and the most affected by fatalities.

ALLOA ACADEMY'S DUX MEDALLISTS IN WORLD WAR I

People look at the names on the Dux Board in the school hall[20] and know that these were the highest achieving pupils of each year. Did the boy Dux medallists go on to do great deeds in the war, perhaps **greater** than all their classmates? So much had, after all, been expected of them.

1898	Matthew Blair			
1900	Henry Anderson			
1904	William T. Buchan	Captain	RAMC	13 Glebe Terrace
1905	William R. Blair	Captain	7th Argylls	51 Grange Rd
1906	Ninian Home-Hay	Lieut.	RAMC	Ludgate House
1907	David Allan			
1908	James C. Brown	Lieut.	RE	Edgehill
1909	John S. Thomson	Private	2nd Gordons	Keilarsbrae
1911	Robert Millar	Sub Lieut.	RNVR	4 Hill Place
1912	Charles M. Hepburn	Captain	7th Argylls	Hillcrest
1913	Alex G. Wardlaw	Signaller	RNVR	15 Coningsby Pl
1914	Sydney S. Rennie	Private	Intelligence Corps	55 Hill St
1915	Christian B.F. Millar	[studying Medicine at Edin.University]		4 Hill Place
1916	James Lindsay	Signaller	RNVR	4 Queen St

The present state of research suggests that four Dux medallists did not serve and two died in action.

The first Dux to be killed was Alexander Gillespie Wardlaw from Coningsby Place. He had been the cleverest boy in the school, but he joined the navy as just an ordinary seaman signaller, having given up his studies at Glasgow University and joined the Royal Naval Volunteer Reserve. He was only twenty-one when he was put on a Q-Ship, one of those disguised merchant ships which in fact carried concealed heavy guns to try to beat the German U Boats. His ship, HMS *Paxton*[21], was torpedoed by the German submarine *U-46* on 20 May 1917, about 100 miles west of Fastnet Rock, and Alex Wardlaw was not among the survivors.[22] He is commemorated on the Portsmouth Memorial to the Missing at Sea.

The other Dux who died was John Snaddon Thomson, who had already gained First Class Honours at Edinburgh University and had become a Classics Master at Mackie Academy, Stonehaven, before joining up as a private in the Gordon Highlanders at Easter 1916. He was killed in the trenches in the Battle of Passchendaele, aged twenty-six, on 4 October 1917.[23] He has no known grave but is commemorated on the Tyne Cot Memorial to the Missing, outside Ypres in Belgium. His cousin of exactly the same name, also an Alloa Academy FP, died of his wounds, aged twenty, at No. 3 Canadian

General Hospital, Doullens, on 29 April 1918.[24] The Alloa Academy Roll of Honour shows that **two** John S. Thomsons were killed. They lived in the same house, 'Deolali', in Keilarsbrae, Sauchie.

ENDNOTES

1. Larbert includes Stenhousemuir and Denny includes Dunipace
2. It is impossible to get an accurate figure for Falkirk. A roll of honour was never constructed [until 2013] and those who drew up the inscription on the war memorial claimed 'over 1,100 Falkirk bairns' had died, but that figure included men from the surrounding area, including some from as far away as Bo'ness
3. This analysis could be done for Alloa [5.9], Causewayhead [6.2], Clackmannan [6.2], Denny [5.9], Sauchie [6.4] and Tullibody [6.3]
4. *Alloa Journal* 26 Dec 1914 p. 3 col. 1
5. *Alloa Journal* 7 July 1917 p. 2 col. 4
6. *Alloa Journal* 15 Oct 1915 p. 3 col. 1
7. *Alloa Journal* 20 Nov 1915 p. 3 col. 3
8. *Alloa Circular* 6 Oct 1915 p. 2 col. 6 had a fairly long and respectful piece on the three Maitland boys, showing that even the less prominent local families got a decent report in these circumstances
9. *Alloa Journal* 6 October 1917 p. 3 col. 3 and Burgh of Alloa Roll of Honour
10. One of these two families, the McEwans of Back O'Dykes, included a father and four sons serving
11. *Alloa Advertiser* 23 Sept 1916
12. Andrew McEwan is **not** listed at that address in either the 1901 or the 1911 census
13. *Alloa Advertiser* 18 May 1918 p. 2 col. 1
14. *Alloa Advertiser* 18 May 1918 p. 3 col. 4
15. See Chapter 14; he was awarded an MBE for it in February 1920. *Alloa Journal* 28 Feb 1920
16. For example, according to the Burgh of Alloa Roll of Honour; Lauchlan Gibb was boy 1st class, and Alexander McMillan and Robert Snowdowne were boy-seamen, and they survived: how old would they have been at that rank? To demonstrate that assumptions should not be made about age, rank or the accuracy of the Roll of Honour, it lists Cornelius McLaren as a boy-seaman [who was killed], yet his obituary in the *Alloa Journal* 4 Aug 1917 p. 2 col. 2 noted that he was in fact a telegrapher on a submarine and was in his 20th year
17. *Alloa Journal* 29 April 1916 p. 2 col. 5 reported on how well he had done in his class at Dartmouth, coming 4th out of 75 cadets

18. *Alloa Journal* 27 Oct 1917 p. 3 col. 3. The national census in April 1901 has him down as 8 months old
19. *Alloa Journal* 27 Feb 1915 p3. col. 7 shows that there could indeed be such a case. A 13-year-old boy from a local school enlisted in the 2nd Argylls as a junior bandsman and the issue was brought before the School Board because 'the Attendance Committee had refused to accept an application for exemption [from attending school] on his behalf'. They seemed to be well aware that a lot of boys of this age were 'desirous of enlisting' and it might open the floodgates if an exemption was given. The Chairman of the Committee felt that 'there does not seem to be any public interest served by children under fourteen enlisting' but this pupil was only three months away from leaving school anyway, so, after discussion, the School Board agreed to do nothing! We have no name for this youngster; did he ever go on to serve in action?
20. People think this is the original Dux Board because the names go back to 1898, but in fact it replaced a marble one in the late 1940s
21. This ship was originally called SS *Lady Patricia* before being requisitioned by the Admiralty and re-named as 'Q-25' or HMS *Paxton*. It was built by Ardrossan Drydock and Shipbuilding Company for an Irish buyer in 1916. See The Long, Long Trail website and www.wrecksite.eu for more details. HMS *Paxton* was only commissioned as a Q-ship on 1 May 1917, so it lasted not quite three weeks in action
22. *Alloa Journal* 2 June 1917 p. 2 col. 3
23. *Alloa Journal* 20 Oct 1917 p. 3 col. 4
24. *Alloa Journal* 18 May 1918 p. 3 col. 3 + p. 1 col. 3. The CWGC Register says he was 21 but the family obituary says 20

CHAPTER 13

ALLOA SOLDIERS IN BATTLE

More men from Alloa (297) served with the 7th Battalion of the Argyll and Sutherland Highlanders than with any other regiment and there are more names from that battalion (seventy-two) than any other on Alloa's war memorial.[1] In trying to answer the question of what were the key campaigns in which Alloa soldiers fought, it seems that we should look to where the 7th Argylls fought.[2]

Apart from the formal photographs of different companies of the battalion in front of Alloa Town Hall, there were few pictures of anything connected with the local regiment in the Alloa press, but this one image from June 1915 shows how much the fate of soldiers in the 7th Argylls mattered to the people of Alloa.

(*Alloa Circular*)

Like most regiments, the 7th Argylls published its own commemorative history after the war was over. It is a small book dedicated 'To the undying memory of the officers, non-commissioned officers, and men who fell during the Great War'. It contains a list of all 256 officers who were on active service, a year-by-year account of the Argylls' battlefield experiences, a list, with accompanying photographs, of 124 of the officers, followed by a much longer year-by-year list of all the 'other ranks' who were killed.

It is a poignant book in some ways (fifty of the officer photographs were of men killed in action and the list of names of 'other ranks' who were killed amounts to 795) but it also follows the conventions of the time, with the authors avoiding criticism of their own regiment and of anyone else by adopting a rather laconic style that reads more like a series of diary entries than any profound comment on the nature of warfare. However, here and there are more expressive passages, as shown by this description of the time the Argylls spent on the Somme; 'A more bleak and desolated countryside would be hard to imagine. The blackened and flattened ruins of Pozières, Courcellette and Contalmaison, the pathetic wooden noticeboard that alone marked the spot where Orvillers had been, the sombre blotches of charred, twisted and stunted trees where woods had once been green, the mud...all these combined to make war in that area a dismal horror.'[3] The 7th Argylls also kept a War Diary which gives a terse account of their exploits, including a day-by-day breakdown of casualties.

The local press was anxious to include reports of gallant military actions by 'our boys' but were not always able to obtain specific details. The first letters home and news of casualties often started to arrive two weeks or so after an event, so it is possible to get some idea of the scope and nature of the engagements in which the soldiers were involved.

Two epic battles in which they were involved stand out in the history of the 7th Argylls ; the month at the start of the 2nd Ypres Offensive in 1915 and the week at the end of the Somme Offensive in 1916.

2ND YPRES OFFENSIVE: FIRST GAS ATTACKS APRIL 1915

The 7th Argylls (a part of 10th Brigade) had their first experience of trench warfare on the Western Front in March 1915, when they held the line at Ploegsteert, south of Ypres. They had moved slightly further south and were preparing to make an attack on the German lines at Houplines near Armentieres when they heard of the first chlorine gas attack on 22 April 1915 to the north-east of Ypres. By a series of forced marches the Argylls arrived in the Ypres front line at 1.30am on 25 April,[4] to support the Canadians who had resisted the initial gas attacks.[5]

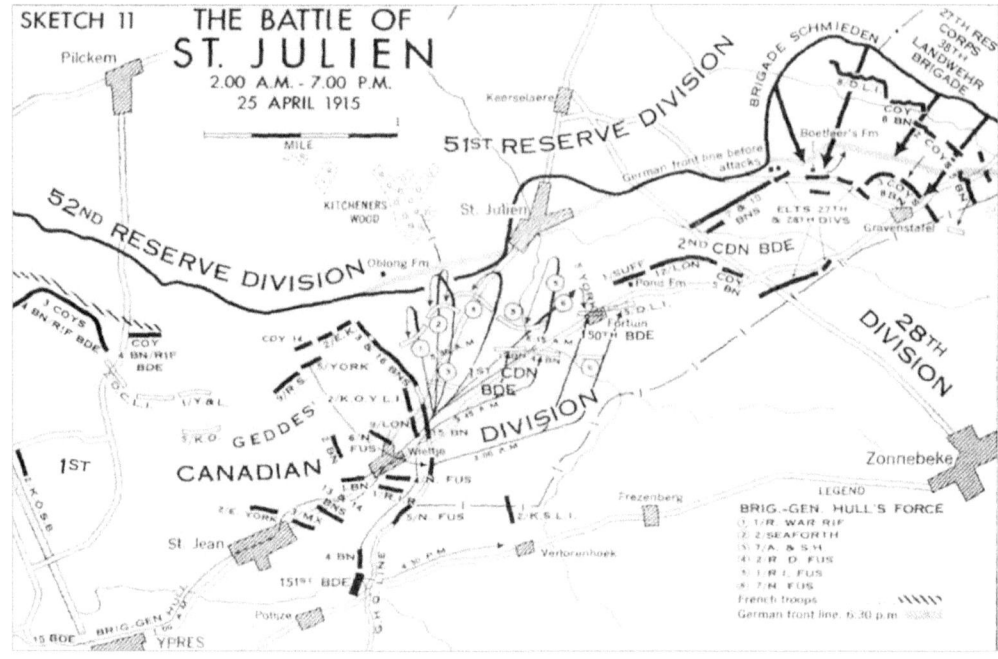

(Ministry of Public Works and Government Services, Canada)

It was a cold and rainy night and the battalion attacked the village of St Julien from the south-west, sustaining heavy casualties from well-positioned German machine guns 'in the upper storeys of some farm buildings'. As the Battalion's War Diary reported of one of their efforts; 'A Company went forward in small parties, the ground was very open and swept by a heavy fire. Few of them succeeded in reaching the firing line'.[6] The Argylls lost six officers and 100 men in that attack. As McWilliam and Steel comment; 'The 7th Argylls, the only non-regular soldiers in the 10th Brigade, were ordered to support the Seaforths and Warwickshires. They were exhorted by their Brigade Major, twice wounded, to 'Stick it out, Argylls'. They did that and lost 425 men and twelve officers that morning.'[7] These figures are confirmed in the War Diary and were total casualties, not just those killed in action. With a likelihood of having to face up to gas attacks, the battalion were issued with their first gas masks that week; just a pad of cotton waste enclosed in bags of mosquito netting, soaked in a soda solution. 'As a protection, they inspired little confidence.'[8]

The Alloa newspapers of 5 May were the first to give any information on this battle and it was quite generalised. The *Circular* commented that 'Although official information is not yet to hand, it is evident from letters and postcards received during the past and present week by relatives and friends of those on active service at the front, that the 7th Argyll and Sutherland Highlanders have passed through a severe engagement, as a result of which there are many casualties.'[9] Further down the same page, in a tribute to the loss of a local man, Lieut. Archie Gifford Moir, the *Circular* astutely commented that '...no authentic list of casualties has appeared, but when the officers have suffered in such numbers, it must be expected that the rank and file will provide a heavy casualty list...'[10] The *Advertiser* had the more dramatic headline of *The Disaster to the 7th Argylls*, and commented that 'the battalion suffered severely'.[11]

The 7th Argylls were there and elsewhere in the Ypres front line, including Hill 60, right until 7 May. On 1 May they were 'badly shelled by heavy guns during afternoon and had nine casualties'; and on 2 May were gassed with the result that 'Many of the men were quite useless from the effects of these gases, and some twenty-five men afterwards admitted to hospital suffering from these effects'.[12] After rest, the 7th Argylls went back into the line on 23 May and suffered a particularly heavy gas attack the following day, which 'bleached the sandbags, it withered the grass, it corroded the buttons on the men's tunics and jammed the mechanisms of their rifles'.[13] Their War Diary reported that 'At 3 am on 24th, while holding the fire trench, the enemy used their poisonous gas, with our battalion suffering very heavily, nearly 200 rank and file having to leave the trench. The trenches were heavily shelled the whole day.'[14] The Argylls suffered severe losses; nineteen out of twenty-four officers were casualties and both their Commanding Officer and second-in-command were killed.

By 8 May the *Journal*'s editorial back in Alloa was expressing everyone's worst fears about the Argylls' first military engagements, that 'Not since the beginning of the war has a gloom spread itself over this district to equal that which has been experienced this week... the dire results of Germany's scientific barbarism have now come too close to our own door...'[15] By 12 May the Alloa press was able to print news about a fairly substantial list of the April casualties, and were much better informed about the nature of the battle; commenting in many cases that the casualties were '...suffering from the effects of the poisonous gas used by the Germans'. The *Circular* devoted almost two columns to individual local casualties of the gas attacks[16] and by 9 June it confirmed that twenty-one local men had been killed, twenty-four wounded and fifteen gassed.[17]

As a consequence of the Argylls' losses, 'Major Schuster [Royal Irish Fusiliers] arrived to re-organise a composite battalion consisting of what was left of the 7th and 9th Argylls'.[18] On 29 May, they were taken out of the line for the next six months while the gaps in the ranks were filled. That gives a clear indication of the scale of loss suffered by the 7th Argylls in their first real taste of trench warfare around Ypres in 1915.[19]

THE SOMME: CAPTURE OF BEAUMONT HAMEL NOVEMBER 1916

The Battle of the Somme started on 1 July 1916, but the 7th Argylls, now part of 154th Brigade, were in trenches further north near Arras, along with the rest of the 51st Highland Division. They were only moved on 21 July to the Somme, where they took part in various actions at High Wood and Mametz Wood[20] before being sent back up to around Armentieres by October 1916. By the beginning of November the 7th Argylls were back in the Beaumont Hamel area of the Somme, just north of the River Ancre. Beaumont Hamel should have fallen on the first day of the offensive, but there they were, four months later and it was still in German hands. However, starting at 6.00am on 13 November 1916 and continuing through most of 14th as well, the 51st Highland Division attacked and captured 'the supposed impregnable fortress of Beaumont Hamel, with its almost ridiculous depth of intricate barbed wire entanglements, its fabulously deep cellars and caves, and its picked garrison of the best of the enemy's troops.'[21] The 7th Argylls War Diary gave a brief account of the first two days of action before ultimate success was achieved:

On 13 November 1916:

'At 11.15am A + D Coys under Capts Cunningham and Strang were ordered up to reinforce the 152 Inf. Brigade and took up position in dugouts Q10a. At 6pm the remainder of the Battn. were ordered up to reinforce 152 Inf. Brigade and took up position in dugouts Q10a. At 8pm A + D Coys were moved forward into BEAUMONT HAMEL to reinforce the 8th Arg and Suth High-ders in the old German 3rd line which was being consolidated... The village was wholly in our possession and third German line completely taken by 6pm.'[22]

The War Diary then outlined the continuing attack and some of the confusion on 14 November:

'At 3.00am B + C Coys under Captains Mitchell and AL Stewart were ordered forward into advanced line E. of BEAUMONT HAMEL. At 7.30am B + C Coys advanced to occupy MUNICH TRENCH. They moved up the hill in two waves of sections in file supported on either flank by bombing parties moving up BEAUMONT ALLEY + LEAVE AVENUE. The progress was very slow on account of the state of the ground, but at 8am MUNICH TRENCH was occupied with slight opposition and some prisoners were sent down... at 1.30pm forward Coys reported that they had to vacate MUNICH TRENCH on account of the shelling from our own guns and had withdrawn to the head of LEAVE AVENUE which they had consolidated and had thrown out advanced posts in shell holes. Machine guns were reported active in FRANKFURT TRENCH.'[23]

The Regimental History summed up the battle:

'It was literally an uphill fight. To walk over the ground after the battle was to be filled with amazement that men found it possible to get into contact with the enemy at all. Yet...they carried the whole objective strictly according to the timetable...' and 'It is worthy of note that on the 15th the 7th Argylls were 400 yards further forward (their flanks completely in the air) than any other troops on that part of the front.'[24]

The map below (taken from a website[25]) is more interested in the advance of the 1st KRR and 1st R Berks in the 2nd Division, but it also shows the position of 152nd Brigade as it attacked in an east to slightly north-easterly direction. The 7th Argylls (in 154th Brigade) were in their support; the position of their targets, Leave Avenue and Munich Trench, can be seen in the German trench system.

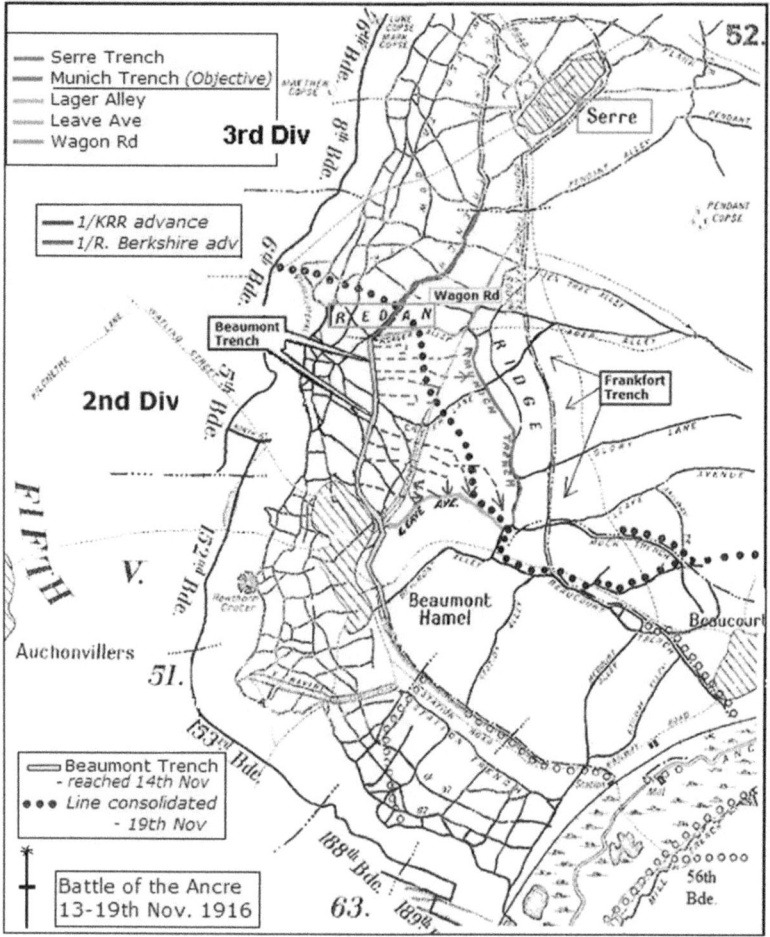

The *Journal* had news of this battle by 25 November, less than a fortnight after the actual event. Its article, under a heading of 'Local Argylls in Action', started by referring to the Argylls' previous moment of glory; '...the memorable 25 April 1915 when the Battalion received its disastrous baptism of fire at St Julien and resulted in over 400 casualties', but commented that since then it 'has been practically immune from serious loss'.[26]

It recognised, however, that its turn had come in November 1916, and the *Journal* was well aware that 'gallant work in the recent British advance' meant that 'local casualties are somewhat heavy', commenting 'Alas! that this brilliant feat of arms should have been accomplished at such cost.' As usual, the press seemed to acquire its information mainly through details sent back to Britain about officer casualties; and it extrapolated from there. There was a fairly precise and extensive piece about the circumstances of the death of a local officer, Capt. Robert Strang,[27] in the battle (possibly via letters from fellow officers or the military clergyman who conducted his funeral, since his name is specified in the account) and this enabled the press to build up a better general picture than would otherwise have been the case.

On 25 November, the *Journal* included an annotated photograph of the officers of the 7th Argylls which was helpful to readers who were anxious to work out which of them had been killed.[28] However, there was surprisingly little further information about this glorious battle in the local press in subsequent weeks.

The anniversary of 13 November 1916 was still commemorated by surviving soldiers from the 7th Argylls until the 1930s as 'Beaumont Hamel Day', in recognition of that famous victory.[29] At the end of the war, 51st Highland Division chose to locate their war memorial overlooking Y Ravine, Hawthorn Ridge and Beaumont Hamel, in recognition of their achievement at this spot. The memorial was unveiled by France's supreme military commander, Marshall Ferdinand Foch, on 28 September 1924,[30] on the very same day that Britain's supreme military commander, Field Marshall Sir Douglas Haig, was unveiling Alloa's war memorial in Bedford Place.

An early picture of the 51st Highland Division's memorial in the still desolate Somme landscape, which later became the memorial site of Newfoundland Park. The figure faces east, looking over Y Ravine towards Beaumont Hamel and the enemy positions.

The sculptor was the Clackmannanshire-born George Henry Paulin, who also designed several local war memorials such as those in Dollar, Coalsnaughton and Muckhart.

The 7th Argylls had many more opportunities for heroic effort in World War I; indeed, their war memorial in Princes Street, Stirling records eighteen occasions where their military contribution was considered significant enough to be awarded a regimental battle honour.[31]

ENDNOTES

1. Burgh of Alloa Roll of Honour. The Supplement of 4th October 1924 records that 132 soldiers from Alloa who were in the Argylls died, but they were not all in the 7th Battalion
2. Alloa's local battalion should more properly be called the 1st/7th Argylls. It was a Territorial battalion, but as it expanded during the war there was a 2nd/7th and 3rd/7th as well.
3. 7th Battalion Argylls Regimental History p. 24
4. Map found at http://cefresearch.com/matrix/Nichol...n/Chapter3.pdf
5. 7th Battalion Argylls Regimental History p. 10
6. War Diary of 7th Argyll and Sutherland Highlanders 25 April 1915
7. *Gas, The First Battle For Ypres*, 1915 by J. McWilliams and R.J. Steel [1985] p. 165
8. 7th Battalion Argylls Regimental History p. 10
9. *Alloa Circular* 5 May 1915 p. 3 col. 4
10. *Alloa Circular* 5 May 1915 p. 3 col. 4
11. *Alloa Advertiser* 8 May 1915
12. War Diary of 7th Argyll and Sutherland Highlanders 1 May 1915 and 2 May 1915
13. 7th Battalion Argylls Regimental History p. 16
14. War Diary of 7th Argyll and Sutherland Highlanders 24 May 1915
15. *Alloa Journal* 8 May 1915 p. 2 col. 4
16. *Alloa Circular* 2 June 1915 in column called 'The War'
17. *Alloa Circular* 9 June 1915 in column called 'The War'
18. War Diary of 7th Argyll and Sutherland Highlanders 29 May 1915
19. For more information see *Gas, The First Battle For Ypres*, 1915 by J. McWilliams and R.J. Steel [1985]
20. 7th Battalion Argylls Regimental History p. 18
21. 7th Battalion Argylls Regimental History p. 20
22. War Diary of 7th Argyll and Sutherland Highlanders 13 Nov 1916
23. War Diary of 7th Argyll and Sutherland Highlanders 14 Nov 1916
24. 7th Battalion Argylls Regimental History pp. 20 +22
25. Map found on internet at answers.net.nz/Other/W2.htm
26. *Alloa Journal* 25 Nov 1916 p. 2 col. 5
27. Capt. Strang's father was the Provost of Alloa during the first years of the war
28. *Alloa Journal* 25 Nov 1916 p. 3 col. 3
29. After the war, Pipe-Major John McLellan [1875-1949] who served with the 51st Highland Division in World War I composed a march for the bagpipes in honour of this famous victory. It was called 'The Taking of Beaumont Hamel'
30. It was no surprise that Marshall Foch did the unveiling. He had personally paid a glowing tribute to the 51st Highland Division in 1918 just after the Schelte-Sambre battle. His tribute was reported at length in *Alloa Advertiser* 23 Nov 1918 p. 4 cols. 3-4
31. 7th Battalion Argylls Regimental History p. 56 [plus photo]

CHAPTER 14

REMEMBERING THE BRAVE

It is invidious to read the list of all the men of Alloa who served then select a few who might be regarded as the 'real' heroes, while all the rest are forgotten. The Roll of Honour published by Alloa Burgh Council after the war includes at the end a list of all the medal winners in a sort of ranked order, though only for gallantry medals, not service/campaign medals. However, even the introduction to the medals list indicates how the Burgh Council grappled with what to say to show due respect to the medal winners without demeaning those who had none. In the end they wrote, rather elegantly, 'The men who faced the foe, conscious of the righteousness of the cause were heroes all... Nevertheless in the Great Struggle some did acts of conspicuous heroism and endurance, and these the King delighted to honour.' This chapter on Alloa's bravest men is therefore based on that list. After the war was over, the local press wanted to know which Alloa serviceman had been the first to win a medal for gallantry. It turned out to be Farrier-Sergeant John Paterson of 6th Dragoon Guards, who won the DCM in April 1915[1] and survived the war.

These are the statistics from the Burgh of Alloa Roll of Honour, for the award of gallantry medals to servicemen and women who came from Alloa:

Victoria Cross (VC)	2	(one posthumous)
Distinguished Service Order (DSO)	3	
Military Cross (MC) and bar	2	
Military Cross (MC)	20	
Distinguished Flying Cross (DFC)	2	
Military Medal (MM) and bar	3	
Military Medal	40	
Distinguished Conduct Medal (DCM)	9	

Distinguished Service Medal (DSM)	2	
Meritorious Service Medal (MSM)	10	
Mentioned in Despatches twice	7	
Mentioned in Despatches	29	
Mons Star	32	(10 posthumous) no officers in the original 32
1914-1915 Star	278	(113 posthumous)]

VICTORIA CROSS

This is Britain's highest award for gallantry; to win it, the heroic action that earns it must be 'in the face of the enemy'. 628 VCs were awarded during World War I; 159 were posthumous. It was considered remarkable that such a small town as Alloa had two VC winners.

James Lennox Dawson VC

James Lennox Dawson was originally from Tillicoultry but moved to Alloa at an early age and attended Alloa Academy between 1903 and 1909[2]; he was Admission No. 104.[3] He lived at 35 Paton Street. He was a matriculated student of Glasgow University in 1909/10 and 1912/13, studying different branches of Chemistry. However, he had regular re-sits for his exams, and even though he had not completed his degree he became a Science teacher at Hill's Trust School in Govan.[4] Following the outbreak of war, he enlisted in the 5th Scottish Rifles in October 1914 and was serving in the trenches with them at Bois Grenier from March 1915, but was compulsorily transferred to the Royal Engineers in May 1915. He was part of a special section involved in gas warfare. He was a Corporal at the time of winning the VC at Loos but had become Acting Company Sergeant Major in 187th Company of Royal Engineers by the time of the public announcement of his VC, before taking a commission in March 1916[5] and rising to Lieutenant (temporary Captain) by the end of the War.[6]

James Lennox Dawson, detail from photograph (*Glasgow Bulletin*)

His citation reveals just how brave his action was. It read:

> 'For most conspicuous bravery and devotion to duty on October 13, 1915, at Hohenzollern Redoubt. During a gas attack, when the trenches were full of men, he walked backwards and forwards along the parados, fully exposed to a very heavy fire, in order to be the better able to give directions to his own sappers, and to clear the infantry out of the sections of the trench that were full of gas. Finding three leaking gas cylinders, he rolled them some 16 yards away from the trench, again under very heavy fire, and then fired rifle bullets into them to let the gas escape. There is no doubt that the cool gallantry of Corporal Dawson on this occasion saved many men from being gassed.'

The Alloa press were naturally ecstatic about the news that a local man had got the VC, the *Circular* commenting that 'There was quite a furore of gratification throughout the town yesterday morning when it became known...'[7] The *Circular*'s representatives visited him at his house and 'found him loath to talk about his action, which he appeared to look upon as a simple act of duty calling for no reward or special recognition.'[8] He received his VC from King George V in an informal ceremony, due to the King's ill health, on 15 December 1915, when the King 'heartily commended his coolness and pluck'.[9] Dawson then came to Alloa on leave for most of the rest of December and received a hero's welcome. He was met at Alloa Station by a military band and a 150-strong military guard of honour. He was then given a procession round the town in a horse-drawn carriage through mass crowds of cheering spectators,[10] followed by an official reception in Alloa Town Hall on 23 December, where Lord Mar presented him with a gold watch.[11]

During his time of leave[12] he visited all the local Alloa schools and had photographs taken outside his parent's house in Paton Street. He also visited his old school in Govan and was photographed with the pupils. He was given such a rousing reception that he was heard asking the Headteacher 'For goodness sake keep them in until I get away'.[13]

He returned to the front, where he suffered gunshot wounds to one of his hands in July 1916 and spent some time in Rouen Red Cross Hospital.[14] There are no other references to his subsequent military career in the Alloa press. The Burgh of Alloa Roll of Honour recorded him at the rank of Lieutenant. He returned to Glasgow University in 1920 and gained a BSc, having written to Professor Milligan expressing the wish to have the degree of BSc in Pure Science granted without having to present himself

Dawson's family home in Paton Street (*Glasgow Bulletin*)

at the forthcoming degree examinations, as a wartime concession.[15] He subsequently re-joined the army as an education officer. He served many years in the Indian Army and died in 1967 in Eastbourne, East Sussex. His VC was bequeathed to Glasgow University and is kept in the Coin Room of the Hunterian.

His VC has the date of his action engraved on the back of the cross; his name is engraved on the back of the bar.

Interestingly, his War Medal and Victory Medal, both of which have his name and army number engraved around the edge, have him at the rank of Major. So too did the *Advertiser* in its Supplement of 28 June 1919, when it reported on the Local Heroes Welcome-Home.

Dawson's medal collection (*The Hunterian Museum, University of Glasgow*)

John Crawford Buchan VC

The public story of John Crawford Buchan began well before his heroic death in 1918. He seems to have been quite a character from an early age. He was a pupil at Alloa Academy between 1905 and 1909 (Admission No. 286).[16] He was in fact signed off on the register on the same day as James Lennox Dawson; 10 September 1909. They were very close contemporaries at school, only ten months separating their ages; indeed, John Buchan's elder sister Jessie was in the same class as James Dawson.

Alloa Academy had a Literary and Debating Society in the first sixty odd years of the 20th century. It was attended by the senior pupils and a few interested staff. The pupils were generally the very pro-school group who felt they were getting a little more from their education by being able to debate issues like Votes for Women and Irish Home Rule and mix with the staff more informally. However, there were also social occasions in the evening. At one of them in 1910 it was recorded that 'Mr John Buchan gave a most amusing ventriloquial entertainment, with his funny little figure. ...'[17] Six months later at their annual social event it was mentioned that 'A neat and original little sketch was played by Messrs Buchan and Young and Miss Jessie Buchan, and Mr Buchan also gave a humourous ventriloquial exhibition...'[18] He capped this at the annual musical evening in December 1911 when 'Mr John Buchan, in his inimitable ventriloquial entertainment, kept the company in roars of laughter'.[19]

So, for a couple of years, while he was a senior pupil at the school, John Buchan entertained his fellow pupils with his slightly off-beat talent for ventriloquism,[20] before leaving school to try his hand firstly at law, then as a journalist. He had a helping hand with the latter because his father and uncle were joint proprietors of the *Alloa Advertiser*, so he hoped to be able to offer them his first articles. There is, however, no mention of him in the local press in the early years of the war, although his elder brother David got a few references for his military career, and both his elder sisters because of their VAD work at Arnsbrae Hospital. The first time John's name cropped up was when he received his commission in the Argylls on 25 January 1917,[21] and one might wonder what he had been doing until then.

J.C. Buchan (*Alloa Advertiser*)

In April 1918 he was reported as 'wounded and missing in action' (since 22 March) and a little more of his background now started to appear in the local newspaper articles.[22] It was noted that he had been on holiday in Switzerland when war broke out and was unable to get a passport to return to Britain for a whole year, facing instead a period of 'unrestricted civil internment'.[23] It has been suggested that he was a YMCA camp worker before the war and initially had pacifist tendencies. This story was of course not covered in the local press, which would have been far more interested in promoting his heroic and patriotic credentials. Upon his return to the UK in August 1915, he instantly enlisted in London and joined the Royal Army Medical Corps as a private. It is unclear whether his time in the RAMC included overseas battlefield service, before he received his commission. He had been at the front as a Second-Lieutenant since 4 October 1917, 'coming through several minor engagements unscathed'.[24] He then took part in the fierce fighting to resist the German attack known as the Ludendorff Offensive in March 1918. It was here, towards the east of the Somme Area, that he lost his life on 22 March 1918, the day after the heroic action that led to his award of a posthumous Victoria Cross. It was only towards the end of May that news of his VC came through. The *Advertiser* commented that 'His conduct on that occasion seems to have been courageous and gallant beyond all praise…',[25] and the citation confirms this.

His award was gazetted on 22 May 1918 (Page No. 6058)[26] and the fairly long citation reads:

'For most conspicuous bravery and devotion to duty. When fighting with his platoon in the forward position of the battle zone, Second-Lieutenant Buchan, although wounded early in the day insisted on remaining with his men, and continually visited all his posts, encouraging and cheering his men in spite of most severe shellfire, from which his platoon was suffering heavy casualties.

Later, when the enemy were creeping closer and heavy machine gun fire was raking his position, Sec. Lt. Buchan, with utter disregard for his own personal safety, continued to visit his posts, and although still further injured accidentally, he continued to encourage his men and visit his posts. Eventually when he saw that the enemy had practically surrounded his command, he collected his platoon and prepared to fight his way back to his supporting line. At this point the enemy, who had crept round his right flank, rushed towards him shouting out 'Surrender'. 'To hell with surrender' he replied, and shooting the foremost of the enemy, he finally repelled this advance with his platoon. He then fought his way back to the supporting line of the forward position, where he held out till dusk.

At dusk he fell back as ordered, but in spite of his injuries again refused to go to the aid post, saying his place was beside his men. Owing to the unexpected withdrawal of troops on the left flank, it was impossible to send orders to Sec. Lieut. Buchan to withdraw, as he was already cut off, and he was last seen holding out against overwhelming odds.

The gallantry, self-sacrifice and utter disregard for personal safety displayed by this officer during these two days of most severe fighting, is in keeping with the highest traditions of the British Army.'

21 March 1918 was a miserable day for the British 5th Army, when most units retreated in the face of the sudden and unexpected German onslaught. Buchan's action was a small beacon of success in an otherwise forgettable day and the citation itself, while being unusually honest about the battlefield confusion of those two days, may be forgiven for perhaps over-emphasising the resolute fighting spirit and sense of duty that Buchan was showing when everyone else was running away.[27]

The *Alloa Journal* reported that there was doubt about whether such an 'impassioned utterance' as 'To hell with surrender' could have come from the mouth of such a temperate fellow as Lieut. Buchan.[28] His sister apparently had been angry when she heard what he had said because their mother had taught her boys never to swear.[29] The *Journal* however, argued that 'in supreme moments of life, when nervous tensions are high, both speech and actions sometimes take unaccustomed channels...'[30]

Tributes continued to be paid; a mixture of congratulation for the heroism of the deed, combined with sympathies to his father and siblings for his apparent loss in battle, though this had still not been confirmed.

The Burgh Council 'made a suitable reference in the minutes'[31] to the heroic deed and it is evident that some Councillors were looking for a way to create a permanent memorial of the event. Dr Ferguson, Convenor of the Library Book Committee, had become aware that *Sphere* magazine in London had commissioned an heroic sketch of John Buchan's action for the 22 June 1918 issue, so he brought an imaginative proposal before the Council. The result was that the Council purchased **the original** *Sphere* drawing by Fortunino Matania and somehow obtained the original copy of the Army order, signed by General Holman,[32] recounting how Buchan had won the VC; and they were put together in a finely carved oak mount, framed and hung in the library in the Town Hall.

The project was financed from the Common Good Fund, on the grounds that

Buchan's gallant behaviour was an inspiring example for Alloa's citizens and they would all benefit from seeing the memorial.³³ The Burgh Council lost no time in getting this commemorative work under way and there was a fine original photograph and a full account of its unveiling in the *Advertiser* dated 15 February 1919. For about eighty years this memorial continued to hang in the former library and later former reading room (now the Tommy Downs Room) in Alloa Town Hall, but in 1999 the original illustration and Army order were removed and replaced with copies to prevent further damage from light exposure.³⁴

John Buchan was finally declared 'missing believed killed' in December 1918. His body was in fact found quite some distance from the site of his action east of Marteville and he had possibly been moved there to receive medical treatment. He is buried at Roisel Communal Extension Cemetery.³⁵

His father and eldest sister Meg went to Buckingham Palace in March 1920 to collect the Victoria Cross from King George V. The King presented over 300 different awards at the ceremony and it was witnessed by over 400 friends and relatives of the various recipients.³⁶ The presentation of John Buchan's VC to his father was however, a private ceremony; the King was well aware of the grief that could overcome parents when being handed their dead son's medal. The King was probably correct; by that time many say that David Buchan was a broken man, having lost three of his five sons in the war. John Buchan's VC remained within the family

John Buchan's CWGC headstone at Roisel, with its VC cross

until November 2000, when his niece presented it to the Argyll and Sutherland Highlanders Museum in Stirling Castle to be displayed with their VC collection.[37]

A 1989 photo of John Buchan's VC in its original case

DISTINGUISHED SERVICE ORDER

8,981 DSOs were awarded in World War I, usually to officers of the rank of Major and above. It was often awarded for leadership skills in the battlefield area (ie often to the much maligned staff officers) rather than as an award for a specific act of bravery in a battlefield situation. It all depended on the rank of the soldier when it was awarded. In certain circumstances the DSO could be awarded to a more junior officer for battlefield bravery and then it was regarded as a 'near-miss VC'. Alloa's three winners of the DSO were all fairly high-ranking – Majors or Lieutenant-Colonels – when they won the award.

Robert Gifford Moir was awarded his DSO in June 1918 when already a Colonel in the 2nd Argylls, but he had won an MC in June 1915 when he was still a Lieutenant[38] and in charge of the grenade contingent of his battalion.[39] He received his MC from the King in early 1916 and was promoted to Captain.[40] The *Scotsman* pointed out that 'He has experienced a good deal of hard and dangerous fighting. So far he has escaped unwounded'.[41] The citation for his DSO hints that his leadership skills over possibly a prolonged time were being rewarded,[42] noting that he 'kept his battalion up to a high standard of fighting spirit...' This man, it should be remembered, was a career soldier who had only left the local Territorials in February 1914 to go to Sandhurst,[43] had served and been promoted throughout the war, was twice mentioned in dispatches and was seriously injured (his right arm was fractured in two places) in July

R.G. Moir (*Argyll and Sutherland Highlanders Museum, Stirling*)

1918.[44] He was sufficiently highly regarded in Alloa at the time for a military march to be composed and named after him. The *Journal* noted that the inclusion of this piece in the Alloa Band's repertoire in July 1918 may have helped to 'draw the exceptionally large turnout to the West End Park'.[45] A brave man indeed, who also served in World War II and rose to the rank of Brigadier. His medals are on display in the Argyll and Sutherland Highlanders Museum in Stirling Castle.

LOCAL FATHER AND SON DECORATED BY THE KING

The above is a photo taken at Buckingham Palace of Captain A. P. Moir, and his son Lieut.-Colonel R. Gifford Moir, who were decorated by the King at the Investiture last Friday. The former received the M.B.E, and the latter the D.S.O. Mrs A. P. Moir and Miss Gifford Moir are the ladies in the picture.

This charming picture appeared in the *Journal* for 28 February 1920

It shows Lieut. Col Robert Gifford Moir, who had just collected his DSO from King George V at the same time as his father was awarded an MBE for his services in organising the home front in Alloa during the war.[46]

Robert's mother and sister 'did their bit' in the war, his mother occasionally helping to launch ships and his sister Margaret often being one of the main vocalists at wartime fund-raising events.

James Younger was acting Lieutenant Colonel in the 14th Black Watch in September 1918 when he got his DSO.[47] He had moved by then from the campaigns in the Middle East and was serving in the eastern section of the Somme. He may have been an officer towards the rear of the lines, but the citation noted that 'During the operation at Moislains on September 2 1918, when a strong enemy counter attack was developed and a heavy barrage put down by them, he at once went forward through the barrage and steadied and reorganised the battalion. He was severely wounded in doing so but continued to command until relieved. He behaved most gallantly.'[48] He was also twice mentioned in despatches.[49]

Lt Colonel Peter Cram of the 4th Queen's Own Cameron Highlanders had already been appointed Major in February 1916,[50] so he was a high ranking officer for most of the war. He went to France on 23 March 1915,[51] he was wounded in October 1915 whilst still a Captain,[52] was mentioned twice in dispatches[53] and his DSO was gazetted on 3 June 1919. There was no citation in the *London Gazette*, but that was true of all the other DSOs on that page (p. 6818). Sometimes there was no citation due to an involvement in a more undercover operation (in Ireland, for instance) but it was often simply due to the backlog of awards to be granted. Very many DSOs were being gazetted as late as 1920 for acts of bravery or leadership that had taken place in the last six months of the war. He received his DSO from the King in late November 1919.[54]

MILITARY CROSS

37,104 servicemen in World War I won the Military Cross, but only 2,984 won it with a bar (ie earning the same gallantry medal again by performing a second specific act of bravery under fire or in the presence of the enemy). An additional 172 servicemen won either two or three bars. It is noteworthy that the two Alloa men who were awarded the MC and bar each won both of them in the same year.

Captain Charles Park MC and bar

Charles Enverdale Park came from Edinburgh as a young lad to live in Dirleton Gardens, Alloa. All the children of the family enrolled at Alloa Academy Primary Dept. on the same day (24 November 1890), when Charles was five.[55] His Admission number was 454, but he left to go to Sunnyside Primary School, before being re-admitted five years later as No. 903.[56] On leaving school he did an engineering apprenticeship. He was working in South Africa but returned to Britain before war started and was manager of an engineering works in Wantage. When war was declared he enlisted as a private in the 9th Seaforth Highlanders,[57] but by early 1915 had become a Lieutenant in the same regiment.[58] He transferred to the Royal Engineers and went to France.

The local press, as was so often the case, had little detailed information on what he had done to win his first Military Cross in June 1916. The *Advertiser* was no more specific than saying that 'In an action in which his battalion took a prominent part, he displayed both coolness and bravery. Recently he had the opportunity of again distinguishing himself on the battlefield and he took full advantage of it... with the result that he was recommended for the Military Cross by his Commanding Officer.'[59] That was hardly very enlightening and the *Journal* was unable to add much more, apart from noting that the award of the MC had been announced in 'The King's birthday honours list...for distinguished service in the field'.[60] Even by the end of July 1916, when he actually received his MC from the King, the *Advertiser* could find nothing new to say about either the recipient or the action in which he won the award, though they published quite a nice photograph of him.[61]

Charles Park
(*Alloa Advertiser*)

Charles won the bar to his MC for his gallant actions on the Somme in November 1916. Without actually quoting the citation, the local press did at least this time know what he had done. Both the local papers wrote that the award of the bar to his MC was due to 'Bravery for rescuing a party of 16 men from a mine where they had become entombed, the rescue being performed under sniping and machine gun fire. We further learn that Lt. Park's company was in the big push on the Ancre [where] he along with another officer and five men captured 49 prisoners...'[62] He was a Temporary Second Lieutenant at the time of both his heroic actions.

Nothing more is known of his subsequent wartime career. Having won his two MCs, his name does not appear again in the local press. It appears that he was promoted to Captain by the end of the war, since that was the rank he was given in the Burgh of Alloa Roll of Honour.

Captain Fred Proudfoot MC and bar

Fred Proudfoot was another former pupil of Alloa Academy (Admission No. 484)[63] but he was not a local man, or even Scottish. Fred's father was the Alloa Postmaster, but came from Carlisle to take up these duties in 1907. He had four sons, of whom Fred was the youngest: another of them, Arthur, won his own Military Cross on Easter Monday 1917, on the same day as Fred won his first one.[64]

Fred had joined the local battalion of the 7th Argylls in peace-time as a Territorial, when he was only sixteen. He was a sergeant aged twenty when the war broke out and went over to France with them in December 1914.[65] He took part in their April/May 1915 engagements at St Julien and Hill 60, and was severely wounded in the right arm.[66] He was commissioned into the 9th Black Watch in September 1915, and the *Advertiser* of 1 July 1916 noted that he had passed first class at the School of Musketry.[67]

He received a bayonet wound to the right foot in April 1917; this may have been at the same time as the action that gained him his first Military Cross. He spent a time in Le Touquet Hospital in April 1917.[68] It was only in June 1917 that the citation was published for that MC. It read: 'For conspicuous gallantry and devotion to duty. He assumed command of and gallantly led his company forward in the face of heavy fire. Later, although wounded, he successfully led his men to the second objective.'[69]

The local press in September 1917 was full of the news of the announcement of a bar to Fred's Military Cross,[70] but they had no specific information on what he had done to earn it. That only emerged when the *Gazette* published the citation in January 1918. It read: 'For conspicuous gallantry and devotion to duty. When the officer commanding the attacking troops had become a casualty, he took charge and handled two companies in a most masterful manner. He led them with the utmost courage to the capture of all their objectives, under heavy hostile fire of every description, consolidating his position through a strong counter-attack, which he beat off with heavy loss to the enemy, and personally led two successful attacks on concrete gun emplacements, which were delaying the whole advance. He displayed exceptional gallantry and fine leadership.'[71]

He collected **both** of his MCs from King George V in a ceremony at Buckingham Palace on 25 July 1918.[72] Fred was promoted to Captain in October 1917 (confirmed in July 1918).[73]

In June 1989 I was fortunate enough to visit Fred's daughter, Mrs J.M. Fowler, to interview her about her father's career. Fred Proudfoot had married Jessie Buchan, an elder sister of John Buchan VC,[74] and Jessie had inherited her dead brother's VC which had now passed to Mrs Fowler, whose brother had inherited their father's two MCs. She told me that like many old soldiers he did not talk much about his wartime life, perhaps just remembering more light-hearted escapades like the story of the gramophone he and his fellow officers liked to have in their dugout, which got packed up in a box labelled 'Whisky', so that someone would always think it was important enough to be carried carefully to the officers' next destination. There was another story of the officers finding a skeleton and Fred getting dressed in a white sheet and carrying the skeleton in front of him to frighten a group of fellow officers at their dinner, though one of them shot at Fred. She remembered him making a more reflective comment,, in reference to a regimental group photograph taken at the time of the Somme, that 'there were only two officers left; that was all, of the company.'

Captain Jeffrey Home-Hay MC DFC

The Home-Hays of Linden House, The Walk, Alloa were a prominent local professional family. The father, John, was a well-respected Doctor with a big family; Jeffrey was the second son, with three brothers and two sisters. He was a former pupil of Alloa Academy (Admission No. 678).[75] After leaving school he trained locally as an engineer with Jeffrey's Shipyard, but went to Canada to take up farming with his elder brother John.[76] He joined up in December 1914, in the Machine-gun section of the Second Contingent of the Canadian Force in Winnipeg.[77] Incredibly, it is still possible to see a copy of his attestation papers for the Canadian Army (see page 260).[78]

He went to the Western Front and served as a private for nine months in the trenches before applying for a commission. By February 1916 he became a Second Lieutenant in the Argylls[79], but was not there long before he transferred to the Royal Flying Corps and, after six months training, by January 1917 was back on the Western Front as a pilot[80] He soon made his mark; the local press were proud to announce that he had won the Military Cross in June 1917[81] and that he was already a Flight Commander of his own squadron.

His citation was printed in the *Journal*: 'For conspicuous gallantry and devotion to duty. He showed consistent ability and courage in observing for and ranging our artillery on enemy guns and trenches. His accurate information was of the greatest value to our batteries.'[82] Rather than quoting the citation verbatim, the *Advertiser* rather more enjoyably and graphically reported what he had done: 'He swooped down on an enemy battery on its way to the front, and at great personal risk dispersed the gunners, and afterwards informed his own artillery of the exact location of the battery which was subsequently smashed by British big guns.'[83] He received his MC from King George V at Buckingham Palace.

After six months' further service he was transferred back to Salisbury Plain to train pilots[84] but that cannot have lasted long, because by June 1918 he was back in the

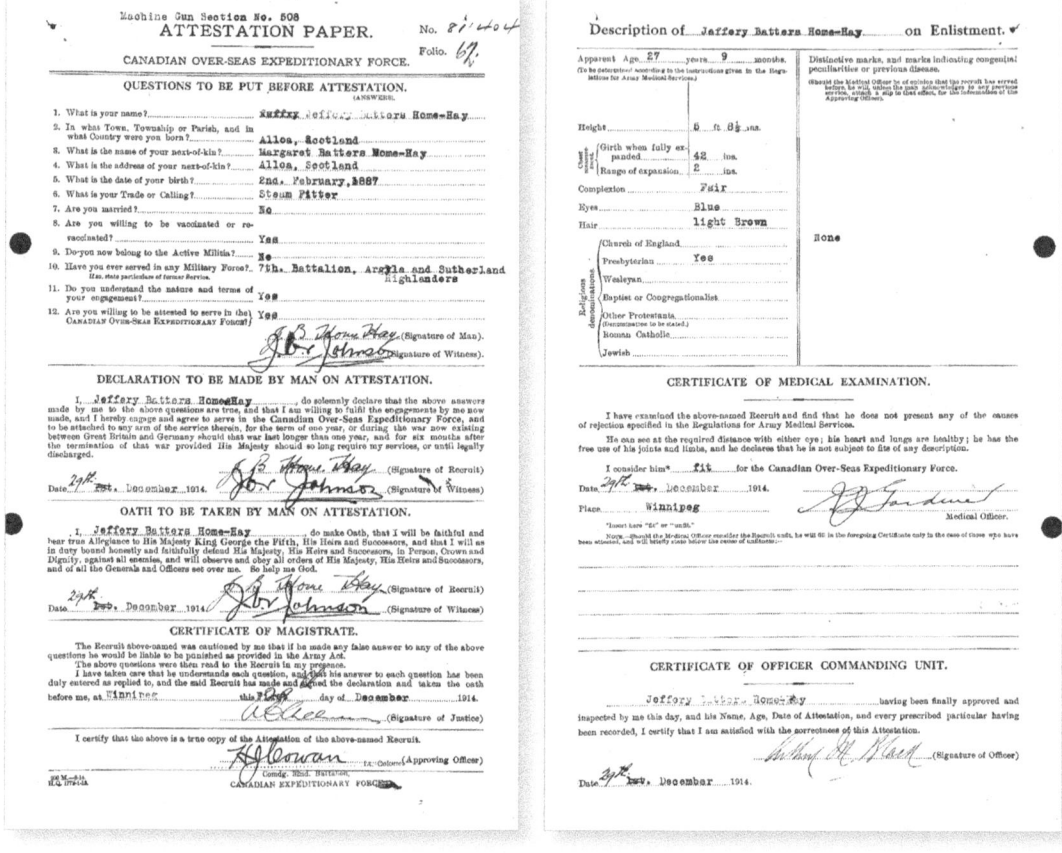

battlefield areas of the Western Front[85] and by 3 August 1918 he had been awarded the Distinguished Flying Cross.[86] He must have been a very early recipient of this new medal, which only started in June 1918 and was only awarded to about 1,100 men in World War I.

The DFC is similar to the MC in the level of gallantry required to win it; the citation suggested just how brave Jeffrey was and shared some similarities with the action when he won his MC. It read:

'This officer displayed admirable coolness and resource while leading a raid on an enemy railway station. His formation was heavily attacked by seven enemy aeroplanes but keeping it well in hand, he fought his way to his objective; proceeding well over the station he successfully bombed it. In the course of the severe fighting two enemy machines were shot down out of control, one of which he himself brought down. He has taken part in eight other raids and his consistent gallantry is a valuable asset in maintaining the morale of his new squadron.'[87]

He was reported missing after being shot down on 2 August 1918, but a fellow officer reported that his aircraft had come down under control and that there was every likelihood of him being a prisoner.[88] It was confirmed by late September that he was a POW at Karlsruhe.[89]

A Canadian newspaper gave a little more information about him, writing:

'He led air raids on such towns as Mannheim, Karlsruhe, Mets, and Offenburg by the 104th squadron. While engaged in an attack on Karlsruhe the radiator of his plane was riddled by a German airman. He managed to land safely, but in German territory, and was taken prisoner and kept a captive till 15 December 1918.'[90]

Jeffrey Home-Hay may have become 'lost to history' in the UK, but Canada was very proud of him and there are a couple of websites about Canadian flying heroes which give much more detail about him, including the information that he was a genuine 'ace' having shot down seven enemy aircraft.[91] The same website shows how August 1918 was a pretty good month for him, before he was shot down himself, since five of his seven 'kills' occurred between 11–15 August, with two on the same day. He shot down all of these enemy planes whilst flying an Airco DH9a.[92] None of this information seems to have been available to the Alloa newspapers at that time.[93] He only collected his DFC in November 1919, once he was back in Canada, receiving it from the Prince of Wales at Regina, Saskatchewan.[94]

MONS STAR

The Burgh of Alloa Roll of Honour contains the details of the thirty-two local recipients of the first campaign medal of the war, which was given to any soldier who had served in the European battlefield area between 5 August 1914 and 23 November 1914. 365,000 Mons Stars were given to soldiers who were generally the 'regulars'; men in the original BEF (British Expeditionary Force) that went out to France, starting about two weeks after war was declared.

The men from Alloa who gained this medal were therefore NOT in the local regiment, the 7th Argylls, a Territorial battalion which was not part of the original BEF and did not embark for France until 16 December 1914.[95] It is curious that the fairly high local loss rate for the Mons Star – almost one in three were awarded the medal posthumously – is *lower* than that for those Alloa soldiers who went out later and were only entitled to the 1914–15 Star, (loss rate almost 1 in 2.5). There is a widespread belief that most of the original BEF was wiped out by Christmas 1914, but for Alloa at least (assuming some degree of accuracy in the Burgh of Alloa Roll of Honour), two thirds of the local men who went out to fight in the first three months of the war survived to get their medal in 1919.

Over 2.3 million soldiers, or their next of kin, for a posthumous award, received the 1914–15 Star.

THE WAR GRAVES IN ALLOA'S CEMETERIES

All of the servicemen mentioned so far in this chapter on bravery were officers. That seems 'rough justice' to all those in the 'other ranks' who are neglected. However, as noted earlier, this account has just followed the medal ranking given by the Burgh of Alloa Roll of Honour and it would take another whole book to tell the stories of how all the other eighty-four Alloa men's bravery awards were won. It is also worth mentioning that, apart from the three DSO winners, **all** the heroic soldiers mentioned so far in this chapter started as 'common soldiers' before being promoted through the ranks.

However, Alloa did in fact have four soldiers from the 'other ranks' who each won a pair of medals for gallantry.[96] There was virtually no explanatory information about the soldiers or their actions in the wartime local press apart from, in some cases, the announcement of their awards. Their names were:

Corporal John B. Gow MM and Bar	Royal Engineers	14 Greenside St
Private Frank K. Mason MM and Bar	2nd Argylls	17 Kelliebank
Lance Corporal James Thomson MM and Bar	7th Black Watch	8 Craigward
Lance Corporal James Brown MM DCM	3rd Sherwood Foresters	5 Drysdale St

To partly rectify the omission of the bravery and sacrifice of the 'common soldier' it seems fitting that this chapter should be concluded by a reminder that readers can pay their respects at the graves of First World War soldiers in Alloa. It is not necessary to understand bravery by looking at medal hauls – standing in front of the war graves of young men also shows what they sacrificed. Greenside Cemetery has two First World War graves with the traditional Commonwealth War Graves Commission headstone and Sunnyside Cemetery has twelve.[97]

GREENSIDE CEMETERY

Private William Dawson

William Dawson fought in the 42nd Canadian Infantry Battalion. The first thing that people notice about this soldier's grave is that he died on Christmas Day 1917, which somehow seems more poignant than dying on any other day. Most soldiers killed in World War I were buried close to where they fell, because there was no repatriation of bodies. So why was this soldier buried in Scotland? The answer is that he died of wounds; he had come back to the UK for medical treatment, before he died. He was then entitled to be buried in his local cemetery. We do not know when he had emigrated to Canada, but his father still lived at 'Ross House', 29, Ochil Street and there may have been a family plot in Greenside Cemetery already. The first local newspaper reference to him, his obituary in the *Journal*,⁹⁸ gave the following details: 'At No. 12 Canadian General Hospital, Bramshot, on 25th inst. from wounds received in action, Lance Corporal William Dawson, Royal Highlanders (Can)...' The *Advertiser* the following week had a good photograph of him but contained no additional information.

As with all servicemen who served with the Canadian forces in World War I, his attestation papers are freely available to view on http://www.collectionscanada.gc.ca. They reveal the additional information that he joined up in Montreal on 26 February 1915, and under the heading of 'Trade or Calling' he wrote 'Engineer'. He was already over twenty-five years of age when he signed up, he had a fair complexion, blue eyes and was 5ft 4½in tall. Further internet research reveals that his name appears on page 442 of the Roll of Honour of the Quebec Regiment of the Canadian Infantry Forces and also on page 226 of Canada's First World War Book of Remembrance. He has not been forgotten.

Private George Monteith

George Monteith had been 'a native of Alloa' but lived in the nearby village of Kincardine-on-Forth by the time the war started.⁹⁹ His war service was in the Seaforth Highlanders. He died on 23 February 1918 after a long illness. His last days were in Paisley War Hospital and his body was brought by train to Alloa where it received a full military funeral with a guard of honour made up of soldiers from the Gordon Highlanders.¹⁰⁰ His funeral cortege was accompanied from Alloa Station to the cemetery by the Gordon Highlanders Battalion Pipe Band under the charge of Pipe-Major Findlator VC, then three volleys of shots were fired over his grave and the Gordons' bugler sounded 'The Last Post'.¹⁰¹ The final reference in the local press to his sad loss was in the *In Memoriam* column a year later, when there was a remembrance note from his mother and sisters.¹⁰² Neither the local press in their reporting nor the gravestone indicated how old he was when he died.

SUNNYSIDE CEMETERY THE WAR GRAVES OF FIRST WORLD WAR SERVICEMEN

Private P. Allan	Royal Army Service Corps	28 June 1920
Private T.G. Bennett	Argyll and Sutherland Highlanders	15 November 1918
Private A. Clarke	Royal Army Service Corps	29 April 1915
Piper W. Gamack	Argyll and Sutherland Highlanders	20 August 1915
Private W. Hunter	Seaforth Highlanders	21 November 1918
Private P.S. Paterson	Argyll and Sutherland Highlanders	18 February 1918
Private E. Percy	Argyll and Sutherland Highlanders	1 July 1918
Rifleman J.M. Robertson	The Kings (Liverpool Regiment)	17 November 1918
Private R.G. Stewart	Argyll and Sutherland Highlanders	23 February 1917
2nd Lieut. J.P. Walker	Argyll and Sutherland Highlanders	18 September 1916
2nd Lieut. R.P. Waller	Royal Air Force	22 May 1918
Private W. Wilson	Machine Gun Corps	12 June 1919

ENDNOTES

1. *Alloa Journal* 25 Jan 1919 p. 3 col. 2. He came from 34 Park Lane, just off Castle Street, an area now absorbed into the glass works O-I Manufacturing UK Ltd.
2. Alloa Academy Rector's Log Book 10 Dec 1915
3. Alloa Academy Secondary Admission Register
4. Letter from Michael Moss, Glasgow University archivist 1992
5. *Alloa Advertiser* 11 March 1916 p. 2 col. 5
6. *VCs of World War I 1915* Peter Bachelor and Christopher Matson [2011]
7. *Alloa Circular* 5 Dec 1915 p. 3 col. 1
8. *Alloa Circular* 5 Dec 1915 p. 3 col. 1
9. *Scotsman* 16 Dec 1915 p. 6
10. *Alloa Circular* 22 Dec 1915 p. 3 col. 3
11. *Scotsman* 24 Dec 1915. In October 1919 he picked up another gold watch which had been left by the Lord Provost of Partick to the first Partick resident who won the VC. Dawson was the only candidate; even though he was not a native of Partick he had worked there so he got the watch. See *Alloa Journal* 11 Oct 1919 p. 3 col. 1 for this story
12. *Scotsman* 13 Dec 1915 claims that his furlough was extended by the military authorities at the request of Provost Strang
13. *Alloa Circular* 15 Dec 1915 p. 3 col. 2. The photographs were taken by the photographer for the *Glasgow Bulletin*
14. *Alloa Journal* 1 July 1916 p. 3 col. 3

15 Information on Hunterian Museum website
16 Alloa Academy Secondary Admission Register 1903-1915. He also spent seven years in Alloa Academy Primary dept – Admission No. 1245
17 Alloa Academy Literary and Debating Society minute book 23 Nov 1910
18 Alloa Academy Literary and Debating Society minute book 19 April 1911
19 Alloa Academy Literary and Debating Society minute book 20 Dec 1911
20 *Alloa Journal* 25 May 1918 p. 3 col. 2 for a bit more of the story of JC Buchan's ventriloquism. His two puppets were Johnny and Sammy.
21 *Alloa Advertiser* 10 Feb 1917 p. 3 col. 1
22 *Alloa Advertiser* 13 April 1918 p. 3 col. 4
23 *Alloa Advertiser* 25 May 1918 p. 3 col. 2
24 *Alloa Advertiser* 25 May 1918 p. 3 col. 2
25 *Alloa Advertiser* 25 May 1918 p. 3 col. 3
26 *London Gazette* 22 May 1918
27 *Alloa Advertiser* 1 June 1918 p. 3 col. 2 carried an article from the *Glasgow Citizen*, reminiscent of the eulogising by the 'common soldier' over Captain Bruce's death in 1914, which reported the words of an unnamed soldier who witnessed Buchan's heroic actions, adding in that Buchan **personally** helped him 'through the thickest of fire' at the end of his day
28 *Alloa Journal* 25 May 1918 p. 2 col. 4
29 Interview with Mrs Fowler, daughter of John Buchan's sister, 21 June 1989
30 *Alloa Journal* 25 May 1918 p. 2 col. 4
31 *Alloa Advertiser* 15 June 1918 p. 3 col. 3
32 Why the Army order should be signed by a general in the 4th Army when Buchan was in the 5th Army, I'm not quite sure. It seems that the Army order was sent to Capt. A.P. Moir. See *Alloa Journal* 13 July 1918 p. 2 col. 2
33 Alloa Burgh Council minute book 30 July 1918
34 The memorial was removed in advance of redecoration of the room several years ago and is currently in the care of Clackmannanshire Council Museum and Heritage Service
35 *VCs of World War I The Spring Offensive 1918* Gerald Gliddon [1997]
36 *Alloa Advertiser* 6 March 1920 p. 3 col. 2
37 Pipe-Major John McLellan [1875-1949] who served with the 51st Highland Division in World War I composed a military march for the bagpipes in his honour. It was simply called Lieut. J.C. Buchan VC
38 *Alloa Journal* 26 June 1915 p. 3 col. 3
39 *Glasgow Bulletin* 30 June 1915 p. 8 col. 1
40 *Alloa Circular* 19 Jan 1916 p. 3 col. 3
41 *Scotsman* 28 June 1915 p. 5
42 *Alloa Journal* 21 Sept 1918 p. 3 col. 3
43 *Alloa Journal* 7 Feb 1914 p. 3 col. 3
44 *Alloa Journal* 3 Aug 1918 p. 3 col. 1
45 *Alloa Journal* 20 July 1918 p. 3 col. 5
46 Capt. Moir must have been told of his MBE at least six months earlier because he was present

at the launching of *Allie* in July 1919 and the Alloa Advertiser report [2 August 1919 p. 3 col. 2] which included the list of guests gave his name with the post-nominal MBE

47 He was promoted to that rank in February 1918. See *Alloa Journal* 25 May 1918 p. 3 col. 3
48 *Alloa Advertiser* 16 Aug 1919 p. 2 col. 5. Also citation in *London Gazette* [p. 9684] 30 July 1919
49 Burgh of Alloa Roll of Honour p. 75
50 *Alloa Journal* 19 Feb 1916 p. 3 col. 4. Also *London Gazette* 17 Feb 1916 [p. 1795] which back-dated the promotion to 5 Nov 1915
51 Details from his medal card found in National Archives File W372/5/7454
52 *Alloa Circular* 6 Oct 1915 p. 3 col. 1
53 *Alloa Advertiser* 14 June 1919 p. 3 col. 1. For his first 'mention', see *Alloa Journal* 1 June 1918 p. 3 col. 4
54 *Alloa Advertiser* 29 Nov 1919 p. 2 col. 6
55 Alloa Academy Primary Dept. Admission Register. He was too old to be recorded in the first Secondary Admission Register
56 Alloa Academy Primary Dept. Admission Register
57 *Alloa Journal* 25 Feb 1915 p. 3 col. 4
58 *London Gazette* 23 Feb 1915 p. 1838
59 *Alloa Advertiser* 10 June 1916 p. 3 col. 3
60 *Alloa Journal* 10 June 1916 p. 3 col. 3
61 *Alloa Advertiser* 29 July 1916 p. 2 col. 3. To be fair to the *Advertiser* there were hundreds of MCs awarded in the King's birthday honours list on that day and **none** of them had citations; not even the first one on the list, which was awarded to the King's eldest son
62 *Alloa Journal* 25 Nov 1916 p. 3 col. 6, *Alloa Advertiser* 25 Nov 1916 p. 3 col. 3. The *London Gazette* has the citation on 21 Dec 1916 [pp. 12436-37] which adds that they worked for one hour under intense fire to rescue the men
63 Alloa Academy Secondary Admission Register
64 *Alloa Journal* 2 June 1917 p. 3 col. 3
65 *Alloa Journal* 2 June 1917 p. 3 col. 3
66 *Alloa Advertiser* 14 April 1915 p. 3 col. 2
67 *Alloa Advertiser* 1 July 1916 p. 3 col. 1
68 *Alloa Journal* 14 April 1917 p. 2 col. 4
69 *Alloa Journal* 23 June 1917 p. 3 col. 4
70 *Alloa Journal* 8 Sept 1917 p. 2 col. 5, *Alloa Advertiser* 8 Sept 1917 p. 3 col. 2
71 *Alloa Advertiser* 12 Jan 1918 p. 3 col. 2
72 *Alloa Advertiser* 27 July 1918 p. 3 col. 3
73 *Alloa Advertiser* 27 July 1918 p. 3 col. 3
74 St John's Church Marriage Register 18 June 1918. The wedding was a month before his medal investiture. Meg Buchan and Arthur Proudfoot were the witnesses. See *Alloa Journal* 22 June 1918 p. 2 col. 3
75 Alloa Academy Primary dept. Admission Register. He was too old to be recorded in the first Secondary Admissions Register. RAF records in the National Archives [AIR 76/217/29] have his date of birth as 31 Jan 1888, but all other records say it was 2 Feb 1887

76 *Alloa Journal* 23 June 1917 p. 3 col. 4
77 *Alloa Circular* 17 Feb 1915 p. 3 col. 5
78 http://www.theaerodrome.com/aces/canada/attestation/home-hay.php which has curiously miss-spelt his first name, but then the Alloa Academy Admission Register spelt it Geoffrey anyway
79 *Alloa Circular* 2 Feb 1916 p. 3 col. 4
80 *Alloa Circular* 2 Feb 1916 p. 3 col. 4
81 *Alloa Journal* 23 June 1917 p. 3 col. 4, *Alloa Advertiser* 23 June 1917 p. 3 col. 3
82 *Alloa Journal* 28 July 1917 p. 3 col. 2
83 *Alloa Advertiser* 23 June 1917 p. 3 col. 3
84 *Alloa Advertiser* 22 Dec 1917 p. 3 col. 3
85 http://www.theaerodrome.com/aces/canada/home-hay records his first 'kill' being in June 1918
86 *Alloa Advertiser* 3 Aug 1918 p. 3 col. 4. Wikipedia says it was gazetted on 21 September 1918
87 *Alloa Journal* 21 Sept 1918 p. 3 col. 3
88 *Alloa Journal* 7 Sept 1918 p. 3 col. 3
89 *Alloa Journal* 21 Sept 1918 p. 3 col. 3
90 Manitoba Free Press, Winnipeg, 12 July 1919
91 http://www.theaerodrome.com/aces/canada/home-hay.php
92 http://www.theaerodrome.com/aces/canada/home-hay.php. The DH9a was effectively a bomber aeroplane, not a fighter
93 There is a fair amount of information about Captain Home-Hay's military career on Wikipedia; some of it is wildly inaccurate, so it is difficult to know how much of the rest to trust. He was never orphaned (see evidence in the Burgh Council letter book of a letter [No. 398] to his father dismissing him from his clinic duties on 29 October 1918). Wikipedia says he was mentioned in despatches in January 1919, but the Burgh of Alloa Roll of Honour does not record this, nor does his official RAF record [National Archives AIR 76/217/29]
94 *Alloa Advertiser* 8 Nov 1919 p. 3 col. 2
95 7th Battalion Argylls Regimental History p. 9
96 The DCM was the DSO equivalent for 'other ranks', the MM was the MC equivalent
97 There are also, of course, many family grave-stones in Alloa's cemeteries which refer to their lost sons who were buried in France or Belgium. All three Buchan boys and all three Waller boys are mentioned on their respective parents' grave-stone, C.F. Younger is on his family memorial, Robert Strang on his, and many more
98 *Alloa Journal* 29 Dec 1917 p. 2 col. 1
99 His name is on the Kincardine-on-Forth war memorial, not Alloa's; and the Burgh of Alloa Roll of Honour does not include his name
100 *Alloa Advertiser* 2 March 1918 p. 3 col. 1, *Alloa Journal* 2 March 1918 p. 3 col. 2 spelled his name incorrectly
101 The Gordon Highlanders were **not**, of course, a local regiment. The reason why their military pipe band crops up so often, both at military funerals in Alloa and in the victory celebrations in November 1918 and June 1919, is that the 53rd Young Soldier Battalion of the Gordons had a training camp at the neighbouring town of Tillicoultry during the war
102 *Alloa Advertiser* 22 Feb 1919 p. 2 col. 1

Conclusion

I hope this book makes sense. It's the most comprehensive research I have been able to do on the key aspects of life in wartime Alloa 1914-1919. There is, in this type of research, however, always a great concern – is there a crucial area which I should have investigated and which I have omitted? Have I sold the town short? I know that Alloa's wartime leisure entertainments included a girls' club and a cage bird society, but there was no evidence available that would have enabled me to construct a reasonable picture of their activities and how the war impacted on them. There was also nothing to be found on the work of local trade unions or railway transport (even though Alloa had two railway companies operating in it) or Alloa Ladies Clothing Society.[1] Then, what about health? Alloa's townsfolk were clearly experiencing increasing stresses in those hard-pressed times, but the shortage of evidence relating to this meant that there was nothing of any substance to enable me to form an overview. The same applies to any attempt to investigate the impact of the Spanish flu epidemic in 1918-1919.

Some may ask whether the village of South Alloa, so close by name and distance, should figure in this story. The answer is no; none of the twelve men from South Alloa who died in the war were listed in the Burgh of Alloa Roll of Honour. They have their own war memorial, which is now on the A905 road, almost opposite the primary school (now a kitchen showroom) that nine of them used to attend.[2] None of them went to Alloa Academy for their secondary education, although they could have gone to the Grange School. As young men they and South Alloa's surviving servicemen may have caught the ferry over each morning and worked in the industries of Alloa, but Alloa did not claim them as its own and therefore they are outside the remit of this book.

However, one little story which started in South Alloa may have been of interest in the town of Alloa itself. The story can be found in David Bytheway's book[3] and the local press in Stirling and Alloa. In August 1920 the obsolete British destroyer *Mallard*,[4] which was due to be broken up at the newly-formed South Alloa Ship Breakers, broke free from her moorings at South Alloa during a gale. The ship drifted up river and in the early hours of Sunday 15 August it hit the railway bridge. The collision demolished pier No. 10 and damaged pier No. 9. Two girders were brought down and crashed into the river; the railway track was left dangling between piers. At first there was confusion about the nationality of the destroyer. The *Stirling Observer* in its first report of the collision said that the bridge had been brought down by a German destroyer that had been surrendered at the end of the war.[5] A week later, under a heading 'The Bridge Stirling Dislikes', the *Observer* included a photograph of the damage and a short article where it had not corrected its earlier error, still believing that it was a German vessel.[6] It was estimated that it would cost £15,000 to repair the bridge and the Caledonian Railway Company threatened to sue the new ship breaking company, which almost immediately went out of business. It seems that, for the people of Alloa, war-related matters would not go away.[7]

I have ended this book in the 1920s with stories like this, as well as with the creation of the various war memorials to Alloa's losses, because they show that the war did not just end on 11 November 1918; its impact and effects were felt for decades. It is a matter of some concern to me to emphasise this point as fully as possible. The impact of the war on Alloa **cannot** be told simply by considering the years 1914 to 1918 and via stories of buying war savings bonds, church ladies making 'comforts' for soldiers and the townspeople putting up with meat shortages. The war's effect on Alloa's population must surely have been emotional, deeply personal and often grief-stricken. Glimpses of this pain and the stoical endurance of Alloa people can be seen every now and then among the evidence, but then it gets lost beneath the welter of factual detail about their everyday lives. I wanted to avoid being drawn into the 'imagine what they must have been thinking' type of history that is so prevalent in studies which try to evoke a picture of life in any wartime town or village.[8] It seems more honest to say that I do not know what was actually on their minds, but this is what they did. Without hard evidence for it, one suspects that for Alloa the war's legacy was a population who struggled for many years to regain that 'even keel' of normality that summed up the apparently secure social structures of that pre-war 'age of innocence'. Perhaps the real and abiding impact of the war on Alloa was that it was never able to be like that again.

ACKNOWLEDGEMENTS

J.D. Henderson for always coming up with a response to any weird question which I emailed to him.
Susan Mills, Head of Clackmannanshire Council Archives, for the serious amount of time and effort put into the proof reading of this work.
Clackmannanshire Archives and Local History Service for the use of extracts from the *Alloa Advertiser, Journal* and *Circular*. The microfilms of these newspapers are in their care.
The Mitchell Library, Glasgow
Archivists at the Argyll and Sutherland Highlanders Museum, Stirling Castle; The Scots Guards Archives, Wellington Barracks; Winchester School; The Scottish Brewing Archive, University of Glasgow; and Alloa Golf Club
Stirling Archives, for access to the Kirk Session records of several local churches
National Archives of Scotland, Edinburgh
For photographs; Anthony Cervi; J.D. Henderson; W.J. Crowe; The Hunterian Museum, University of Glasgow; The Red Cross; Clackmannanshire Council Museum and Heritage Collection; The National Portrait Gallery
John McClelland
In spite of all the help received from those above, it is my book, not theirs, and any mistakes are mine alone.

ENDNOTES

1. Incredibly, such a society did exist; it was run by Mrs Mary Smith Procter of 21 Claremont, [wife of a director of Paton's Mills] to supply clothing to destitute females. It did little of note during the war apart from inheriting £700 from two bequests from the Forrester Patons, making it the richest poor persons' clothing organisation in the county! It invested some of the money in a 5 per cent war loan and the tax returns showed that it was still getting interest of £29 pa in 1927. National Archives IRS/21/338. *Alloa Journal* 28 Dec 1918 p. 2 col. 4 reported that it was providing coal and clothing for 58 local pensioners
2. *Alloa Advertiser* 22 Nov 1919 p. 3 col. 6 for report of the unveiling of this war memorial
3. David Bytheway *Back on Track* (2008) pp. 52–53
4. This ship did not have a totally ignoble war. It had been involved in October 1918 in heroically saving lives from the *Leinster* disaster in the Irish Sea. The captain of *Mallard*, Lieut. Rowland Lloyd, was awarded the OBE for his part
5. *Stirling Observer* 17 Aug 1920 p. 5 col. 6
6. *Stirling Observer* 24 Aug 1920 p. 5 col. 2. This article thanked Messrs Buchan Bros for the use of the photograph; strange, really, because it did **not** appear in the *Alloa Advertiser*, which was owned by Messrs Buchan Bros!!
7. People may ask; 'How near did Germans ever come to Alloa during the war?' We have already noted the internment [by the **Stirlingshire** constabulary] of the crews of the German steamer and sailing ship which were berthed at South Alloa when the war broke out, but there was no suggestion in the local press that these men ever crossed the River Forth to actually set foot in Alloa. During the war, there were two German POW camps in the vicinity, at Bandeath and Glendevon, but the local press never reported that the prisoners performed any sort of jobs in Alloa. Bandeath Naval Depot, just up-river from South Alloa, was the home of about 250 German POWs for many of the war years; they were finally moved out by the end of December 1918 see *Alloa Journal* 21 Dec 1916 p. 3 col. 2. Glendevon water works was rebuilt during the war by German POWs [many of whom then fell ill with Spanish Flu]. See *Alloa Journal* 15 March 1919 p. 3 col. 2. A few German POWs escaped from Glendevon in April 1918 but they were all rounded up. See *Alloa Journal* 4 May 1918 p. 3 col. 2
8. See for instance on p. 1 of *No Finer Courage* by Michael Senior (2004). He writes about a cricket match in the village of Lee on 3 August 1914, saying that 'The minds of the cricketers were pre-occupied by thoughts of mobilisation and enlistment.' How does he know that? There are no footnotes, so what evidence does he have that those thoughts were on their minds?

BV - #0049 - 200325 - C34 - 245/170/15 - PB - 9781999890056 - Gloss Lamination